Patent Engineering

Scrivener Publishing
100 Cummings Center, Suite 541J
Beverly, MA 01915-6106

Publishers at Scrivener
Martin Scrivener (martin@scrivenerpublishing.com)
Phillip Carmical (pcarmical@scrivenerpublishing.com)

Patent Engineering

A Guide to Building a Valuable Patent Portfolio and Controlling the Marketplace

Donald S. Rimai

Scrivener Publishing

WILEY

Co-published by John Wiley & Sons, Inc. Hoboken, New Jersey, and Scrivener Publishing LLC, Salem, Massachusetts.
Published simultaneously in Canada.

For general information on our other products and services or for technical support, please contact our Customer Care Department within the United States at (800) 762-2974, outside the United States at (317) 572-3993 or fax (317) 572-4002.

Wiley also publishes its books in a variety of electronic formats. Some content that appears in print may not be available in electronic formats. For more information about Wiley products, visit our web site at www.wiley.com.

For more information about Scrivener products please visit www.scrivenerpublishing.com.

Cover design by Donald S. Rimai and Roland Schindler. The figure is from U.S. Patent 7,823,996, issued to Benjamin Rimai *et al.* (2010)

Library of Congress Cataloging-in-Publication Data:
Names: Rimai, Donald S., author.
Title: Patent engineering : a guide to building a valuable patent portfolio
and controlling the marketplace / Donald S. Rimai.
Description: Hoboken, New Jersey : Wiley-Scrivener, 2016. |
Includes bibliographical references and index.
Identifiers: LCCN 2015048490 | ISBN 9781118946091 (hardback)
Subjects: LCSH: Patent laws and legislation--United States. |
Patents--Economic aspects--United States. | BISAC: LAW / Intellectual Property / General.
Classification: LCC KF3116 .R56 2016 | DDC 346.7304/86--dc23 LC record
available at http://lccn.loc.gov/2015048490

ISBN 978-1-118-94609-1

This book is dedicated to my son Dr. Benjamin Rimai. You inspire me to reach beyond my grasp.

Contents

Preface

For 33 years, I conducted research in digital printing at Eastman Kodak. While this field was certainly chronologically mature, having been around since Chester Carlson first invented xerography in the 1930s and having been the subject of much research and development by many companies over that period, the advent of modern digital electronics presented both novel opportunities and challenges in this technological area.

Several years before I retired from Kodak, I was asked to transition from the role of an independent researcher to that of an intellectual property manager for digital printing. In that position, I was involved with generating and maintaining patents that protected Kodak's proprietary technology, asserting patents against allegedly infringing companies, prosecuting patent applications, implementing cross-licensing agreements, and related activities. During that period of time, I had the privilege of working with world-class engineers, scientists, and technicians, as well as an outstanding legal team comprising attorneys, patent agents, and paralegals.

The technology advanced by Kodak's technical team members was highly innovative and allowed electrophotography to go from being limited to office copiers to its rivaling both silver halide photography and offset printing in quality, reliability, and speed, while being able to integrate the capabilities of the digital era with hard-copy printing. Invention disclosures were submitted by the members of the technical staff and patent applications were filed and prosecuted by the attorneys. Kodak was highly successful in both the quantity of applications filed each year and the number of patents received. However, despite these successes, it was apparent that there was opportunity to greatly enhance the extent and the value of the patent portfolio by broadening the intellectual property actually covered by and increasing the assertability of the patents, while making the patenting process less expensive and more efficient.

While addressing the need to significantly improve the patenting process, two outstanding individuals were assigned to work with me. One was attorney Roland Schindler and the other was engineer-turned-patent agent Chris White. Both saw the need and opportunity for improvement as I did and both were enthusiastic about trying to make the improvements wherever possible. Together, we developed a methodology that allowed us to address these needs. As a result, we were able to generate a far greater number of patent applications that were broader in coverage and more extensive and assertable than those previously filed, while enjoying a high success ratio of issued patents to applications filed. We also found that, by implementing this methodology, the technical team members, who often were reluctant to divert their attention from their assignments to pursue patent applications – a task many of them considered painful – became much more cooperative as we were able to remove the most painful aspects of filing and prosecuting applications.

This book describes the methodology designed and implemented by Roland, Chris, and me. It is intended to give the readers, in this day of global competition, the tools that will enable them to use the concepts discussed herein to give their companies a competitive advantage in the marketplace, as well as to generate a patent portfolio that can significantly enhance the revenues and value of their companies.

Don Rimai
Rochester, NY
November 15, 2015

Acknowledgements

When writing a book, the goal is to discuss a topic in a clear and concise manner. The author gratefully acknowledges the considerable efforts of his wife Nancy Rimai for her painstaking reading, commenting, and proposing changes that have allowed this book to achieve its goals. The author would also like to thank Chris White, Kelly White and Roland Schindler for their input into this manuscript. I would especially like to thank Roland and Chris for sharing their expertise in patent law with me. The author would also like to thank Mr. Ray Owens, Esq. for the numerous discussions that we have had over our many years together. These discussions greatly enhanced my understanding of patent law and related issues.

About the Author

Dr. Donald S. Rimai recently retired from Eastman Kodak, where he worked as a researcher and intellectual property manager in digital printing and adhesion science. He is expert at developing patent portfolios and helping inventors patent their inventions. He is an Eastman Kodak Distinguished Inventor with more than 150 U.S. patents and over 120 scientific publications. Don has published five books and edited two conference proceedings, is a Fellow of the Adhesion Society and of the American Physical Society, and has won the Charles Ives and Chester Carlson Awards. Don holds a BS from Rensselaer Polytechnic Institute and MS and Ph.D. degrees from the University of Chicago. In 2014 Dr. Rimai received the Inventor of the Year Award from the Rochester Intellectual Property Law Association.

1

An Introduction to Patent Engineering

Patents have long been recognized as a vital tool in the business world. Patents are designed to give the owner or assignee of the patent a monopolistic position in which to practice the technology described in the patent. In years past, a few patents may have provided adequate protection. That is no longer the case. In today's world, a solid patent portfolio that is the result of engineering and executing a focused patent strategy is vital to protect your business interests.

Moreover, patents should not be considered solely as defensive legal documents. Rather, they should be considered part of the marketable product stream emanating from your company. If the patent portfolio is good, it can be worth billions of dollars. If it is poorly designed, it can simply be an expense that divulges your technology to your competition.

It is the goal of this book to enable you to develop patent portfolios that both protect your vital technology and have commercial value without burdening your company with undue expenses. To begin this discussion, let us consider your night immediately prior to your big product introduction.

The Night before Product Launch

Your company is about to launch a new product. Perhaps that product will also launch your entrepreneurial company. Alternatively, that product may enhance the profitability of your established company.

The product has many key features that are lacking in competitive offerings. You should be able to capture a large segment of the market and offer your products at a premium price. You have filed patent applications, or perhaps even already obtained issued patents, on the key features. Yet, despite this, you are stressed. Why?

You know that no marketing window is open in perpetuity. It is only a matter of time until competitive products are offered, perhaps with additional features or at a lower price. You hope that your patents will prevent this, but do they?

In too many instances, the answer to the above question is no. Companies patent or attempt to patent what they perceive as solutions to problems. These solutions are often specific to their own technologies and do not extend to technologies of value to other companies. They also do not block competitors from developing and marketing competitive technologies that solve the same problems in different manners. In fact, a patent stemming from a patent application may not be allowed or issued. In this situation, the information put forth in the disclosure contained within the application teaches your competitors exactly how to solve the problem without affording you any protection. You have educated your competitor—at your expense.

It is important to realize that this is where most businesses make their mistakes. Most businesses patent technologies that are specific to their products. This is fine, as long as people want your specific product. The problem is, more often than not, people do not buy products—they buy solutions to their problems. When a person needs to sit down, which matters more—picking a bar stool over a bean bag, or getting off his aching feet? You may have patented the chair, but it's only a matter of time before someone comes along with something better or cheaper. It can take years, even decades, for an industry to hit that combination of cost and functionality that makes consumers accept a new product paradigm. If you want to keep your business relevant long after your product has been surpassed, you need to stop patenting the product and start owning the problem. This is accomplished not by filing random patent applications but, rather, by filing patent applications that emanate from developing a patent strategy that allows your company to "own the problem" rather than simply specific solutions to a problem. The process of developing and executing that strategy is called "patent engineering".

The Value of Patents

In the early 1980s, Xerox accepted a pile of stock shares from Apple in exchange for allowing Steve Jobs to go cherry-picking in Xerox's now-legendary Palo Alto Research Center (PARC). Jobs took what PARC had learned about graphical user interfaces and birthed a new era in computing, providing computers that were far easier to use than the DOS-based computers people had before.

Apple may have created a new market for personal computer use, but it did not get the patent coverage it needed to defend its space. When Microsoft muscled in and established a dominant market position with its Windows products, Apple was reduced to suing Microsoft in the fuzzier arena of copyright law, alleging that Windows stole their "look and feel." Without hard patent documentation, the courts took one look at this case and decided that there was no cause of action. Apple was defenseless.

The Apple case was dismissed, and as a result, Microsoft Windows nearly destroyed Apple Computers. The only way Apple was able to regain a presence in the computer marketplace was to create a whole new user market by developing a brilliant, consumer friendly ecosystem, first in its desktop and laptop products, and later in its music players, smart phones, and tablets.

Smart phones had spent more than a decade in development before the iPhone came along and blasted the market open. The first smart phone was introduced by IBM in 1993, but it was expensive and impractical. For years, the marketplace was littered with failed attempts. There were lots of good phones that were bad computers, as well as bad phones that were good computers. There were a few devices that managed to do both well, but they were far too expensive for mass consumption. When it was introduced, the iPhone was like a revelation—a good phone and a functional computer in a sleek, affordable and (perhaps most important) attractive package.

For a while, Apple regained market dominance with its iPods, iPhones, and iPads, but they were only the first-movers in a new arena. Soon, second-mover competitors, like Google and Microsoft, entered the market with cost-competitive products that had a similar balance and user feel. By waiting until after Apple had created the market, these second-mover competitors were able to take advantage of both Apple's research investment and the feedback of Apple's customers. As a result, these second-mover products were able to have a price advantage over the breakthrough products and still yield a competitive return. In America today, there are more

Android-based smart phones sold than Apple smart phones, even though the first iPhone reached the market more than a year before the first Android smart phone. Android's primary advantage is clear—its phones just cost less.

And now we arrive at the real reason you are feeling such stress on the night before the product launch. You know that even though your product is incredible, your competitors do not have to copy its exact features to create a product or service that will attract your customers. All they have to do to compete with you is reduce the importance your product's advantages while offering advantages of their own that will resonate strongly with consumers. Windows 3.1 might not have been as refined and efficient as the Apple Macintosh operating system with which it competed, but Windows was good enough to offer most of the advantages of Apple's more-intuitive computing experience both at a lower cost and in the open environment of the IBM PC architecture trusted by millions of corporate IT professionals. The advantages of Apple's interface were clear; Windows' advantages simply outweighed them.

So what can you do to protect yourself? Like it or not, you know patents can be valuable and if you have not started filing, you probably will soon. Still, you're not sure what makes a patent valuable. Is it the specific technology? Is it the number of patents you own? You need to know, because whether you own a large multinational corporation or run a small business out of your garage, your competitors are looking for any opening that they could use to force you to pay them large sums of money, force you out of business, or both.

You need a patent strategy, one that looks beyond the minute details of gear A and slot C, one that prevents you from throwing money away on useless patents with little value. To protect your bottom line, you need a big-picture patent strategy that will help you reap financial benefits from what may be your most valuable product—your intellectual property.

Implementing a Patent Strategy

So where do you start? The good news is that implementing a proper patent strategy—otherwise known as "patent engineering,"—is both time efficient and cost effective. In this book, you will learn that the strategy is all in the details as we guide you, step by step, through the choices you can make long before your patent application is ever filed.

We will show you how to boost your inventors' patentable output in the time they are already spending on your products. We will guide you through the patenting process, highlighting the places where you can maximize your patenting dollar. Most importantly, we will teach you to think about product development in a whole new way. We will show you how to look beyond the nuts and bolts of your specific technologies and instead to lay claim to something far bigger and more profitable than any product could ever be—the problem they solve. You will have more than a product. You will have a solid plan that will allow you to prosper for years to come. Now, introduce your product with confidence.

How does one control the market in today's rapidly changing world? An important aspect to this is to change the way that companies implement patent strategies. Traditionally, a company, facing a technological problem, would develop and patent a solution to that problem. That may have worked in years gone by. However, in today's highly competitive and rapidly advancing world, such an approach is not viable. A new approach to developing patent portfolios is needed. To understand the present requirements of a patent portfolio, let us go back to the fundamental reasons that your company seeks to own patents and develop a patent strategy for today's world that addresses these fundamental requirements.

Goals of a Patent Strategy

The goals of a modern patent strategy should recognize that:

1. Patents prevent your competition from doing something that you do not want them to do.
2. You do not want your competition to offer products that compete effectively with your products.
3. To offer new features you must solve new problems. Such features can include, but are not limited to, totally novel products or improvements to existing products such as lower costs, better reliability, or improved ease of use.
4. By owning intellectual property that covers the best alternative ways of solving these problems you block your competitors from competing effectively with you.
5. A good patent portfolio should be considered part of the value-adding products of your company.

To achieve these goals, an effective patent strategy can no longer focus on the specific solution to a technological problem. Rather, it must strive to own the entire problem. It is the goal of this book to provide the reader with the knowledge and tools to develop and implement that strategy.

Examples and Consequences of Two Patent Strategies

Let us illustrate the concept of owning the problem with two examples. In the first case, the company failed to own the problem, even though it had a massive patent portfolio that effectively blocked competitors from using its specific solutions to that problem.

The first case involves the electrophotographic office copier, which later gave rise to the laser printer commonly used today. By 1980 the plain paper copier had become a common machine in most businesses. It was able to quickly and effectively produce adequate copies of typed documents, such documents principally comprising alpha-numeric characters. These copiers and printers operated by applying toner, transported in a development station, to a photoreceptor in an image-wise manner and then transferring the toned image to paper. However, the ability to produce graphics such as pictures having solid areas and gray scales was poor. It was simply not possible, at the time, to deposit the toner in adequate and controllable amounts to print high-quality pictures.

At about this time, scientists and engineers at Eastman Kodak devised a method for developing the solid areas and gray scales that allowed pictures to be printed. This required a development station comprising a rotating magnetic core concentric to a rotating, electrically biased shell, over which the toner flowed.

The device was complicated and expensive. The magnetic core required multiple magnets of comparable and controllable strength. The tolerances between the magnetic core and the shell were tight and required precise machining. Rotating both the core and shell required multiple motors whose speeds had to be precisely controlled. This made for a massive subsystem that required rigid supports. Process control was also required and special materials for use as electrophotographic developers were also needed.

Despite these complications, for many years this was the only method that was known to produce pictures using electrophotography and Kodak aggressively developed a patent portfolio to protect this technology. In essence, they precluded competitors from practicing the specific technological solution to the problem. Unfortunately, Kodak lost sight of the problem, which was to produce high-quality pictures. As a result, Kodak did not own the problem, but just one specific solution to the problem. The consequences rapidly ensued.

The competition, which existed in both the United States and abroad, sought and developed alternative solutions to this problem. In many instances, these solutions were less complicated and less expensive than Kodak's technology. As electrophotographic printers became more common, including low-priced printers suitable for home use today that print good pictures, Kodak was relegated to producing high-priced machines for the commercial market. Even there, they came under pricing pressures as so-called "mid-volume" printers that cost less became faster and more reliable.

Had Kodak sought instead to own the problem of producing high-quality electrophotographic pictures, it could have dominated the printer market today and companies that sought to compete in that market would have had to pay royalties to Kodak for the rights to use that technology. As it turned out, these other companies actively pursued patents in their respective technologies. Moreover, they did not need Kodak's technology and, accordingly, were not interested in patent exchange agreements in this area. Kodak was blocked from effectively competing in a technological area that it pioneered because it did not own the problem.

In contrast to the above example, let us illustrate the value of good patent portfolios with another example, namely the oxygen or O_2 sensors used in every automobile in the U.S. market today. The O_2 sensor is a device of which few automobile purchasers have ever heard. As opposed to other electronic features, traction control capability, audio or navigation systems, or climate control systems, no one buys a car because it has a certain O_2 sensor. Still, no car can be sold in the U.S. market without several O_2 (oxygen) sensors and any manufacturer that does not have access to this technology will be out of business.

The O_2 sensor, first invented and patented about 40 years ago, has evolved to address problems brought about by increasingly stringent regulations governing fuel consumption and emissions, at the same time that consumers have been demanding additional features that increase the price and complexity and consume energy and add weight to automobiles. Moreover, many consumers today demand automotive performance that rivals that of cars in the 1970s that got only 8 miles per gallon and polluted heavily, but which also get 30 miles per gallon today. To fully appreciate how these conflicting requirements play into the necessity of formulating patent strategies that aim at owning the problem rather than specific solutions to problems, it is beneficial to divert from discussing patent strategies and first discuss the evolving technology present in automotive engines.

An automobile typically comprises an internal combustion engine where gasoline is atomized and sprayed into one of a series of cylinders.

Air is also inputted into the cylinders. Each cylinder contains a piston attached to a crankshaft. At the appropriate time, a spark is generated that ignites the gasoline-fuel mixture, forcibly pushing the piston and generating the energy that allows the automobile to move. Traditionally, the gasoline would be atomized and mixed with air in the carburetor using vacuum generated by the engine and sprayed into the cylinder through an intake valve that would open and close at the appropriate time. A spark plug would ignite the mixture, with the timing of the spark controlled by a rotating mechanical switch, i.e. the distributor. After ignition, the spent gases would exit the cylinder through an exhaust valve that would open at the appropriate time. These components were all connected to the crankshaft via a timing belt or chain, thereby creating a mechanically timed and operated engine.

Gasoline is a mixture of hydrocarbons consisting of chains of approximately eight carbon and eighteen hydrogen atoms. If gasoline is burned completely and stoichiometrically, carbon dioxide and water are produced. A gallon of gas weighs approximately six pounds and, if completely burned, produces about eighteen pounds of carbon dioxide.

The problem is that we do not live in an ideal world and cannot guarantee the complete combustion of the gasoline. It is important to realize that air, rather than oxygen, is fed into the engine's combustion chamber. Air comprises 21% oxygen and 78% nitrogen. At the elevated temperatures encountered during combustion, some of the oxygen reacts with the nitrogen to generate nitrous oxides, thereby reducing the amount of oxygen present to support the combustion of the gasoline. This results in unburned or partially oxidized hydrocarbons and odorless but toxic carbon monoxide (CO), as well as other noxious gases, being exhausted from the engine. Controlling these emissions adequately is just not feasible with carburetor technology.

How does the automotive industry adjust its products to the seemingly contradictory demands today? Today's consumer is certainly more quality and safety conscious. Cars are also expected to last a lot longer than was typical in the 1970s. Moreover, the average consumer today wants more luxuries in a car, including air conditioning, entertainment electronics, and navigational and communicational devices. Stereos, DVD players, GPS devices, power adjustable seats with memory capability, WiFi, computers, etc. have become common place even in moderately priced cars. These features add to the cost of car production. However, competitive pressures are forcing prices down, thereby creating economic constraints on how much an automobile manufacturer can spend on technology that controls emissions and mileage.

These devices and today's improved performance requirements consume energy, which can cause increased emissions and decreased mileage from internal combustion engines. Even more problematical is that the emissions and mileage can vary as the consumer decides how frequently and for how long certain devices are used. For example, an air conditioner can certainly use a lot of energy to run.

Seemingly in direct contradiction to these demands, consumers and ever more stringent Corporate Average Fuel Economy (CAFE) standards are demanding better gas mileage. This is most readily achieved by building smaller, lighter, less powerful cars. But many consumers are demanding SUVs and other larger, more powerful vehicles. Safety requirements mandate equipment including, but not limited to, seat belts, airbags, side impact bars, antilock braking systems (ABS), traction control, skid control, controlled crumpling structures, and rear viewing cameras. These safety features add both weight and cost and can adversely affect reliability when costs, fuel mileage, and quality are major issues. And, lest one forget or dismiss any of these issues, the Yugo, attempting to access the low price market with a small, basic car, was driven off the shores by a lack of demand because of its perceived low quality and lack of reliability. The marketplace is not very forgiving. It is apparent that the only way that these seemingly contradictory requirements can be met is by being able to control the operation of internal combustion engines so that they operate in a clean and highly-efficient manner.

The answer to these seemingly mutually contradicting requirements is that the automobile of the 21st century is vastly different from that plying the highways in the early 1970s and before. The modern automobile is designed using aluminum and plastic instead of steel to lighten the car and improve corrosion resistance. Front and side impact airbags are standard. Cars are designed to crumple in a controlled fashion during a collision, thereby absorbing energy and better protecting the occupants. Fuel tank shut-off valves are commonly used to reduce gasoline spillage in case of a roll-over. And the modern automobile has more space-age electronics than would be even conceivable a few decades, or even a few years ago. Both fuel delivery and ignition timing are controlled by microprocessors. The carburetor has given way to the fuel injection system, with the amount of fuel and the timing of its delivery carefully controlled. This has been made possible by incorporating an ever increasing number of microprocessors that control the combustion of the fuel within the engine. These microprocessors rely on a myriad of sensors to provide accurate operating conditions so that the amount of fuel and the spark voltage and timing can be adjusted.

One such sensor is the oxygen or O_2 sensor. O_2 sensors are devices that few purchasers of automobiles have ever heard of or requested. It is certainly not an option such as a DVD player, or a device such as a supplementary restraint system (SRS), i.e. an airbag, that is well known. Yet, the O_2 sensors, which are invisible to anyone but a mechanic or possibly to an owner when a check engine light appears, are required in every car made today in order to meet emissions and CAFE standards. Located in the exhaust pipes of a car, these sensors have to operate under hot and corrosive conditions, providing feedback to the microprocessors on an ongoing basis.

Oxygen sensors first made their appearance in cars in the late 1970s. Originally, a single O_2 sensor was installed in the exhaust manifold of a car just in front of the catalytic converter. The sensor detected the oxygen concentration in the exhaust gases and, assuming that the amount of oxygen present was a measure of the completeness of the combustion, adjusted a solenoid valve in the carburetor to lean down or enrich the gasoline-air mixture. Unfortunately, this often led to cars with rather anemic performance. Moreover, as the mixture was leaned down, there would be more oxygen present to react with the nitrogen, to yield more nitrous oxides. This problem was further exacerbated by the fact that the leaner mixtures caused the engines to run hotter, which further increased the nitrous oxide concentrations. Enriching the mixture reduced mileage and caused an increase in carbon monoxide emissions. Clearly, further improvements were needed to correct this problem.

Modern automobiles use computer controlled fuel injection systems, with monitoring signals from various sensors, including O_2 sensors. These sensors supply the information to the computers thereby allowing the computers to rapidly and reliably adjust the processes, including the amount of fuel injected, to optimize performance.

Presently, automobiles contain at least two O_2 sensors, with one located immediately before and one immediately after the catalytic converter. An O_2 sensor functions as a battery. The center is open to the atmosphere and the outer portion is located within the exhaust gases. Oxygen is absorbed onto both surfaces of the sensor and, because of the differences in oxygen concentration between the air and the exhaust gas, a voltage is produced that depends on the concentration of oxygen in the exhaust. The voltage from the sensor is fed into the computers controlling the car's operation, which are far more sophisticated, control many more subsystems, and operate at much higher speeds than those used in the 1970s, and the amount of air being fed into the cylinders is adjusted in response to that signal.

As time went on, demands that had to be met by the O_2 sensor changed. Originally used to control a solenoid in a carburetor that crudely adjusted the amount of fuel that was atomized after the engine reached normal operating temperatures, now these sensors must adjust fuel mixtures with both cold and warm engines. The sensor evolved to contain an internal heater, enabling it to switch on more rapidly.

The types of gases that had to be monitored also changed from only CO to various nitrous oxides and hydrocarbons. The response times of the sensors had to increase to allow them to respond more finely to variations in the output gases. Original sensors had a life expectancy of about 15,000 miles. Soon thereafter the expected life increased, first to 30,000 miles and ultimately to the life of the vehicle.

This evolution has led to problems and solutions, all of which gave rise to opportunities to obtain patents. The problems that had to be addressed with respect to the O_2 sensors included, not just the basic design of the sensor, but improvements to the sensors, increased capabilities of modern O_2 sensors, their interfacing with other features in modern automobiles, and their use in enhancing automotive performance. The O_2 sensor problem is quite extensive.

Most automobiles today have at least two microprocessors—one of which controls ignition and the other controlling fuel delivery. The two microprocessors interact to determine the precise amount of fuel and air required and the timing of the spark. The distributor is gone, its role taken by a computer, and the carburetor has been replaced by computer controlled fuel injection systems. Braking and traction are controlled to minimize skidding, again through the automobile's two main computers. Even steering and the transmission are electronically controlled these days.

Indeed, the microprocessors themselves have greatly evolved and the types of input signals and the speed and sensitivity at which these signals have to be produced increased. To address these demands, changes in the components ranging from the relatively simple connectors used to attach O_2 sensors to the microprocessors to the sophisticated software that allows their signals to be processed have occurred. These areas all gave rise to an evolution in O_2 sensor patents despite the fact that the original sensor was invented a long time ago.

In principal, an O_2 sensor is a fairly simple device with a well-defined function, namely to ensure the proper combustion of fuel. The device was first invented over 40 years ago. Yet, the number of patents (a total of 700 according to this table) issued with respect to this technology, as seen in Table 1.1, continue to increase unabatedly. Let us address why this is the case.

As can be seen in Table 1.1, the U.S. and Japanese automobile manufacturers hold most of the patents that refer to oxygen sensors in the claims,

Table 1.1 The number of O_2 sensor U.S. patents for various automotive manufacturers. Source: United States Patent and Trademark Office (USPTO).

Company	No. of O_2 Sensor Patents	Years Spanned
Bosch	54	1976–2013
General Motors	65	1978–2010
Ford	286	1976–2013
Chrysler	25	1989–2001
Toyota	120	1976–2013
Honda	37	1985–2013
Mercedes	0	–
Fiat	0	–
Volvo	2	2000–2001
BMW	1	1996
Hyundai	15	2001–2013
Nissan	95	1976–2007

as does Bosch. These companies generally produce their own fuel and ignition systems. European manufacturers, who tend to be smaller and buy their sensors from Bosch, may have less need to file for patents as they are not making or using their own sensors, but, rather, obtaining them from a supplier.

Why are there so many patents focused on this one device? Why was there not just a single patent issued in 1976? The answers to these questions, in many ways, form the focus of this book.

Certainly, the original sensors were patented in 1976, according to Table 1.1. Some of the multiple patents may be the result of some design variations, given that the USPTO allows only one invention per patent. If the examiner* determines that claimed designs can function independently, a divisional application will be required.

However, that does not fully address the questions, especially as patent activity has continued over a period of 40 years. Moreover, obtaining and maintaining patents is both time consuming and expensive. Why do these

* The "patent examiner", or "examiner" for short, can be considered the employee in the USPTO who will be assessing your patent application and deciding whether or not it defines a patentable invention.

companies continue to invest resources into a device that was "invented" 40 years ago?

If one examines the individual patents, one finds that most of the patents cover features other than just the basic device. There are patents that cover the connectors. There are patents that cover the feed-back control system linking fuel delivery to the O_2 sensor output. There are patents that cover using O_2 sensors with fuel injection devices. The list of inventions is as long as the list of patents, and is far more significant than merely patenting a specific device.

One reason companies continue to apply for and receive patents related to this technology is that patents expire after a period of time. Certainly, those issued as recently as the latter part of the 20th century are now in the public domain, with anyone allowed to practice them. However, the issue is far deeper.

It needs to be stressed that the problem addressed by oxygen sensors is very significant and that no modern cars can be sold in the United States if they did not have and properly utilize such sensors. Without access to this technology an automobile manufacturer would be forced to shut down.

Some manufacturers address this issue by buying these devices from a company that focuses on producing them, with that company holding the patents. Other automotive companies produce the sensors themselves.

One can easily imagine how much it would be worth to one such manufacturer to be able to eliminate another major producer of cars from the competition. Each automotive company must have a sufficient O_2 sensor patent portfolio to ensure that it is not locked out of being able to use the sensors. No one is obligated to give, sell, or lease a license to patented technology that he owns to anyone else. Absent an adequate patent portfolio, a manufacturer would have to either license the technology or buy the devices from another producer, paying whatever price the second producer chooses to charge.

It is worthwhile to note that the automotive companies are investing heavily in patenting areas of interest to others—so-called "brown space". Brown space is particularly valuable because of its broad interest to other companies, which might be willing or required to pay licensing fees to or enter into patent exchange agreements with the patent owner in order to have access to the technology.

It is not sufficient to simply have a patent on a solution to a problem. The early O_2 sensor patents covered that. Those patents are long expired and, while they protected the device itself, they did not protect the use of the device or how the device and its functionality evolved over time. Rather, in order to remain competitive and continue to sell their products, companies should also have patent coverage on the technology that their competitors need.

Failure to develop such a patent portfolio can result in your company being prevented from selling its products due to your competitors having blocking patents or in your company having to pay large sums of money for licenses to use your competitor's technology.

To obtain such patents requires that a solidly executed patent strategy that results in a strong and valuable patent portfolio be developed. Sometimes, companies can own patents even for products that they do not intend to produce, but that others may want to manufacture. Such patents can be exceedingly valuable. In some instances, the patents may be worth more than the products a company intends to make.

In their patent portfolios, these proactive automotive companies are not just preserving solutions to certain problems. Rather, they are attempting to own the problem, or at least own sufficient portions of the problem so that other companies cannot block them from using crucial technology. Owning the problem rather than just a specific solution to the problem is key to developing a valuable patent portfolio.

Goal of This Book

This book presents methods of building valuable patent portfolios that allow your company to thrive in an increasingly competitive and regulated world—a world where consumers are more cognizant and demanding and where access to information by those consumers is more readily accessible. More specifically, this book teaches you how to generate such patent portfolios without bankrupting your company. It discusses whether or not to file outside the United States and, if so, how to select the countries where a company's patents would be of most value.

Building a solid patent portfolio that gives you control of the marketplace and that has high intrinsic value in its own right is not accomplished by aggressively and expensively filing a plethora of patent applications covering every aspect of your technology. Rather, it is accomplished by first identifying the critical problems and their solutions. Alternative solutions are also identified, as are problems encountered when attempting to implement those solutions (so-called "enabling technologies"). All of these solutions, both fundamental and enabling form the basis of a sound patent strategy.

However, a sound patent strategy goes well beyond that. It also identifies the solutions to the problems in competitive products and seeks patents encompassing those solutions. Such patents are often far more valuable, even if simpler and more limited than your key patents, because through them you can block a competitor who relies upon access to that technology.

Your patent portfolio may have value that extends beyond your specific product offerings, even encompassing products that would not be considered competitive with yours. These patents can be of great value to your company as they may be needed by noncompetitive companies, which then have to pay you licensing fees to gain access to your technology.

These goals cannot be obtained by accident or by simply patenting specific technological improvements that your company has discovered. Rather, it comes about by engineering a comprehensive patent strategy.

It is recognized that no one will be awarded every patent for which one applies. Sometimes, the examiner finds "related art" that may or may not be relevant. Whether or not an applicant can circumvent that art often depends on the extent of the teachings in the disclosure. At other times, related art such as prior patents may be possessed by other companies.

This book does not pretend to be a text on patenting one's own invention. Patents are legal documents and writing patents should be a job for an expert. However, ensuring an adequate disclosure and sufficient background is the responsibility of the inventor.

Finally, this book is about engineering a comprehensive patent strategy for maximizing the value of your investment in generating patents. Patents can prevent a company from being sued if a proper strategy has been pursued. The sale or licensing of patents can greatly enhance the revenue of a company. However, a poorly designed strategy may be of little value at best. Moreover, because an applicant must divulge his invention in sufficient detail in his patent application so as to allow someone else to practice the invention, a poorly designed patent strategy can teach much and result in little protection of the technology.

To succeed, you need to own patents that provide more than a good solution to a problem. You need to possess a sufficiently strong patent portfolio that gives you the power to own the problem.

2

Patents and Patent Strategies—What They Are and Why You Need Them

The World Changed

In years gone by, clever inventors, often working on their own, would devise a new method or piece of equipment that would have distinct advantages over that that had been previously available. Simple devices such as the pol on an ax (the weighted portion of the ax head opposite the blade that counterbalances the blade) provided more mass and better balance to the ax than that of earlier designed axes. This allowed the large trees found in the New World to be cut efficiently. The claw on a hammer that allowed a carpenter to pull, as well as drive, nails is an example of another such improvement.

Such inventions, though simple in concept, were extremely useful. Moreover, they represented distinct technological advances that tended to be fairly unique and differentiated from any proposed alternative methods that could be used to compete with these inventions. As such, it was often possible to obtain a single patent that was readily understandable and that provided adequate protection for an invention.

This is no longer the situation in the 21st century. James Burke in his books *Connections* [1] and *The Day the Universe Changed* [2] described how technological advances generally do not occur because of an isolated inspiration. Rather, an individual, cognizant of seemingly unrelated technologies, with a stroke of brilliance is able to relate those technologies to one another and solve a problem in a novel and beneficial way. As the number of such technologies, as well as the rate in which they occur, increases, the need to protect one's intellectual property changes.

Single patents no longer provide adequate protection. Rather, it is necessary to generate a patent portfolio that totally envelops your intellectual property. Such generation does not occur by accident. Rather, it is the result of carefully developing a patent strategy.

As an immense side benefit of generating such a portfolio, you also create a product that has great value in and of itself in the marketplace.

It is the purpose of this book to teach you how to formulate and execute such a strategy, as well as to argue why it is necessary. Finally, we will discuss how obtaining such a portfolio can be done without burdening you with undue expenses. To understand why the change from obtaining isolated patents to generating a patent portfolio is necessary, let us consider how the world has changed in the past 40 years.

40 Years Ago

The world in 1972 was a far different place than it is today. The United States was only just completing its nearly thirty-year recovery from the devastation wrought by World War II. People bought cars made in Detroit by a tiny handful of American companies. European cars were relatively scarce, Japanese cars even rarer, and Korean automobiles were entirely unknown. The cars were large, had an engine life expectancy of about 50,000 miles, and were often sold to the consumers with numerous defects that had to be fixed under the terms of the warranty after the sale. Gas consumption was not a topic most people cared about even though many cars only got eight to ten miles per gallon. Why worry? Gas was inexpensive and readily available and, as far as most consumers and manufacturers were concerned, there was no need to change.

Computers, in 1972, were large, expensive power hogs whose impressive mass belied their limited functionality. To even make the computer work, the consumer had to buy a myriad of add-ons, including punch card machines, punch cards, card sorters, card readers, and software written by the engineers at the computer company. Made primarily by IBM and a small number of other manufacturers, these machines were sold only to a limited market—industries, universities, and government agencies. The thought that a single individual would actually own a computer was pure science fiction.

The World Today

Then the world changed. Asian manufacturers burst onto the scene, flooding the market with lower-cost, and sometimes higher-quality, products that quickly undermined America's dominance. This change, although rapid, had been long in the making. It began after World War II, when the Marshall Plan called for rebuilding industries in both the Allied nations and former Axis powers Germany and Japan. Often, these factories were constructed with the same materials and tools used in new American factories, but not present in existing American factories that had not been destroyed during the war, giving their host countries an extensive modern manufacturing infrastructure. These factories were more efficient than their existing U.S. counterparts, saving on cost, effort, and materials.

The spread of industrialization outside the United States was not limited to the countries being rebuilt under the Marshall Plan. Other nations, most notably China and South Korea, began to industrialize, taking full advantage of their vast, low-cost labor forces. Lower production costs led to lower product prices, effectively undercutting the American products already on the market.

Even as the market shifted away from American manufacturing dominance, people were embracing digital technologies that would revolutionize the way they saw the world. Tandy Radio Shack introduced the first home computer, the TRS-80, in 1977 [3], and the Atari 2600 brought video games into people's living rooms that same year [4]. The 1973 oil crisis revealed major weaknesses in automotive design while devices developed for the military, such as global positioning systems, started appearing on hiking trails and in homes. In the 1980s and 1990s, IBM, the primary manufacturer of industrial computers, was swamped with competition in the new consumer electronics market as companies like Apple, Microsoft, and Dell made computers affordable and easy to use. Added to this was the birth of the Internet, which changed the way people gathered information and communicated throughout the world. By 2002 the world as we knew it had been transformed and American companies were left struggling to survive in a global marketplace.

Today's markets change with unbelievable speed. The cutting-edge smart phone you buy today will be obsolete in six months or less, leaving producers who rely primarily on product sales less than half a year to recoup millions of dollars in product development and marketing costs—less time to recoup their costs if a competitor imitates their technology. For a business to survive in the melee, it must be able to protect and defend its innovations in markets throughout the world.

The Role of Patents

Enter the patent system. Since 1790 the United States Patent and Trademark Office (USPTO) has issued over 8,600,000 U.S. patents, as shown in Figure 2.1 with the rate of issuance increasing exponentially over time.

While patent systems have existed in various forms throughout modern history, the current system was established with the United States Court of Appeals for the Federal Circuit (the "CAFC" or "Federal Circuit") in

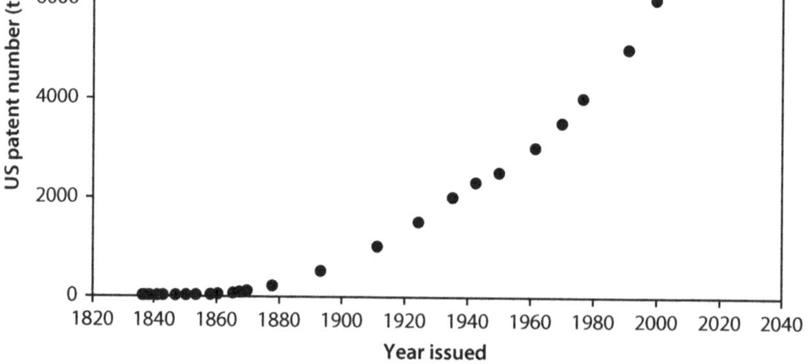

Figure 2.1 United States patent number reached for each year. Data from the United States Patent and Trademark Office (USPTO.gov).

1982. This court is unique among the thirteen U.S. Federal Circuit Courts of Appeal because it has jurisdiction in specific subject areas, rather than geographic regions. Prior to the establishment of the CAFC, patent cases would work their way through the lower courts, eventually appealing to the Court of Appeal of a particular geographic region. These courts often lacked the technical expertise to assess a patent's validity and often ruled that issued patents were invalid.

Therefore, prior to the establishment of the Federal Circuit, it was relatively safe for a business to infringe upon a patent issued to another company, knowing that there was a good chance the patent would be found invalid. Companies were also less inclined to go through the expense of filing applications for patents that held dubious value at best, while companies holding patents were less apt to run up legal expenses asserting their patents against others in a court that would probably rule their patents invalid.

This changed with the birth of the Federal Circuit. The new court standardized definitions of "patentability" across all regions of the U.S., and was much more likely to rule that a challenged patent was, in fact, valid. By giving patents new teeth, the Federal Circuit gave companies financial incentive to file for patents and assert them against competitors.

So what is a patent? Simply defined, a patent is a legal document containing the description of a technical solution to a technical problem. While it may describe a new method, device, or chemical compound, a patent can only be issued for a concrete solution to an actual problem.

Ideas, by themselves, are not patentable. Your neighbor could say, "It would be nice if something reduced skidding when I am using the brakes in my car," but without a specific technical solution, this is nothing more than wishful thinking.

In contrast, the concept of antilock braking—using a sensor to detect the relative rotational speeds of the brakes while braking, coupled with an actuator to reduce pressure to a brake cylinder if one wheel is rotating more slowly than the other—is a practical, applicable solution to the problem. A patent is not a technical paper nor is it organized for any kind of exposition. Instead, it is a massive transfer of information—a brain-dump, if you will—about your claims.

Because the U.S. has few hard and fast requirements for organizing a patent, every patent practitioner has an individual preferred method. That said, a typical patent consists of six major parts: title, abstract, background, descriptions (including optional short description, detailed description of figures, and detailed description), claims, and figures. The information presented in a patent constitutes what is often referred to as a "disclosure".*

Of those six, the claims are what give the patent its heart, as well as its teeth. While the descriptions explain how to make and use the invention, the claims act as a title deed, defining the actual property you own, and can prevent others from trespassing on it. Everything else, though vitally important, exists solely to give the claims context and support, either by defining the problem solved or by specifying how the problem has been solved.

At its core, the patent system is the government's way to further the progress of technology and innovation in order to benefit its citizens. By issuing a patent, the government gives the patent-holder exclusive use of the patented inventions for a period of time (a "term") in exchange for teaching anybody who might be interested how the invention actually works. In this way, everybody wins. The public gets to benefit from new technology while it is relevant, and inventors get space in the marketplace to try to monetize their inventions without worrying about having their innovations stolen by competitors. The term of a patent is between 15 and 25 years, allowing patents to be valuable long after the specific products that were envisioned when the applications for the patents were filed may have become obsolete.

A portfolio of patents with strong, flexible claims can provide its owners with a number of ongoing legal and financial advantages, including the right to exclude others from practicing the invention(s) claimed in their patent(s). Also, should a competitor willfully infringe the patent—that is, use the claimed technology knowing that it is patent-protected—the patent owners can then recover three times the damages that they would be entitled to if the infringement were inadvertent. This is a heavy penalty, and it gives competitors who need access to a patented technology for the success of their own business powerful incentive to enter into a licensing agreement with the patent's owner, which can be lucrative in its own right. This ability to stop competitors from using your technology without your express permission makes patent protection a powerful and valuable tool in today's global marketplace.

* It should be noted that the term "disclosure" encompasses more than simply the information contained within a patent or patent application. Any information presented to even a single member of the public constitutes a disclosure. This includes, but is not limited to, publications in scientific or trade journals, presentations at shows, the demonstration or sale of a product, or even the casual mention of the technology to an individual.

It is important to note that being a named inventor on a patent is not the same thing as being its owner. Many companies require that their employees give them all rights to any inventions created during their time of employment as a standard part of their hiring agreements. This means that at the time of filing a patent application, those inventors must "assign" (transfer) to their employer all rights to the invention: the employer then becomes the "assignee" or the patent's owner. In situations where there is no external assignee, however, the inventors retain rights of ownership. While inventorship of a patent/patent application remains static, the assignee of a patent or patent application can, and often does, change any number of times as the intellectual property is traded and sold.

Inventors

Even though the inventors may not be a patent's owners, they are vital to its production. Under U.S. patent law, all individual inventors must be identified on the application. Naming a non-inventor as an inventor or—even worse—failing to name an actual inventor can dramatically reduce the value of any patents that might be issued from the application.

As a result, it is vital that patent applicants understand what qualifies someone as an inventor. Many of us, when confronted with the concept of an "inventor," immediately call up visions of Dr. Frankenstein working on his creature or a character in an H.G. Wells novel tinkering with arcane gadgets that are too complicated for ordinary mortals to understand. The truth is far more mundane.

Under patent law, anyone who has contributed to the mental conception of a technical solution, or has creatively helped convert that concept into a practicality, is an inventor (people providing financial, marketing or other ancillary assistance do not count). In other words, if an individual has made an inventionable contribution to even a single claim, he must be listed as an inventor. Alternatively, someone who has explained how a technology works or who has suggested the problem that ultimately gave rise to the patentable solution but who has not contributed to a claim is not an inventor no matter how valuable his input was to the inventors.

While inventors might be members of teams of brilliant PhDs who devote themselves to creating medical technologies that save millions of lives, they might also be ordinary people, like nurse Tamra West, who used Velcro-style fasteners and foam pads to create a device that keeps patients safely in position while on the operating table [5]. Anyone can be an inventor, from professional engineers and tech gurus, to Ron Popeil, famous for his rotisserie cooker [6] and bagel slicer [7], or Hedy Lamarr,** right on down to the three-year-old who lives next door,*** as long as the basic defining requirements are met.

Inventions

Defining what constitutes an "invention" is somewhat trickier. We have already established that a patent cannot be issued for a mere idea, but we have not defined what makes a technical solution patentable.

Legally speaking, an invention is a novel and non-obvious solution to a defined problem. In order for it to fulfill the "novel" requirement, the solution in question cannot have been known prior to its disclosure in the patent application. To be "non-obvious", there can be no obvious way to connect known technologies of any area in a way that would point to that solution.

As an example, let us consider a pencil and its eraser. For a moment, imagine that rubber erasers and pencils, as separate entities, are both known but that no one has ever tried to bond the one to the other. Let us further assume that, as a separate entity, the rubber eraser is known to erase pencil marks but not those made with ink. Then, in a moment of pure inspiration, an engineer at the pencil company comes up with three proposed technical solutions:

- A product comprising, for the first time known to man, a pencil with a protruding rubber eraser affixed to its top by a metallic band.
- A method for wrapping the metallic band around a wooden pencil so that the rubber eraser can be affixed to its top in a protruding manner.
- A method of erasing pencil marks on a substrate by inverting the pencil and rubbing it vigorously against the pencil marks.

The engineer has come up with solutions that should be both marketable and revenue producing. The question is, which, if any, of these counts as an invention?

** Co-inventor of U.S. Patent No. 2,292,387 for radio techniques now used in WI-FI. See Musil, Steven. "Happy 100th birthday, Hedy Lamarr, movie star who paved way for Wi-Fi." CNET, Nov. 9, 2014. Retrieved 2014/12/18 from http://www.cnet.com/news/happy-100th-birthday-hedy-lamarr-movie-star-and-wi-fi-inventor/

*** British patent GB2438091(B) was issued Feb. 24, 2008 to Sam Houghton of Buxton, Darbyshire for an invention he made when he was three. See http://www.mirror.co.uk/news/uk-news/sam-houghton-5-is-the-youngest-patent-303180, retrieved 2014/12/06.

A patent examiner, upon seeing these solutions, would immediately discount the first two. The rubber eraser and the pencil are both known technologies; even in this new scenario, they are merely functioning in a normal way. While the concept of using of a metallic band to attach the eraser to the pencil might be new, the use of a metallic band to attach spokes to the hub of a colonial wagon wheel is already known (it is "prior art"), making the invention obvious. Moreover, the requirement that a portion of the pencil and a portion of the rubber eraser protrude from the metallic band would also be deemed obvious, as it already known that a rubber eraser must be able to make direct contact with the pencil marks on the substrate to erase them.

As a result, the first and second proposed inventions would be dismissed as "obvious," even though the concept of an eraser-bearing pencil was not formerly known and would, therefore, be considered novel. The third solution could not even be considered novel, as rubber erasers are known to function precisely in this manner. Three solutions—no inventions. Can anything be salvaged?

Now let us suppose that, in order to ensure sufficient adhesion of the rubber eraser to the pencil by the metallic band, the diameter of the rubber eraser had to be between 5% and 15% larger than that of the pencil. Moreover, let us assume that, in order to effect a bond between the rubber eraser and metallic band, the rubber eraser had to be compressed to a diameter smaller than that of the pencil while the metallic band was being wrapped around them.

The details of this method are neither known nor obvious, and by incorporating them in the inventor's second solution, the method for attaching the eraser to the pencil by compressing the rubber in this way becomes an invention in its own right. Because it compresses the materials to attach the metallic band, rather than using heat expansion as in the case of the wagon wheels, the attachment method itself is now considered to be novel and non-obvious and, therefore, a patentable invention.

Aside from the invention issue, this scenario brings up an excellent question—why would any company want to split a solution into multiple parts? It seems redundant at best. By obtaining patents on the method of making the product as well as the product itself, a company can dramatically increase its patents' value. Should a patent have been awarded for the first solution, the company would have guaranteed protection against any other entity producing, importing, selling, or otherwise profiting from an eraser-bearing pencil product, with damages accruing from the date the patent's owner first notifies the infringer. By focusing the second patent on the method of production, however, the method patent gives its owners additional fire power when targeting infringing manufacturers by allowing them to seek damages from infringers for a period of up to six years prior to them serving notice of infringement [8].

The third proposed patent, had it been awarded, would have given its owners power over the actual use of the eraser-bearing pencil, targeting the customers of the manufacturers and distributors of these devices. Method claims in this case might also allow the owner to seek damages covering a period of up to six years prior to notification of infringement. Furthermore, this patent, if granted, can undercut the business of both the manufacturer and the distributor by threatening to engulf their customers in a massive infringement suit. This puts pressure on such manufacturers and distributors to seek appropriate licenses from the owner of the patent, opening up a new source of income unrelated to the production and sale of the actual product. This, in turn, would increase the value of the patent portfolio in the marketplace.

Then, one day, the engineer who created the eraser-bearing pencil discovers that the rubber bit on the end of the implement will erase dry ink, as well as graphite. Though he does not fully understand it, he believes that this is due to the increased leverage provided by the pencil's length, so he proposes a method claim centered on this new, mechanical insight. While the company has no interest in expanding into the pen business, it is still in the company's best interests to file on this new technology.

Assuming patents were awarded for the engineer's pencil solutions, the company already has a patent on attaching the eraser to a writing implement, effectively blocking competitors from attaching erasers to pens with a metallic band. However, by filing on these applications, the company has taught its competitors its basic technology, giving them the information they need to design their products around these patents, thereby negating any protection afforded by its existing patents. By expanding its patent portfolio to include related non-pencil technologies, the company ensures its continued presence in the writing implement market and opens up the possibility for lucrative licensing agreements with complementary businesses.

Of course, this example is only hypothetical. Actual solutions and inventions can be far more complicated, which is why patent applications should always be drafted under the guidance of qualified patent practitioners.

Timing is also an important issue. Had the pencil company immediately taken its claims to a patent attorney the moment the engineer stuck an eraser on the end of the pencil, it is probable that a single patent application would have been filed that would not have resulted in a patent being issued. The only people who would have benefited would have been the pencil company's competitors, who would have used the published patent application to learn about the pencil company's product, enabling them to produce a competitive work-around without the hassle and expense of performing their own R&D.

Preparing to File

Once you have determined both the invention and its inventorship, you are ready to file a patent application. With the help of a qualified patent practitioner, you must describe both the problem you are solving and your way of solving it, as well as those novel aspects for which you are seeking exclusive rights (the claims). Each patent application is limited to a single invention; if the examiner determines that an application claims more than one invention, he will ask the inventor to select which claims should be prosecuted**** at that time. Anything else must be separated into one or more additional applications (so-called "divisionals"). Alternatively, the examiner may find that the claims do not describe an invention at all, because there is sufficient literature that allows the invention to be anticipated. At this time, while the inventor cannot modify the description, or disclosure, part of the application, he can revise the claims to take the examiner's concerns into account. If the examiner ultimately finds that the claims do describe an invention, the patent will be allowed with a period of exclusivity limited to about 20 years from the date of application.

In some instances, a company may decide not to file a patent application on a technology. This can be because the company believes that it can keep the invention confidential (a so-called "trade secret"), as is the case for the Coca-Cola syrup formulation. The risk to the company is, of course, that if someone is able to determine the content of the trade secret, the company has no legal protection. Alternatively, a company may choose not to patent an invention because it does not want, or cannot afford, to make that kind of financial investment. This can lead to situations where the company cannot practice its own invention because other companies have swooped in to patent the technology that would allow the invention to be practiced (we will discuss this in a later chapter). Very often a company does not patent its inventions because it does not plan to practice them or because it lacks

---

**** The process of obtaining a patent, referred to as "prosecution" is discussed more fully in Chapter 7.

a coherent patent strategy. This can become a very costly mistake, as discussed in the book, *Rembrandts in the Attic* [9].

Even when a company chooses to file on its inventions, it incurs risk. While patents provide important legal benefits to their owners, there is no guarantee that a patent application will result in an issued patent. That said, all patent applications are published eighteen months after their submission, whether or not a patent has been allowed. In this case, the inventor has given the public access to the invention, but has obtained no protection against its infringement.

While no strategy can guarantee that a patent will be allowed, there are steps that can be taken at every point in the application process that enhance the probability that the patent examiner will say "yes." These will be discussed throughout this book.

The Five Patent Commandments

No one will be awarded every patent for which one applies. Sometimes, the examiner finds prior art that may or may not be relevant to the proposed solution. In those cases, whether or not an applicant can circumvent that art often depends on the extent of the teachings in the disclosure. At other times, related art such as prior patents may be possessed by other companies. Even with the risks, developing a solid patent strategy and portfolio is essential for preserving the interests of your business. Recall that, as discussed in Chapter 1, while it is important to protect your company's innovations, it is also important to have patent coverage on the technology that your competitors need. Ultimately, the value of a patent does not need to correlate with the value of your company's products. With these principles in mind, we have come up with five patent commandments for your company to live by.

1. *File early and file often*
   Filing early is important because patents are granted to the first person to file an application claiming a particular technology, rather than the first to invent that technology. Simply put, if someone in your company invents something but does not file promptly, it opens the door to any other company that may have invented the same item at a later time but filed first to obtain that patent. Filing often is also simple to understand. Technology advances and patents expire or can be found, if challenged, not to be valid. A company

needs to constantly buttress its strategic intellectual property by upgrading its patent portfolio.

Consider once again the automotive O_2 sensor. The original patents that protected the fundamental device have long expired. However, manufacturers have enhanced their portfolios by filing patent applications for improvements such as internal heaters that allow the O_2 sensor to start feeding back a signal from a cold engine to an electronic control unit (ECU) more rapidly, thereby reducing noxious emissions, methods and devices for controlling fuel and air intake to improve stoichiometry, methods of integrating the signal from the O_2 sensor into the ECU, the use of multiple O_2 sensors, and the like. The importance of both this technology and the patents that cover it is evident by the large number of companies that continue to obtain patents in this area.

2. *If you cannot fix it, feature it*

   Does a problem that eludes a solution offer an advantage in some other way? Consider the earlier hypothetical example related to the rubber dry ink eraser. Suppose, for example, that a group of engineers in your company's pencil division decides that it would be more cost effective to use a heat shrinkable polymer to hold the rubber eraser to a pencil. While the polymer supplies sufficient support to the pencil to hold the eraser while exerting a shear force to erase ink and pencil marks, if someone applies a modest tensile force such as would be the case encountered when removing the pencil out of his pocket by pulling on the eraser or polymer, the polymer sleeve slips off the pencil, leaving the eraser and pencil in two separate pieces.

   Naturally, the eraser is no longer capable of erasing dry ink marks. Despite repeated attempts, the engineers in the pencil division have not been able to correct this problem. However, this creates an opportunity to obtain patent coverage and market a product, because your company now has an eraser that can erase both pencil and dry ink marks and, if it becomes worn out or otherwise damaged, it is replaceable—because it is removable. In effect, the problem that could not be fixed has been converted to a feature because it solved a technical problem, namely replaceability.

3. *If you have problems worth fixing, you have patents worth filing*
   Your company has invested a lot of money into solving problems whose solutions offer marketable products or services to your customers. Presumably, if these goods and services are profitable for your company, they would be profitable to other companies. This is even more so as those companies can benefit from your solutions to these problems if the solutions are not protected by a suitable patent portfolio. If your advancements are not worth the few thousand dollars required to obtain patent protection, why did your company invest in that technology?

4. *If you have to explain it twice to a competent peer, you have to file it*
   If an average fifth-grader could figure out your solution by looking at the prior art, that solution is likely not inventive. Conversely, if an engineer or patent practitioner cannot figure out your solution by looking at the prior art, it may well be inventive. This commandment is the primary, daily guard against inventors' tendency to underestimate their inventive potential, and plays out in several ways.
   If an inventor goes looking in a textbook or journal for a solution to a problem or a "critical challenge" and does not find that solution, file on it. If the inventor does not know, and with his knowledge of the field cannot find, that someone else has solved the problem, chances are good that the inventor is the first to solve that particular problem. That is a good clue that a patent application on the solution should be filed and that a patent has a good chance of being issued. Do not let your inventors think that they are not inventing just because solving new problems is their job.
   If an inventor has to explain the solution to a competent peer twice, and the peer agrees it is a good solution once he understands it, file the application. A competent peer in terms of this commandment is someone with comparable skills, education, and experience to that of the inventor.
   However, the peer is not someone who has been working on the specific problem or even in the specific technological area. For example, an engineer working for 10 years on automotive transmissions would be a peer of the engineer who

has been working for 10 years in the automotive industry on the problem of emission control.

There is often a question of whether or not the solution to a problem is obvious or not, as obviousness precludes patentability. If a solution has to be explained twice to another individual who has comparable skills to those of the inventor in order for that individual to understand the solution to the problem, as opposed to simply presenting it a fait accompli, it is probably not obvious. Basically, that individual did not understand the solution the first time it was explained, so the solution is not obvious. In this situation, the competent peer is standing in as a proxy for the fifth-grader, and is someone more knowledgeable and discerning. Give your inventors time to discuss their ideas with peers outside their immediate specialty, and encourage them to listen to the responses. A "great idea!" is not just a compliment, but it also can indicate a potential patentability opportunity.

5. *If you have to explain it to a patent practitioner once, file it*
   If a competent inventor thinks it is worth telling a patent practitioner about his solution to a problem, it is probably worth considering filing an application (This does not include the inventors who submit invention reports to try to bulk up their resumes). Our experience is that many serious, experienced engineers do not usually think about patents. This will gradually change as you use the strategies described herein. However, especially as you begin to roll out the strategy, if your inventors actually notice that an idea might be worth considering for patenting, take them at their word. Chances are they are right. Plus, accepting the idea and giving it full consideration will encourage that inventor to bring more ideas in the future. If the inventor believes it is worth explaining the solution to the problem to a patent practitioner, and the practitioner does not think the solution is immediately apparent upon presentation, that solution has a good chance of being patentable.

Throughout this book, we will show you how to build these five commandments into a valuable patent strategy.

It is again emphasized that this book does not pretend to be a text on patenting one's own invention. Patents are legal documents and writing patents is a job for a qualified and registered patent practitioner. What we can and will do, however, is help you imbue the five patent commandments into your existing workflow, thereby building an innovative company culture that results in the creation of a strong, enforceable patent portfolio. More than ever, building such a portfolio will keep your company competitive in an ever-more regulated world—a world where consumers are more cognizant and demanding and where access to information by those consumers is more readily accessible.

We will show you how to streamline your application process and give your inventors the resources they need to prepare for each patent application, helping you generate a strong portfolio without bankrupting your company. We will give you tools to help you decide when, and where, to file your patent applications, and how to work through some of the challenges that you will encounter. Finally, we will help you determine your cast of players, including providing insight into developing your patenting team.

By coupling a flexible patent strategy with a good patenting team, your company will have a significantly better chance of monetizing the value of its intellectual property. Not only will a strategic portfolio give you grounds for suing those trespassing on your property, it can help prevent others from suing you. Even when product sales are down, selling and/or licensing patents can greatly enhance the revenue of your company, driving up both stock prices and market share. Patents are great tools, but to succeed, you need to own more than a good solution. You need to own the entire problem.

References

1. James Burke, *Connections*, Little, Brown and Company, Boston (1978).
2. James Burke, *The Day the Universe Changed*, Little, Brown and Company, Boston (1985).
3. https://en.wikipedia.org/wiki/TRS-80, retrieved 2015/01/02
4. https://en.wikipedia.org/wiki/Atari_2600, retrieved 2015/01/02
5. Will Astor, "Device created by nurse ready to hit market," *Rochester Business Journal.* 5/4/2012 http://www.rbj.net/print_article.asp?aID=191227. Viewed 11/11/2014
6. A. L. Backus and R. M. Popeil, U. S. Patent #7,424,849 (2008).
7. A. Backus and R. Popeil, U. S. Patent #4,807,862 (1989).
8. http://patentlyo.com/patent/2010/03/the-marking-requirement-here-is-how-the-statute-has-been-interpreted.html, retrieved 2015/01/02
9. Kevin G. Rivette and David Kline, *Rembrants in the Attic*, Harvard Business School Press, Boston (2000).

3

Developing a Patent Strategy and Patent Engineering

Most companies today, from small start-ups to major corporations, realize that there is real money in intellectual property. High profile cases such as Apple's suits against Samsung and Google have made it very obvious that there can be just as much profit, if not more, in enforcing patents as in making the product. Because of this, there has been great emphasis on applying for and obtaining patents, with companies scrambling to increase their holdings.

This surge in patent popularity has made it very clear which companies understand the real value of their intellectual property and which ones do not. Adding confusion to the mix is the reality that all of us are competing on a global level; the moment you introduce a great product, competition will spring up throughout the world, often in countries with substantially lower taxes, labor costs, and less government regulation than the United States.

A single U.S. patent will not protect you if a company in Korea decides to copy your technology and sell the resulting product throughout China and India. For many business owners, deciding which patents to pursue and which to leave on the shelf seems harder than inventing the technology in the first place. Your business only has so much capital—how do you go about formulating and executing a patent strategy that will yield a high value portfolio without bankrupting your company? Let us first discuss five patent strategies that, although all too frequently used, generally result in weak portfolios and simply burden your company with unnecessary expenses.

Five Patent Strategies

A single patent is analogous to a rock tossed into a stream. The water in the stream may be diverted around the rock. In some instances the water may even flow over the rock instead of being diverted. If the flow of water is to be stopped or controlled, it is necessary to use many rocks to build a dam. A single rock, no matter how large, will not stop the stream from flowing. It is the same situation with patents.

A single patent may force competitors to seek other ways around your technology, but it will not stop them from introducing competitive technology. In some instances, they may even patent important enabling technology* that prevents your company from practicing your invention, forcing your company to grant patent rights and even pay licensing fees much the way that the water can flow over the individual rock, rather than being diverted around it.

The only way to prevent this from occurring is to develop a sufficiently strong patent portfolio that allows you to own the entire problem, rather than simply a specific solution to a problem.

Absent that ability, your company needs to own enough of the problem so that your competitors must negotiate favorable patent exchange agreements with you if they are to participate in this market. This is akin to the patent portfolios that were previously discussed with respect to the O_2 sensor. In that instance, no individual company owns the entire problem, but, rather, companies own enough of the problem to allow them to produce automobiles. Those that do not are forced to buy sensors from companies such as Bosch, paying the price that Bosch wishes to charge. They may also have to buy the other components and software related to

* Enabling technology differs from the fundamental technology that encompasses a product. Rather, enabling technologies comprise the solutions to the problems that would pose obstacles towards the ability to practice or commercialize the fundamental invention.

interfacing the O_2 sensors with the computers that allow cars to perform acceptably.

Developing a patent strategy that works for you and your company is a vital part of your company's health, both now and in the future. Patent strategies give definition to a company's technological priorities and, as a result, will define the innovative culture at your company at every level.

Most product-producing businesses, regardless of size, utilize one of five strategic methods for generating patent portfolios: solution-specific filing, patent landscaping, spaghetti filing, mish mosh filing, and everyone's favorite, the ostrich approach. Though their core philosophies vary, all five of these strategies have one thing in common: they do not work very well.

Before discussing the five patent strategies frequently utilized by businesses, let us briefly consider how generating a patent strategy can be implemented. Let us start by assuming a team of engineers is in the process of designing a new product. The product may simply have evolved from those already sold by your company, or it might differ greatly and be very novel. In either event, the process is similar.

In addition to your team of engineers, it would be valuable to also have a patent engineer. A patent engineer, discussed in more detail later in this book, is an individual who has a good knowledge of both the technology involved in the product development and a working knowledge of patent law. The patent engineer may or may not be a member of the specific project team. It is important that the patent engineer know the competitors' technologies.

The strategizing process begins with the patent engineer having the project team list the desired attributes of the product and the perceived methods of obtaining those attributes. The team will then discuss interactions between the various systems and subsystems that are necessary components of the perceived product. These typically constitute the problems on which the engineers are working and give rise to a number of problem-solution patent applications. This forms the basis of the patent strategy, but does not constitute the complete strategy by itself.

The key element at this step is to get as much of the product design as possible, including the problems encountered and their solutions, onto the table, recognizing that not everything is known at this time.

This is the point at which the team decides whether or not the individual subsystems are patentable. If the subsystem is sufficiently novel, it may be patentable. If it has evolved from previously-built subsystems, the modifications may be patentable. Next, the problems encountered between subsystems (e.g. systems interactions) and their solutions are discussed. Again, this can give rise to many valuable patent applications.

Generally, in designing a product, assumptions are made that steer the technology along one course as opposed to another. These assumptions should be challenged. In the case of the automobile, at one time it was assumed that a carburetor was needed to meter and aerosolize fuel. Fuel injection was impractical because computers were large, expensive, and relatively slow.

However, as discussed earlier, the availability of modern microelectronics has caused a shift from the original assumption that fuel injection is impractical to the assumption that such technology is eminently practical. Remember, patents can have lives of up to 20 years. Also, assumptions that are reasonable for a given product line may not apply to other products.

On one occasion, engineers working on an electrophotographic fuser described to the author a technology that they said would be able to work well at toner-fusing temperatures. When asked what limited the operation of the fuser to those temperatures (the author was thinking in terms of functional printing rather than printing words), the inventors replied that paper would be degraded at higher temperatures. The author of this book responded "who said anything about paper?" The invention could be very valuable at the higher temperatures needed for functional printing. This was outside of the assumption made by the engineers, i.e. that the device was only for fusing toner to paper.

The next question that should be addressed is what your competition is doing and what technology would they need to fix their present problems or improve their products. If the engineering team has solutions that would be needed by your competition, these should also be incorporated into your patent strategy. Such patents can be extremely valuable, again reminding the reader that patents should be considered as a valuable part of your company's product line rather than just an expense.

It is now important to decide when and which patent applications to file. It is likely that many of the resulting disclosures should be filed concurrently, so as to preclude them from becoming prior art with respect to subsequent filings. There may be additional timing constraints, such as upcoming trade shows in which the product will be demonstrated. Specific information regarding what should be disclosed in patent applications will be discussed in a later chapter. Suffice-it to say here that random filings of individual patent applications may adversely affect your ability to generate a valuable patent portfolio.

Let us now return to the discussion of the five strategies or methods businesses often use to generate patent portfolios. These methods, however, often result in great expense and yield little of value.

Of the five strategies being discussed herein, the most common approach, **Solution-Specific Filing**, relies on a business filing patent applications for the specific technical solutions they have developed for their specific products. This approach is profitable when there is only one possible way of solving your problem—which rarely occurs. You may have patented the chalk and the chalkboard, but as soon as someone invents the dry erase marker, the usefulness and profitability of your patent disappears. While it may be structured, this approach does little to optimize your patent investment and can undermine your company's innovative output by encouraging your Research & Development (R&D) employees to restrict their imagination to the specific product solutions in which your company has invested. This limits the power of your portfolio, making it useful only in cases of direct product infringement.

Patent Landscaping takes place when businesses try to file a lot of patent applications in technology areas that have little patent activity. These patent areas are often referred to as "white spaces" because they are nearly empty of patents. Companies choose this method with the hope of getting "in on the ground floor," patenting technologies that they hope will eventually become profitable. The advantages to this approach are clear—by operating in a less developed technology field, companies can save turnaround time on their patent applications, and keep related legal fees to a minimum. This approach is amazingly effective if you are able to foretell the future. Otherwise, you just end up placing an expensive bet, gambling a lot of money procuring patents that may or may not be of any value.

In cases where the technology is very novel and valuable, patent landscaping can be an excellent strategy. However, due caution needs to be observed. The classic case, perhaps, is that of Chester Carlson, who invented and patented dry electrophotography. This was clearly novel, as competing technology included the wet and messy Verifax process, typewriters and carbon paper, and mimeograph machines. Despite its novelty that ultimately gave rise to both the office copier and laser printer, Carlson had difficulty selling the rights to his invention.** The word of caution when deciding whether or not to do patent landscaping is that hubris can lead to a downfall.

** Carlson tried selling his invention to and was rejected by a number of companies, including IBM and Eastman Kodak. He finally convinced Joseph Wilson, the CEO of a failing photofinishing company known as Haloid to risk entering this business. Wilson subsequently changed the name to a company that, translated from Greek, means "dry writing" -Xerox.

The third approach, **Spaghetti Filing**, is one that is often used by smaller, more inexperienced companies, as well as larger businesses where R&D is kept separate from consumer product development. Under this strategy, business owners file patent applications on whatever technological developments their researchers and engineers come up with, regardless of its relevance to either their market or their business plan. They are assisted in this process by their very dedicated and capable technical staff, which, taking the pride of ownership in their advancements, seek the natural recognition obtained by being named as inventors on a patent.

An additional problem often encountered with spaghetti filing occurs during prosecution of the patent applications and will be discussed in more detail in Chapter 7. The problem is that, with the plethora of intertwined by often unrelated patent applications, contradictory or limiting statements can be made either in the application itself or in correspondence with the examiner during prosecution of the applications. These statements become public record, and can be used by the examiner to deny a patent or by a court at a later date, when your company attempts to assert its patent, which rules that the patent or patent being asserted does not mean what you state in court that it means, or worse, that the patent is invalid. In fact, members of your own technical staff may be compelled to take the witness stand to explain how some other patent precludes the validity of the patent being asserted. The result can be embarrassing and annoying, let alone costly.

While this strategy can produce a massive patent portfolio, it is also very expensive, with a high likelihood that any patents (and/or products) produced will not be valuable to either the company or its competitors.

Related to spaghetti filing is **Mish Mosh Filing**, which is sometimes practiced by companies that feel a need to expand their patent portfolio as quickly as possible—usually in response to concerns about the portfolios of their competitors. These companies, desperate to expand their holdings, resort to soliciting any and all inventions from their R&D people, then filing on whatever they get, regardless of its relevance or quality, including inventions that have been sitting at the bottom of a barrel for a very, very long time.

Much like the spaghetti approach, mish mosh filing produces large, expensive portfolios with little to no practical value and, in general, of minimal focus on any particular problem. This approach is particularly destructive, as the companies most likely to use it are those whose cash flow is threatened in some way. In some aspects, mish mosh filing can be considered to combine the worst aspects of both landscaping and solution-specific strategies by disclosing much information without a business oriented objective in mind.

Finally, we come to the **Ostrich Approach**. This method, though relatively uncommon, is often employed by independent inventors who are not familiar with the patent system and who may be leery of expending capital on legal services without a guarantee of return. It is also followed by both small and larger companies that only view applying for and maintaining patents as unnecessary expenses, to be minimized or eliminated.

The classic example of this is the narrow range of patents held by Eastman Kodak in the area of instant photography. Specifically, Kodak had obtained patents to protect its own instant photography chemistry. This chemistry was different from that used by Polaroid in its product offerings. However, Kodak did not seek patents in the more mundane enabling technologies or for technology that was needed by Polaroid even though Kodak was manufacturing the film packets for Polaroid and, presumably, had the insight and opportunity to develop the technology that could lead to such patents.

When Kodak decided to enter the instant photography business and market its own products, Polaroid sued and was ultimately awarded approximately $900,000,000 in damages and forced Kodak to terminate its business. Had Kodak owned any patents that Polaroid needed, a different result may have occurred.

Adherents to the ostrich approach generally function by ignoring patents entirely. They do not file any patent applications on their technologies, regardless of their perceived value. Many are unaware of their competitors, and those that are aware often assume that their bigger, better-equipped competitors will never notice them. This approach leaves the inventor and/or business owner vulnerable to even the smallest attacks; this is a case whereby a competitor can use a single patent to destroy an entire product line and, potentially, bankrupt a company. The ostrich approach leaves entrepreneurs vulnerable to predators who may steal their technology and use it to their own advantage without compensating the inventor in any way.

There is a better way.

A New Strategy: Problem-Specific Filing or "Owning the Problem"

Imagine that you live in a primitive world where getting the basic necessities—food, shelter, clothing—requires hard labor and constant effort. At the end of every day you come back to your shelter, your muscles worn from the hunt, your fingers raw from gathering, and you look around for a place to rest. Your bed roll is over in the corner, but you are not ready to lie down and rest. All you want to do is sit... but on what can you sit? Out in the forest you would sit on a fallen tree; here, there is nothing but the muddy ground.

One day, you decide to go out into the woods and get yourself a tree. Because your hut is small, you only take a piece of that tree. You bring it home and you are happy, because now you have a clean, dry place to rest your feet. Your friend comes by and asks you to make one for him. In turn, he shows the blacksmith, who wants one for his forge. Soon, you have a thriving little business sawing off chunks of tree stump and selling them to your neighbors as seats. Still, you know that it is only a matter of time before someone else goes and cuts one's own tree stumps, thus muscling in on your good thing. So you have your best idea yet—you decide to go the village elder and tell him that you will give him some of your profits if he tells everyone else that you are the only person in the village who can make seats out of logs. Then you go home, happy in the knowledge that your great idea, and the business that goes with it, is protected.

Imagine your surprise when you go outside one day to find the blacksmith showing off a stool that he put together out of scrap metal. Soon, all the people who had wanted your logs are over at the smithy buying metal stools because, unlike your logs, these stools are easier to move and do not rot when it's wet outside. You go to the village elder, but he tells you there's nothing he can do. You laid claim to seats made out of logs, but the blacksmith's seats are made of metal and are, therefore, not covered under your agreement. Overcome by the competition, your business crumbles, and soon you've nothing left but a pile of old logs.

When it comes to intellectual property, most business owners and/or inventors think the best way to protect themselves is to stake exclusive legal claim to the specific technical solutions that characterize their products (solution-specific filing). The truth is more complex. The value of a patent relies on many factors outside of your control and it is difficult, if not impossible, to forecast which patents will be valuable to your competitors in the future. In short, a patent is valuable if and only if someone else needs to practice the specific technology claimed in the patent. Even then, the value of the patent is a function of its value to the other company if the products it intends to produce require the use of your claimed intellectual property.

Even if a patent is valuable, you have no guarantee that your competitors won't just "work around it." In other words, the value can be quite transient. You may own the patent on log chairs, but if your neighbor does not feel like paying you, he will just find something else to sit on. In this way, owning a single patent is a little bit like leaving a rock in the road—it just gives people an excuse to drive around it.

Companies that choose to follow a solution-specific patent strategy often make the erroneous assumption that they need to obtain a patent on their solution to their problem so that they can practice their technology. Nothing could be further from the truth. A patent gives the owner or assignee of that patent the right to exclude others from practicing the invention. It does not convey the right to the owner to practice the technology.

Let us illustrate the issue, once more, with the example of the chair. Let us assume that the inventor of the log chair consulted with a good attorney prior to filing his patent application. The attorney looked at what the inventor submitted and wrote a claim that specified, rather than a log, a more generic "raised platform suitable for sitting without unduly rocking". The only further description was for such a platform to be made of wood. The attorney also asked whether or not the esthetics of the chair could be improved by applying a finishing coat such as paint or varnish. Having been answered in the affirmative, the patent application includes disclosure and claims, including a claim that does not reference the material from which the chair was made, that discuss applying a finishing coat of paint or varnish to the chair. We will not presently address the question of whether or not the attorney is now an inventor on the patent application. That will be discussed later in this book.

Enter once more the blacksmith. He sees that the wood would rot or become bug infested if left outdoors and he files a patent application on a solution to the problem of how to make a chair that would be suitable for outdoor use. Specifically, he applies for a patent on an iron chair that could be left in the outside environment without decaying. Moreover, if the iron chair were suitably painted, it would not rust.

What is the crux of the blacksmith's patent application? First, as he has solved a problem in a novel fashion, i.e. making a decay resistant chair for outdoor use out of iron, he can obtain a patent on that technology. However, he cannot obtain a patent on painting the chair, nor could he sell painted chairs.

Simply stated, the inventor of the wooden chair disclosed painting the chair. That it was painted for esthetics, rather than rust prevention, is irrelevant. The blacksmith can neither paint his iron chairs nor sell them, if painted, even though he wanted to paint them for a totally different reason (preservation) than that given in the original patent (esthetics). Producing his iron chair, even though patented, would, if painted, infringe upon the first patent. Similarly, he could not even patent painting his chair as the first inventor has full rights to his invention, even if he did not realize all the benefits. In effect, pursuing solution-specific patent applications allowed each inventor to obtain a patent, but did not preclude competition. Moreover, in as much as the iron chair needed to be painted in order to prevent it from rusting, the blacksmith would not have been able to practice his invention without addressing the rust problem in another manner such as applying a more costly and less esthetically pleasing finish such as galvanizing the iron.

Enter a new strategy. **Problem-Specific Filing**, or "Owning the Problem," as we like to call it, as opposed to solution-specific applications, is a patent strategy designed to prioritize filings based on the technical problems that must be solved for your market rather than on the specific solutions your company uses. It forces your inventors to think outside of the company box and look for the places where your technologies intersect with your competitors'. Under problem-specific filing, strategic patents are used to build a powerful defense system that will better protect your business's interests. In other words, "owning the problem" instead of or in addition to owning a specific solution to a problem, takes that one rock in the road and builds it into a wall that oncoming traffic cannot avoid.

This may seem like a complicated concept, but by changing the thinking within your company from solution-specific to problem-specific, you free the minds of your R&D people, allowing them to intuit your competitors' needs and invent technologies for which those other companies will be forced to pay you.

Consider our story. You might have stopped your competitors from making seats out of logs, but they can still make seats because all you have done is claim the wood. Now, imagine how the situation would change if the focus of the original agreement with the elder were slightly different. In exchange for some of the profits, the elder gives you exclusive rights to the making and selling of any raised surface intended for sitting. Then, just in case someone decides to get clever with a swing, you make a second agreement barring anyone else from making or selling any platform held in a horizontal position to the ground.

By looking beyond the details of the solution (the materials from which the seat was made) and claiming the basic technology necessary to all solutions (a horizontal surface upon which to sit), you have given teeth to your agreement with the elder. This time, when you go out and find the blacksmith selling his stools, you have the means to stop him. Who cares if the stool is made from metal or that it is an improvement on your (admittedly) more primitive chair design? It is not possible to make a seat to sit on without including a horizontal surface—by claiming this basic technology, you can effectively block any chair innovation that could ever be made in your village, thus cornering the market. You go to the elder and he, bound by the terms of his own agreement, shuffles over to the smithy and shuts it down. You win, the blacksmith loses, and your chair business explodes.

The difference between the two endings to our story lies in the focus of the agreement. The first focused only on the details of the inventor's solution—the log—while the second, more broad, agreement left room to consider, and, therefore, block, the ways others might solve the same problem under different circumstances. The best way to achieve this kind of broad thinking is by delving into the underlying principles of your problem, as well as its practical manifestations. Even if there are a hundred ways to solve a given problem, chances are good that the solutions share at least some underlying technical characteristics. By building claim coverage around those underlying characteristics, you are more likely to cultivate a patent portfolio that can block competitors from using any implementation of those characteristics—even ones you may not have considered.

A good example of this is the problem of cleaning the air around power plants. While every power plant has a different fuel mix, as well as different environmental concerns, there are only a limited number of ways pollutants in the air can physically interact with the objects that will trap them. You could focus your patents on your particular filter composition, but your competitors will simply pick different materials. However, if you have patent claims that cover those physical interactions (such as absorption, adsorption, and van der Waal's interactions), it will be difficult for your competitors to create a product that does not infringe on something you have claimed, making those patents valuable to both them and you.

By focusing your claims on the relationship between components, rather than the components themselves, your patents will have broader applications that are more likely to cover the technology necessary to your competitors' products. Whether you run a small business or a big corporation, it is very likely that you have patentable subject matter hidden in the connections between your inventions' elements, in addition to the inventions themselves.

Recognizing those connections and securing patent claims to that subject matter is one of the primary ways you can take control of your market, and own the problem. Owning the problem leaves your competitors few, if any, options to design around your claims. Also, any options that remain open to them are more likely to force them into products that are less functional, less convenient, and more expensive. In this way, owning the problem doesn't just protect your interests—it promotes them.

When you own the problem, your patent claims describe the key solution options around critical problems. You have thought ahead of your competitors and secured those claims and the corresponding product features before the competition even fully understands that it has that critical problem. There is always a chance a competitor will devise a radically different approach you did not foresee, but by making use of the skills and knowledge your people already have, you can greatly reduce the probability of such surprises.

Owning the problem is not a one-time activity; rather, it is an ongoing process where you continue to explore the problem you've identified, seeking patent coverage on any product or service, or any improvement of an existing product or service that might be relevant. Some organizations apply for product-related patents only after the product is fully developed and all the solutions are known. Owning the problem means that, rather than waiting until the end, you claim solution options throughout development, increasing both your creative output and the likelihood that you will be first to file.

Guiding Your Technical Team: The Patent Engineer

As beneficial as the concept is, "owning the problem" stands in stark contrast to almost everything most companies "know" about intellectual property. Because of this, it can seem like the concept of owning the problem might be difficult to incorporate into your company's current culture. This is where patent engineering comes in. Most people think of engineers as solving complicated technical problems, and indeed they do.

The products resulting from good engineering can be of immense value to a company or even to the world. Like his industrial counterparts, a patent engineer also tackles complicated technical problems; however, instead of focusing on developing products or technologies, the patent engineer works to optimize the patent application process. By bringing design engineering and patent engineering together, your company is more likely to identify, and creatively solve, the problems encountered by your customers in ways that are not limited by the specific details or applications of your current product line.

The first step in patent engineering, as in any kind of engineering, is to plan for the outcome you want. Choose your patent strategy carefully as your choice of strategy will define your company's ability to innovate and progress. Then, make sure all your players are on the same page. Few things impede a good patent strategy like the disconnection between the way inventors and attorneys define the concept of "invention." Many times an engineer who invents certain technology does not understand what the legally-defined invention actually is. Adding to the confusion is the reality that while the patent attorney who is working with the engineer knows patent law, he may not have a good working knowledge of the invention's technological area and, therefore, may not be able to guide the inventor towards developing solid patent protection around the inventor's technology. Make sure your engineers are educated about the role of your patent practitioners, and vice versa, and give them communication tools that will help everyone work together in harmony.

It is important to note that every player on your patenting team needs to understand your company's patent strategy, as well as the way in which they fit into the bigger picture. If an engineer is working on a few specific problems within a project, he may not have a holistic overview and may not understand how various technical components would have to fit together to form a patent strategy. All too often, premature disclosures are made when patent applications for solutions being worked on by one team of engineers reveal information that prevents or impedes the filing of other important patent applications from another team.

This problem can become even more complicated when a company has multiple projects that may transcend various technologies. For example, a company that produces both ink jet and laser jet printers may have different teams of engineers working in each area. While the methods of putting ink on paper differ for these processes, there can be overlap in the algorithms and methods related to writing the pixels from which the alpha-numeric characters and the halftone dots used to form pictures are produced.

Because color correction algorithms and methods, e.g. edge control, registration of colors comprising the separations from which a full color print is produced, noise corrections, and other examples transcend the technologies, separate teams which have limited interactions with each other are likely to be working on the same technologies at the same time.

Another example is paper handing; it bridges both ink jet and electrophotographic printers and may also have value in other industries such as in lithography. In fact, paper handling can transcend many industries totally unrelated to printing, such as the manufacturing of sand paper, for example. It is important to think beyond the specific products being produced by your company when formulating a patent strategy.

Helping your players understand how they fit into your company picture also helps them understand how their work affects the greater marketplace.

While your designers are in their labs and workshops ironing out the kinks, your competition is working at a feverish pace to come up with products that will directly compete with yours. They are in the same market trying to solve the same problems, and so it is likely that they are encountering and solving the same challenges that you are facing even if they are using different techniques. For example, whereas one company uses a laser scanner to write its electrostatic latent images in its high volume electrophotographic presses, another company uses an LED array. Despite the difference in these methods, however, both companies need to use imaging algorithms to drive their respective writing subsystems. When your players realize that they need to look for common problems faced by everyone working in your marketplace, and find solutions for those, they are more likely to come up with profitable innovations in the areas where there is overlap in both the problems your greater market has encountered and the solutions it has developed.

A Brief Look at Applications, Prosecution, and Claims

Several factors need to be considered when advancing proposed patent applications to the actual filing stage. Upon filing, the patent office assigns the application to an examiner in an appropriate department for that particular technology. The patent application now goes through a process referred to as "prosecution". Prosecution of a patent application will be discussed in more detail in Chapter 7. However, it is necessary to discuss a few details here.

Doing an appropriate literature or patent search is crucial at this juncture of the process in order to state the problem and how the invention solved that problem. This is not to say that the examiner may not find or combine other art in such a manner that results in claims, which are the legal description of the invention, having to be rewritten.

Discussions with the examiner may have to occur. However, without a proper and reasonably thorough initial search that guides the discussion presented in the application, the probability of obtaining suitable patent coverage is significantly reduced.

It should also be noted that well-conducted searches can help you define just how broadly you might be able to claim your invention. For example, a patent that your company, which produces ink jet equipment, may have discloses a novel method of stacking the printed paper that one of your engineers discovered, thereby facilitating drying. Searching shows that this invention is not described anywhere in the literature.

Perhaps it might also be of value for companies that have to dry slurries of abrasive particles applied to fibrous supports when making sandpaper. Money coming into your inkjet company as a royalty from a sandpaper manufacturing company is just as good as money coming into your company from a consumer who buys your printer.

Returning to the pencil example from Chapter 2, the more narrow the proposed invention, as disclosed in the patent application, the easier prosecution generally will be and the higher the probability of obtaining a patent. In essence, if the invention is claimed to be limited to a pencil bearing a rubber pencil mark eraser that can now erase ink, the examiner will be limited in his searching and arguments to such pencils.

Alternatively, if the claim is expanded to include shafts to which a rubber eraser is affixed, the examiner can search for shafts. In addition, if the examiner finds a shaft to which a rubber member is attached, he may reject the patent application even if the rubber member is used for totally unrelated purposes, such as for a rubber bushing, and argue, absent disclosure in the application to the contrary, that the ability to erase dry ink marks is inherent to the rubber being mounted on the shaft.

In addition, the definition of the invention will determine to which department in the USPTO the application is sent. This, too, can affect the probability of obtaining a patent. Patent attorneys may also steer inventors to define their invention narrowly as 1) this results in a higher probability of a successful prosecution and 2) the attorney rarely has the technical expertise to fully understand and help define the proposed invention. It is really up to the technical team to understand and present all aspects of the proposed invention to the attorney so that the attorney is in the best position to do what he has been trained to do—offer legal advice.

Unfortunately, defining an invention too narrowly has a significant downside. The patent obtained may not offer the protection desired. All too often, this is discovered long after the patent has been issued and when a competitive company produces a comparable product to the one that your company is selling. At that time, you approach your attorney and ask what can be done about this and, upon detailed and painstaking analysis, you find that your competitor has worked around your claims and is not infringing. You have spent a great deal of money obtaining a patent only to discover that you still have competition in the very area in which you thought you had exclusive rights to practice.

It should also be recognized that patent law precludes being able to file on a single invention more than once. If one files on a rubber eraser attached to a shaft and that application is rejected, the inventor will have difficulties filing on the more narrow invention of the rubber eraser attached to a pencil, as the term shaft can be construed to include a pencil. Thus, your own application has disclosed the invention and is now prior art.

So how does one handle the conflicting issues of trying to get sufficiently broad coverage to protect the invention, yet not wind up in a situation where no patent is ultimately issued? The answer is to break down the technological advance into a series of smaller inventions and file on all of them. Using our example, separate patent applications are filed on the invention of attaching the eraser to a pencil, to a pen, to a stylus, and to a shaft that is not a pencil, pen, or stylus.

The legal costs associated with a problem-specific strategy would be relatively modest because the disclosures contained within the applications would be almost identical and the differences in the claims, although very significant, would be modest. Separate filing fees would, of course, be required, as would any fees associated with the prosecution of the cases, including appropriate legal fees. A key element in pursuing this strategy, however, is that the patent applications should all be filed on the same day so that none constitutes prior art against the others.

This strategy protects the core invention, which is the eraser atop the pencil. However, it should be understood that, in order for a company to infringe upon a patent, it must be practicing every aspect of a claim in that patent. Simply stated, a company doing 90% of the teachings in a claim, but not the other 10%, does not constitute infringement. This will be discussed in a later chapter, which covers clearances.

Given the fact that a company needs to be practicing every aspect of a claim in order to be considered to be infringing, let us now examine whether or not the proposed patents would actually afford the desired protection against a competitor being able to introduce a comparable product. Consider the verbiage describing the proposed invention of the eraser atop the pencil. Specifically, the proposed invention contains the wording "rubber pencil eraser affixed to the top of the pencil by a metallic band that is wrapped around the pencil and the rubber pencil eraser." To more easily comprehend the following discussion, it is worthwhile to momentarily digress into a discussion about the two types of claims—independent and dependent.

Basically, there are two types of claims in patents. The independent claims—of which there are typically between one and three—state the fundamental invention. There are also dependent claims. The dependent claims represent various refinements of the fundamental invention and can include preferred modes of actually implementing the invention. Dependent claims relate back to either other dependent claims or to an independent claim. We have already established that for an independent claim of a patent to be infringed, the infringer must be practicing every aspect of that claim. For a dependent claim to be infringed, the infringer must be practicing every aspect of the dependent claim as well as every aspect of any claim on which the dependent claim depends.

With this understanding, let us examine the first invention, as written, assuming that what is presented is the independent claim. The invention is the discovery that, once mounted to the top of a shaft such as a pencil, the eraser that previously was only able to erase pencil marks could now erase dry ink marks. You know that restricting the claim to a pencil could seriously limit the extent to which an issued patent can be asserted against competitors marketing similar products, so you have taken that into account in the formulation of a patent strategy. At least as crucial is that the claim requires the use of a metallic band. Any nonmetallic band, such as a plastic band, would totally circumvent the patent, allowing your competitors an easy workaround that does not infringe on your property. Even if a metallic band is used, if it only partially encompasses the rubber eraser, your competitors would not be practicing 100% of your claims and so would still not be infringing on your patent. Rather than limit the primary independent claim, it would be better to move the metallic band to a dependent claim, also filing other dependent claims that address alternative devices for attaching the rubber eraser. Better yet, you could file the attachment techniques and devices as separate patents covering enabling technology.

In order to have an encompassing patent strategy, one should also file applications that cover alternatives that would accomplish the same goal. Questions such as how else one can obtain comparable results or products should be asked. In the present example, could a generic elastomer serve as a dry ink eraser instead of rubber? Could another device be used to attach the rubber eraser? What ideas were left on the cutting room floor when the product design was determined? Perhaps one such idea was for a retractable or replaceable eraser. Such ideas are often dismissed because they do not fit into the product under consideration, but would be quite valuable for different products such as a mechanical pencil or a pen. Again, the goal of a patent strategy should be to own the problem rather than just a particular solution to the problem. Even if your company has no intention of producing mechanical pencils, licensing fees and cross license agreements with other companies that do produce such products can be quite lucrative.

It is very important to consider what would change if the assumptions used in the product design were different. Consider automotive technology. For many years, the sparks and spark timing in internal combustion engines were controlled by a rotating mechanical device known as a distributor. This device contained a switch that was opened and closed by a rotating cam within the distributor.

The switch was commonly referred to as a set of points. The electromagnetic pulse from the opening of the points was fed into an ignition coil that increased the voltage and allowed a spark to be generated across the spark gap of a spark plug in the appropriate cylinder of an internal combustion engine. A distributor was a precise mechanical device that worked well, generally for the life of the automobile in which it was used, as it was effectively able to time the occurrence and the duration of the spark.

Both the timing and duration of the spark are important in an engine typically rotating at speeds up to several thousand RPM. The distributor had an additional advantage of being able to adjust the timing of the occurrence of the spark with varying engine speeds through the use a vacuum advance mechanism and centrifugal weights.

However, once computer technology became compact and inexpensive, the distributor became obsolete. The prevailing assumption that computer technology was not suitable for automobiles changed and, with that change, the method of timing the spark changed. No longer was the expensive mechanical distributor needed when a computer could control the spark.

The key point here is that implementing a solution-specific filing strategy based on assumptions that led to a specific solution to a problem does not allow for the effects that occur when the original assumptions are no longer valid. Patents have lives of up to 20 years. Assumptions change with changing technologies and markets. Keuffel and Esser never dreamed that its profitable slide rule and graph paper businesses would die because of the advent of calculators and desk top computers. This means that one should strive to get the broadest coverage possible if one is to have valuable patent coverage in the future. This generally means that claims—especially independent claims—should be written with as few constraints as possible.

With this discussion, it is important to recognize that no idea should be left behind. Examine each idea outside the proverbial box to determine if implementation is feasible and, if so, under what circumstances. Would your competition accept one of those ideas to introduce their competitive product if they could not practice your patented technology? Would such a product undercut your market? Could there be other applications for products produced using one of the dropped ideas? If technology changes the basic, underlying facts that determined your design, would you have altered your design? Are other designs more amenable to improvements? If any of these are true, your company should consider filing on them. Again, filing applications using similar disclosures on the same day can reduce legal expenses and give you more effective coverage and protection.

In formulating a patent strategy for your company, you should consider the shortcomings and limitations of your competitors' products. Often, your engineers will have examined or used products similar to those that you market or intend to market, but that are produced by your competition. Frequently, shortcomings in those products become apparent. More often than not, the technical expertise in your company will provide the knowledge to improve or correct those shortcomings. Patents owned by your company that address those problems can be of great value as your competition will probably need access to that technology—technology that your company owns!

The more patents you have relevant to a particular competitive product, the more likely at least some of them will be upheld by the courts and may then be used to block your competitor.

That said, it is important to note that while the concept of problem-specific filing can be applied to all situations, its implementation must be customized to each company's particular needs. An implementation strategy that meets the needs for one organization may be overkill for another. Conversely, a strategy that is effective for a specific organization such a university may be totally inadequate for a company that manufactures and/or commercializes products based on its intellectual property.

Additional Goals of a Patent Strategy

A properly designed patent strategy has several goals related to those outlined in Chapter 1. The strategy should maximize the commercial value, i.e. the value of the intellectual property portfolio to other institutions, subject to the constraint of the resources available to support that strategy. This can be a two-edged sword. On the one hand, the more patents a company has, the higher the commercial value would generally be; on the other hand, more patents means more time, effort, and money expended in the process of cultivating and maintaining that portfolio.

Second, a patent strategy should ideally attempt to establish a proprietary market position, whether or not the institution owning that portfolio will ever produce the goods or services protected by the patents in the portfolio. While that may seem a tautology, one of the goals of a properly-crafted patent strategy, regardless of its implementation, is that it must protect the intellectual property, especially the invention. Protecting a single invention is fairly straight forward. However, when teams are working on various aspects of a proposed product, the filing of patent applications related to solving one problem may, if proper care is not taken, adversely affect the ability to obtain patent coverage on other aspects of the problem. It is important that, as applications regarding potential inventions start to take shape, a patent engineer oversee the process to ensure that the strategic inventions be protected.

While you are hammering out the details of your company's customized patent strategy, make sure that special attention is paid to facilitating communication between your people—particularly your engineers and attorneys. Remember, lawyers and engineers speak different languages, and it is easy to fall into miscommunication when the inventors try to communicate their invention to the attorneys. More often than not, this is where companies can end up missing many of the important, but less solution-specific, aspects of their invention, thereby losing out on an excellent opportunity to strengthen their portfolios.

The final goal of a good patent strategy is to reduce a company's exposure to patent infringement suits. Though we live in a litigious society, a good patent portfolio discourages lawsuits by displaying the company's strengths. Should your company own patents that are strategic to your competitors, you will find that many, if not most, will prefer to enter into licensing agreements that bring you income rather than press a lawsuit they are unlikely to win.

While a good patent strategy maximizes a company's ability to use its intellectual property, the reader should recognize that no patent strategy can ensure that the owner of a patent will actually be able to practice the invention. It is always possible that practicing your patented technology would end up infringing upon patents owned by other organizations—a possibility that will, hopefully, be minimized as you practice problem-specific filing. That said, a good patent strategy would allow your company to develop a strong portfolio, giving you effective negotiating power in patent exchange agreements with your competitors.

Another situation that can occur is when government and/or industrial regulations prevent a company from practicing its inventions. For example, recent regulations require that light bulbs have a certain minimum energy efficiency. It is unlikely that any conceivable improvements in the technology going into incandescent light bulbs would allow it to meet or exceed the designated efficiency criteria. Even if a company invented an improved light bulb, it is unlikely that the company would be able to practice the invention and market that bulb. Similarly, patents focused on those improvements may not be of much value because other companies would probably not have use for that technology.

It must be emphasized that no patent strategy that does not adequately identify and file on the enabling technology, i.e. what one actually does in order to commercialize or practice the invention, is complete. It is relatively easy to discern valuable scientific papers. Those are the ones that present significant advancements, as opposed to the papers that report more routine calculations or data. The scientific community awards scientists that publish papers having great impact with appropriate awards such as the Nobel or other prizes.

This is not the case with patents. A patent is valuable when another company needs the patented technology, as witnessed by the Polaroid-Kodak patent infringement lawsuit. It is the ultimate need for the specific claimed technology, rather than the loftier, perhaps idealistic, technical advancement, that makes a patent valuable despite the fact that patents were established by the United States Constitution in order to encourage technological advances.

A Brief Look at Claims, Infringement, and Assertion

The process of seeking damages for the infringement of a patent is called assertion. A proper patent strategy should be formulated with the idea of filing applications with the intent on asserting those patents that are issued against other companies. This does not mean that every single patent must be assertion-friendly, but most should be. What does this mean, in practical terms?

The first question that should be addressed is what other companies are interested in practicing the technology. There are, of course, instances where the technological advances are so revolutionary that no competitors presently exist. Eventually, however, if a market for that product is sufficiently lucrative, competitors will arise. However, more often, companies both large and small compete. If the practice of the invention by a competitor within the foreseeable future is unlikely, filing patent applications and obtaining and maintaining patents could be a waste of money and merely serve to teach others. Even in this instance, however, obtaining patents may be valuable as it does demonstrate to the public a company's creativity and novelty. Whether or not this is sufficient to pursue patent coverage and, if so, how much of a patent strategy should be implemented is a decision best left up to you.

Far more important a question is whether or not the infringement is detectable. This means that you, the assignee, are responsible for enforcing your patents. No one else—no government agency, business, international agency, or anyone else—will enforce a patent. The assignee must shoulder that task. To do so, you must be able to both identify the infringer and show that your patent is being infringed.

As an example, let us consider the proposed second invention concerning the method of attaching the rubber eraser to the pencil. Specifically, the claim, as written, states "by compressing the rubber pencil or dry ink eraser to a diameter less than the diameter of the pencil and wrapping a metallic band around the pencil and the rubber pencil or dry ink eraser while the rubber eraser is in the compressed state..." The claim states that the rubber pencil eraser must be compressed prior to wrapping it with the metallic band. The act of compressing the rubber eraser is done in the factory.

It would be difficult to prove that the compression occurred prior to the act of wrapping, as opposed to during the wrapping process. It would be better to state this claim so that the rubber is acknowledged to be in a compressed state when in the wrapped configuration. As such, you can prove infringement simply by removing the band and showing that the rubber eraser expands to its uncompressed state.

The infringement of patents that cover manufacturing processes or methods are often difficult to prove. Chemical processes for producing a new material, as opposed to the material itself, can be problematic to demonstrate infringement. Infringement of software patents, especially those covering some sort of process control or running of a device can also be difficult to prove. Although patents wherein infringement is difficult to prove should not be the bulwark of a patent portfolio, they do have value as part of the overall portfolio and should not necessarily be neglected. However, when formulating a strategy, it is generally better to give a higher priority to those patent applications in which infringement is readily demonstrable.

In a proper patent portfolio, the claims should adequately protect the invention(s). Again, let us look at the wording of the second proposed patent, which states "... diameter less than the diameter of the pencil..." This would seem to imply that the invention is limited to a cylindrical pencil and cylindrical eraser. If so, a competitor can avoid infringing the patent simply by making a hexagonal pencil and eraser. Would it not be better to change the wording of the claim to include cylindrical and polygonal pencils and erasers, perhaps claiming the perimeter of the pencil and the eraser? These are questions that need to be addressed prior to filing the application.

Brevity may be the soul of wit, but it is the essence of patent applications. It has been stated by a colleague that a claim should be no longer than the width of three fingers [1]. While this may often be too rigorous a constraint and often it is necessary to include more detail in a claim to avoid prior art, it is a good guideline. Do not include more in a claim than is absolutely necessary to protect the invention.

Alternatively, it is unwise to have less in the claim than would be necessary to have the patent actually allowed by the examiner, as this might result in significant discourse with the examiner that becomes part of the file history. It should be noted that, during assertion, the defendant, i.e. the alleged infringer, can examine the entire file history of the patent and its prosecution. All correspondence and communication between the examiner and the inventors are open. This includes all discussions of what various terms actually mean, which is generally synonymous with restricting the extent of the coverage of the patent.

The best patent application is often the one where the examiner reads the application, does his prior art search, finds nothing directly relevant to the application, and allows the patent without further discussion or requiring amendments. On the other hand, the patent application or applications, in the event of filing multiple related applications on the same day, must adequately define and protect the inventions.

When conducting a prior art search and differentiating the present invention from the prior art, it is not sufficient that the invention is different from that previously known. Rather, it is vital that the prior art also does not predict and cannot be used either by itself or in combination with other art, to give the present invention. Prior art searches are discussed in more detail in Chapter 5.

Strong, broad patents are essential to a portfolio's effectiveness. Prior to the formation of the Patent Circuit Court of Appeals, U.S. courts frequently ruled that patents were invalid. This changed, as discussed in the second chapter of the book, with the formation of the Patent Circuit Court of Appeals,*** which was much friendlier towards issued patents; however, this may have once again changed. In 2011 Congress passed a law overhauling the patent system.

As part of this overhaul, the Patent Trial and Appeal Board was launched in 2012. The purpose of this Board is to allow companies to skip the question of whether or not it infringed upon a patent and challenge the legitimacy of the patent itself. As of March 6, 2014, the Board received 1,056 requests to challenge the validity of issued patents [2]. Whether or not this Board is subjected to future constraints imposed by Congress or the Patent Circuit

*** Officially named the "United States Court of Appeals for the Federal Circuit" or CAFC, as discussed in Chapter 2.

Court of Appeals remains to be seen. For the moment, it is enough to say that challenging the validity of issued patents has been and will continue to be a commonly used method of defense in patent infringement lawsuits.

While the contents of a patent portfolio are the primary measure of its health, its size is another important measure of its health. Another commonly used method to defend against an infringement suit is to file a counter-suit, claiming that the original plaintiff is infringing upon the patents of the defendant. These methods are not mutually exclusive and are often used jointly. On whichever side you find yourself, the more patents you have, the more weight a judge is likely to give your legal claims. Again, a good example of this is the Polaroid instant photography lawsuit against Kodak, in which Polaroid asserted that Kodak infringed on eleven of Polaroid's patents. Kodak did not have any patents that it could assert against Polaroid and was, in fact, practicing the claimed art in those eleven patents. Kodak's defense was left to challenge the validity of the patents—patents that covered not the fundamental chemistry but the simpler enabling technology. Despite Kodak's more tenuous position, it vigorously challenged the validity of those patents and the court ruled that two were, in fact, invalid. However, this still left nine others with which to contend. This ultimately resulted in Polaroid becoming $900,000,000 richer and Kodak being ordered to exit the instant photography business—a loss of both the business revenue and the expense incurred with shutting down production and recalling the instant cameras that Kodak had previously sold but that had now been rendered useless to the consumers who had purchased them.

A general rule of thumb is that a court will likely rule one or two patents in a case to be invalid. The Patent Trial and Appeal Board, if its role is not restricted in the future, may or may not be more assertive in ruling patents invalid. However, to date and to the knowledge of the author, no court has ruled that five patents are invalid. If your company wants to assert its patents against a competitor, your chances of success are greatly enhanced if you can assert five or more patents. Moreover, facing multiple patents instead of just one or two may very well bring a defendant company the incentive they need to quit the courtroom and seek out your company at the negotiating table.

Throughout your patent filing process, it is important to ensure that your claims are understandable by a jury. Put yourself in this scenario. Your company has found that a competitor has been practicing your technology and selling products into your market. The result is that your company has lost a lot of money and is presently seeking damages against the infringing company. The defendant company has denied any infringement, claiming that its product is the result of its own R&D, and it refuses to negotiate with your company. Your company is now forced to either drop its assertion or pursue legal recourse in court. Your company has to prove that the defendant company is, in fact, infringing upon your company's patented technology, as described in the claims. The people deciding whether or not your company's patents have been infringed are most likely people with no technical or legal expertise in the area in question, and want the trial to be over as quickly as possible so they can go back to their normal lives. The defendant will be using its technical and legal experts to try to convince the jury that the competitor is doing something different from what is claimed in your company's patents. What the people on the jury understand will determine who wins the lawsuit. As the plaintiff, you have the burden of proof; it is up to your company to prove infringement. You need to make sure you have given yourself the necessary tools to do so.

This is not a simple task, due to a combination of factors. The first is that a patent describes an innovation—something novel. The novelty may be, and often is, the result of highly trained scientists and engineers making an advancement in a solution to a difficult problem. For someone to understand the solution, he must first understand the problem. Second, as stated, a patent is a legal document that has been drawn up by an attorney with the intent of providing legal protection to the owner of that patent. Making understandable to laypeople any language combining the highly-technical with legal jargon is a herculean feat. However, it is a feat that, if accomplished, can pay large dividends.

Make sure that your inventors understand the claims as they are presented in the patent application and that those claims accurately reflect their invention. In the event of a lawsuit, it is highly likely that the inventors will be called to the witness stand to explain their invention to the jury. The wording of the claims must correspond closely to the explanation presented by the inventors.

It may be that the inventors are not available for a court appearance. Certainly, issues including health and mortality come into play. Can someone else explain the invention? Even better, is the claim so clearly written that the layperson can understand it without further explanation? Moreover, is the language sufficiently clear that attempts to obfuscate the claim by representatives of your competitor will fail? If the members of the jury become glassy-eyed listening to arcane testimony about your company's invention, the chance of success lessens. Along this line, your company must lay out exactly what is being practiced by your competitor, along-side the infringed claims, so that the jury can plainly see what is being practiced and how it infringes upon the claims.

These are the goals of the claims. They are not always achievable. Many times claims have to be rather complicated as the technology described is not simple and the law requires the legalese to precisely describe the invention. Inventors should, however, attempt to picture themselves explaining the invention to laypeople when the patent application is being drafted.

We have discussed what should be done to establish a patent strategy that results in a strong and valuable patent portfolio. In the next chapter, we will discuss some of the pitfalls of the patent application process. Not only will we show you how to avoid them, we will show how to use these pitfalls to your advantage during the application process.

References

1. J. Manico, private communication
2. A. Jones, "Wall Street Journal" March 11, 2014, pg. B4. See also P. J. Pitts, "Wall Street Journal" June 11, 2015, pg. A13.

4

Implementing Patent Strategies and the Application Process through Patent Engineering

In the previous chapter we discussed the elements that go into formulating a patent strategy and the consequences of not doing so. In this chapter we will describe in more detail how to execute that strategy and how to determine which inventions are worth patenting and which ones are not. We will also discuss alternative avenues that can be pursued if material does not warrant the expense of obtaining patent coverage, but for which it is still important to keep competitors from obtaining patents that prevent your company from commercializing your technology or undermine the value of your patent portfolio.

Patent Application Process

In order to receive a patent, the inventors—assisted by legal counsel—file a patent application in a patent office. U.S. inventors generally file in the

U.S. Patent and Trademark Office (USPTO). As discussed in Chapters 2 and 3, the application describes the problem solved by the invention and how the invention solves the problem, and it must clearly describe those aspects of the invention for which the inventor is seeking exclusive rights. These descriptions, known as "claims", define the exact property the patent holder will own. While the application contents are vitally important—what you can claim is limited to what you have described or shown in the application—the title, the abstract, the background and the descriptions and everything else other than the claims exist solely to give the claims needed context and support, either by defining the problem solved or by specifying how the problem has been solved. The specification may set the stage, but it is the claims that describe the invention that determine the patent's value.

Claims

Each claim consists of a sentence that defines the technical specifics of the new technical solution. Claims are broken up into one of two categories: independent, which stand on their own, and dependent, which contain specifics that relate back to a previous claim. Claims are numbered starting from one. Independent claims set forth the minimal core of the invention. For example, the first claim of antilock brake patent U.S. 3,930,688* describes the invention as:

> *1. A digital machine method for augmenting braking control of a braked wheeled vehicle employing fluid pressure operated wheel brakes, comprising the step of selectively modulating the fluid pressure applied to the valve of at least one braked wheel so as to cause the braking control to track the knee of the road torque and wheel velocity versus time envelope.*

This claim is an independent claim because it totally describes the essential parts of a particular invention. A person who produces a device that "selectively modulat[es] the fluid pressure" in the way listed in the claim without the patent owner's express permission "infringes" (is an "infringer" of) that claim, and the patent containing that claim. The patent owner can sue an infringer to stop them from using the technology or to recover money the patent owner might have made in the absence of the infringement.

* issued in 1976 to Rockwell International Corporation.

The second claim of this patent (called the "688 patent" based on the last three digits of its number) is a dependent claim. This claim reads:

> 2. *The method of claim 1 in which said step includes the set of iterative steps of preselectively relieving an applied brake pressure to said braked wheel in response to either wheel deceleration thereof being greater than a preselectively large first level or the combination of a wheel deceleration of a lesser preselected second level and a wheel velocity within a preselected first range of upper and lower velocity levels; and preselectively restoring an applied wheel brake pressure to said braked wheel for a period not in excess of a preselected first mode interval in response to said wheel deceleration being less than said second lesser deceleration level and said wheel velocity being at least equal to a second velocity level less than said first range of upper and lower velocity levels.*

The second claim is classified as "dependent" because the method it describes of using iterative steps is a variant, or option, for implementing the invention described in the first claim, i.e., the "method of claim 1." In other words, it is not possible to use the second claim without being able to practice the first. The second claim cannot exist without the first and, therefore, it is dependent.

Now here is where it gets interesting. The patent's third claim states:

> 3. *The method of claim 2 in which said first interval is substantially equal to ten times the response time of said valve.*

Claim 3 is a dependent claim that depends on the second claim which is, in of itself, a dependent claim. Thus, a dependent claim can rely on either independent or dependent claims as long as they precede it in the application. An application can have any number of claims, independent or dependent, though most have at most three independent claims and at most 20 total claims to avoid USPTO fees above those counts.

Dependent claims are important, but it should be noted that in infringement cases, if the claim on which a dependent claim relies is not infringed, the dependent claim is not infringed either, even if it appears that the infringer is practicing every aspect of that claim. For example, if someone uses the practice described in the second claim of the 688 patent to relieve and restore brake pressure but does not "track the knee" as in the first claim on which the second hangs, that individual has not infringed the second claim.

In summary, for an independent claim of a patent to be infringed, the infringer must be practicing every aspect of that claim. For a dependent claim to be infringed, the infringer must be practicing every aspect of the dependent claim plus every aspect of any claim—independent or dependent—on which the dependent claim is predicated.

"Practicing" part of a claim means generally making, doing, selling, using, or importing what that part of the claim describes. Individual parts of a claim are called "features." For example, anyone "modulating the fluid pressure" in the specific way given in the independent claim above infringes that claim. Someone who modulates the pressure just as described in the independent claim, and does so specifically by "relieving" and "restoring" the brake pressure as described in the second claim, infringes both the first and second claims.

As previously mentioned, a typical U.S. issued patent today will have up to approximately twenty claims. In addition, the patent office today limits a patent to a single invention. These limitations were not always the case. Rather, as one peruses older patents, one often finds 40, 50, or even more claims, often encompassing what today would be considered multiple inventions. For example, in previous years, it was common to combine both method and apparatus claims into a single patent. This is rarely allowed today, because the apparatus and methods used to solve a problem are generally viewed as two distinct inventions, as either can be practiced independently of the other. The United States Patent and Trademark Office, while subject to restrictions imposed by Congress, the U.S. Patent Circuit Court of Appeals, and even the U.S. Supreme Court, as exemplified in its 2007 decision of KSR vs. Teleflex [1], has a lot of discretionary latitude.

Because the claims are the legal backbone of a patent, it is important that they be written by someone who is fully proficient in patent law, such as a patent practitioner (i.e., a patent attorney or agent). That said, it is also important that the claims carefully and completely describe the invention, a task that generally resides within the domain of the engineer, designer, or inventor. Combining the technical with the legal issues to create a strong claim set can be a significant challenge; this makes it both advantageous and cost-effective for organizations to consult with an experienced patent engineer whose knowledge can provide a bridge between those realms.

Prior Art and Novelty

In order to obtain a patent, one must file an application with the governmental patent office of the country in which one seeks patent protection.

That office considers whether the claims in the application describe an invention. The office will ask whether the claims describe how to solve a problem. There are no patents for works of literature or for philosophies, for example. The office will then ask whether the claimed solution is "novel." This means that if someone else has ever publicized the solution before you filed, it is not an invention. This is important. If someone has published or publicized the proposed invention in any manner, it is no longer considered to be novel. In this book, "published" does not just mean information included in a book or magazine, but information in any form to which the public has access. Anything available to the public up to and including the day before you file your application is called "prior art." Prior art can include conference papers, prior patent applications or articles, and descriptions of products, devices, or methods that are or have been in the market. The prior art can also include your own work if you have published your invention prior to filing your patent application. Prior art even includes products themselves once they go on sale—you cannot force your competitor to pull a product from the shelves based on a patent application you filed after that product was released.

As we discussed in Chapters 2 and 3, should your invention be published before you file your patent application, it is considered "known" (i.e., not novel) under most countries' patent law and is no longer patentable. This is true regardless of the context in which the invention was published. It does not even matter whether or not the publication was intentional! In the U.S., you have a one-year grace period to file an application for an invention after that invention is published. As soon as an invention is published, that one-year clock starts ticking.

Obviousness

The invention must also not be "obvious." This means that the invention must not be evident to a typical person working in the field, frequently referred to as "one of ordinary skill in the art". Broadly, this means that if a fifth-grader could figure out your solution by looking at the prior art, the solution is obvious and, therefore, not an invention. That said, there is no rule defining what a typical person (or a typical fifth-grader) should or should not understand. Because of this, what constitutes obviousness is often a subject of debate between the patent applicant and practitioner on the one hand, and the examiner in the USPTO on the other.

"One of ordinary skill in the art" generally refers to someone who is a user of the technology. It generally does not refer to member of a group of PhDs who have been working for the better part of a year to solve a problem. The latter consists of individuals of extraordinary skill in the art. Second, it is assumed that an individual of ordinary skill in the art is familiar with all the literature, especially the patent literature, whether or not it is in his particular field, and can combine disconnected pieces together. If a connection can be made between the teachings of an indeterminate number of patents or other sources, whether directly relevant to the field of interest or not, the proposed invention would probably be considered to be obvious. Thus, a method of producing a screen mesh to filter particulates or to make a window screen to block the entrance of insects and other creatures by weaving a pattern of wires in orthogonal directions (assuming that such devices did not presently exist) would be considered obvious in light of the fact that textiles are commonly produced by weaving threads in a similar pattern. However, if the inventors could show that they had to produce a crimp in each strand of wire where it crossed an orthogonal wire to allow the screen to lay flat, and that crimping was not taught and, indeed not relevant to the more flexible threads, then a patent could be granted that included the step of crimping.

Obviousness also applies if the solution to a problem can be arrived at by simply combining known components without changing them. For example, attaching a piece of rubber—which is already known to remove graphite markings from paper—to the top of a device containing a graphite rod capable of producing markings on paper to make an eraser-bearing pencil does not constitute an invention. Even if no one had ever thought of the combination before, each component is performing in a previously known manner making the whole solution "obvious." On the other hand, if attaching the rubber piece to the graphite containing device produced a product that could now erase ink markings in a manner that was not previously known, you would have an invention—the claims would be "non-obvious."**

Requirements for novelty and obviousness are hurdles to jump, not barriers stopping you from obtaining patents. For example, one cannot obtain a patent on a generic fork or spoon, as forks and spoons are known. However, there have been 173 patents granted on the invention of

---

** The reader is reminded that, in this hypothetical example, the rubber pencil-mark eraser was affixed to the top of the pencil to create an eraser-bearing pencil product distinguishable from that of the competition. As each component was to function in its normal manner, the new product would not be patentable. The hypothetical unanticipated result that the eraser could now erase dry ink once affixed to the pencil would make this a patentable invention, as the result would not have been obvious.

the "spork" between 1976 and February 25, 2014. These patents covered advancements in a variety of areas ranging from novel food dispensing and measuring devices to surgical instruments to computerized methods of filling out forms. All 173 of those patents successfully met the requirements of novelty and non-obviousness.

Patent Practitioner

A competent patent practitioner can help the inventor understand if the solution they have created fits the legal definition of an invention. A patent practitioner is anyone licensed by the USPTO to represent patent applicants. Practitioners are skilled at writing claims, writing patent applications, and managing those patent applications as they are processed by the USPTO. Practitioners can be patent attorneys or "patent agents," who are not attorneys but who still represent applicants before the USPTO. Please note that a patent practitioner and a patent litigator are not the same; the latter can only help you with litigation arising from either your assertion of your patents against an alleged infringer or with your defense in the instance of a patent owner asserting his patent against you. The USPTO requires all patent practitioners—both attorneys and agents—to have a technical background. Again, we must stress how vital it is that inventors consult with competent patent practitioners who can help them navigate the legal process in a timely and cost-effective manner.

Patent Application Prosecution

The process of filing a patent application begins with an invention report, usually prepared by an inventor. A patent practitioner will then draft a patent application based on the invention report and, usually, discussions with the inventors and the responsible managers. After you apply for a patent, the application goes through what is known as "prosecution." Prosecution may take several years, during which an examiner at the USPTO (or other patent office) will determine whether the claims define a patentable invention and whether the application meets formal legal requirements. If the examiner answers "no" to either, the applicant and the patent practitioner can attempt to argue against the examiner's findings. Prosecution in the U.S. often involves negotiations with the examiner to determine what claim coverage the applicant should receive in an issued patent.

Eighteen months after having been submitted to the USPTO, the patent application is published. At this time its contents become public knowledge regardless of whether or not a patent is ultimately granted. This means that everything described in the application will become freely available to anyone who is interested—including your competitors. Divulging some of your secrets in this way is part of the bargain as a patent applicant that you make with the government when you file a patent application.

Although divulging your proprietary intellectual property without the guarantee of ever having a patent issued may pose some risks, there are some benefits. You may be able to use your published applications for leverage in negotiations with other companies. Competitors will recognize that many of your published applications will eventually mature into patents. Published applications also encourage inventors by giving them a tangible piece of work they can point to and brag about. Even if a particular application does not lead to a patent, that application will serve as prior art to prevent others from later claiming the same things you described in your application. Moreover, published applications may be useful as prior art against competitors' later-filed patents in a similar technical field. Specifically, if your competitor asserts his company's patents against your company, you may be able to have his patents cancelled ("invalidated") based on the prior art in your published applications, even if the inventions are not identical.

The examiner may decide that the proposed claims constitute more than a single invention. This generally occurs if aspects of the proposed claims can be, at least theoretically, practiced independently of each other. Today, examiners in the U.S. often assume that claims that describe a method for accomplishing a task and the apparatus for doing so do not inherently depend upon each other and, accordingly, do not constitute a single invention. If the examiner does determine that the claims represent more than a single invention, he will send a "restriction requirement" asking the applicant to select those claims that the applicant desires to have initially prosecuted. The other claims can be subsequently prosecuted in a separate application. This application is known as a "divisional". Alternatively, the examiner can determine that the claims are both novel and non-obvious. In this case he will issue a "notice of allowance". The patent owner*** may then pay an "issue fee" to the government and receive a patent.

*** The patent owner may be the inventor(s). However, in many instances, the inventors must assign all rights to their employer, who will then become the patent owner. Assignees can transfer those rights to others, so that entities not directly related to the inventor may ultimately become the patent owner.

Perhaps the most common occurrence in prosecution is that the examiner will "reject" the claims as either obvious or lacking novelty. Almost every patent application receives at least one rejection. If this happens, the applicant can rewrite the claims, taking into account the arguments presented by the examiner, or try to convince the examiner that his conclusions are not correct. If the applicant prevails—and the chances of being successful are fairly high if proper care is taken and due diligence is exercised in writing the claims—the patent office will issue a patent. More details on the prosecution of patent applications will be presented in Chapter 7.

Value of a Sound Patent Strategy

Patents cost money to initially obtain and then to maintain. Costs include filing and issuance fees, as well as those directly billed by the attorneys or agents doing the actual filing and prosecution of the application. There are also indirect costs associated with diverting the time of the inventors from their normal assignments to the myriad of issues associated with applying for patents.

There are substantial benefits that can be accrued if sound patent strategies have been developed and executed. Alternatively, the lack thereof can result in serious threats or loss of revenue to your company.

If your business is profitable, other companies will try to offer competitive products, often at lower prices because they do not have to recoup the investment your company incurred while developing your product. Once your product hits the market, it can often be reverse engineered. Not only have you taught your competitor or would be competitor**** the value of your product, but you have also facilitated his ability to copy your technology. Your competitor is then free to offer a similar product at reduced cost or with enhanced features, thereby giving your customers a better value proposition. Either situation does not bode well for your business.

However, these pitfalls can be avoided using a properly designed patent strategy, such as the strategy of owning the problem, using patent engineering, as described in the previous chapter. As a result of your patent protection, your competitor would be at least delayed in introducing a product with comparable features that does not infringe upon your patent.

**** Competition can arise, not only from companies that presently offer products in your field, but from new companies or companies that, seeing the value of your products, choose to expand their product line into your market

As market windows are transient, this may very well discourage his attempt to do so. Moreover, having to design "workarounds" to avoid infringing on the claims in your patent would add development costs to your competitor's product, thereby impeding his ability to undercut your price. In essence, your competition's resources, like any company, are limited and infringing on your patent can be expensive. Moreover, having to design his product to avoid infringing on your patent can result in added expenses and an inferior product. Either case can be very discouraging for a potential competitor.

If your company has a good patent portfolio that has resulted from implementing a well-designed patent strategy, your competition would have limited options, assuming that it does not want to be sued and face paying substantial damages. First, the competition may choose to implement an alternative design that does not use your claimed invention, or in patent jargon, does not "read on your patents". However, a well-designed patent strategy would have anticipated reasonable alternatives and buttressed your company against that option. Second, a competitor may pay royalties to the owner of the patent in order to be allowed to practice the invention—if the owner is willing to grant such a license. This would make it more difficult for your competitor to compete on price and, in fact, the license may be written to limit the use of the patent, such as restricting the number of items produced or the features contained therein. Third, your competitor can simply forgo the advantages that are protected by your patent. This will often result in a less desirable product with limited profitability. Fourth, your competitor can choose to develop or purchase technology providing a comparable feature. For example, European auto manufacturers chose to pursue the latter approach by buying O_2 sensors from Bosch, rather than developing their own technology, as did the U.S. and Japanese manufacturers. This can be a reasonable approach, especially with the present example of the relatively small European manufacturers not diverting their resources, thereby allowing them to concentrate on developing technology that they deemed necessary to differentiate their products from those of their competition. However, it can put a company at the mercy of another company. This is especially true if the company must buy the technology from a competitor.

A solid patent portfolio is not just for defensive purposes. Rather, it has great value in its own right. Companies such as IBM, Intellectual Ventures, and Eastman Kodak have developed substantial licensing businesses that sell access to patented technologies to other companies. In addition, a company's patent portfolio can allow it to gain access to target markets or technology through cross-licensing. Large companies often trade access to each-others' patents for mutual competitive advantage.

In fact, your patent applications and patents are products, too. The right to sue an infringer of a claim is actually a piece of property [2]! It has value and can be bought or sold just like your house or your car.

From the universe of possible claims, you want to select and secure those that provide you the right coverage for the right investment. You want patent engineering—making complex technologies and smart people work together to build value in your patent portfolio. That value may be in the patents or applications themselves, for example if you sell or license them. That value may also be in damages awarded by a court or market share you protect from infringers using your patents. However you extract value from a patent, the process of getting that patent involves attention to detail and analyzing complex sets of alternatives. Just as you now engineer your products to add value, you can also engineer your patents to add value.

Companies had been filing patent applications for many years. However, in 1999, Harvard Business School Press published *Rembrandts in the Attic* by Rivette and Kline [3]. That book suggested that many companies had valuable patents from which the value was not being extracted. This situation was the patent equivalent of unknowingly having valuable Rembrandt paintings in one's attic. This book triggered increased interest in intellectual property in general, and patents specifically. In the ensuing years, the value of intellectual property has dramatically increased, as companies have recognized the market value of their patents and have sought to extract licensing fees from their intellectual property.

Universities have also begun to actively seek to patent the results of academic research. Some universities have established separate research organizations dedicated to commercializing the technological advances made by the university. For example, the Purdue Research Foundation holds over 820 U.S. patents issued since 1976. Massachusetts Institute of Technology holds over 4,200 patents. The University of Chicago holds over 500. Rensselaer Polytechnic Institute holds over 250 patents. Moreover, as opposed to industry, which seeks to market its products, universities tend to try to license their intellectual property. They are practicing what Rivette and Kline espoused, namely that intellectual property by itself is an extremely valuable product.

Governmental agencies have also gotten into the act, principally by encouraging industrial-university collaboration, including the generation of patents. The goal of such agencies is to encourage industries to partner with American universities to expand the technical expertise available to the industrial engineers and scientists while focusing university research into practical areas. At the federal level, programs such as GOALI,***** administered by the National Science Foundation (NSF) accepted research proposals, filed jointly by industrial and university partners, in which the government would pay approximately half of the costs of an accepted proposal, with the industry paying the other half. Similar agencies exist at the state level. New York State, for example, has established the New York State Energy Research and Development Authority (NYSERDA) to enhance cooperation between the government, industry, and universities. New York has also established a number of centers for advanced technology (CATs) at universities throughout the state, which are focused to help industries take advantage of these opportunities.

Goals and Uses of Patents

The goals, values, and uses of patents have changed in recent decades. Organizations of multiple types and all sizes now seek to obtain and use patents. Major companies may have attics that contain Rembrandts, but many organizations do not. In many cases, the value of the Rembrandts is offset or even degraded by the number of patents that have relatively low value but were, on average, just as expensive to obtain and maintain as higher-value patents. The presence of such low value patents simply clutters up the attic, making it difficult, if not impossible, to appreciate the Rembrandts.

On the other end of the spectrum, small entrepreneurial companies often have few patents even though they have extremely valuable intellectual property. Their patents often cover only their core technologies. Unfortunately, their patent protection may be much less extensive than their management realizes. As many such companies have painfully learned, technological advances are very rapid and last month's state of the art advances may be obsolete or undesirable today. Moreover, patents covering relatively minor advances in the enabling technology may block an entrepreneurial company from selling its products with the very technology it developed. Even larger companies such as Eastman Kodak, which thought that its instant photography business was well protected because it held patents on the basic chemistry used in its products to produce instant photographs, failed to understand the value of having supporting patents covering the enabling technology.

***** Grant Opportunities for Academic Liaison with Industry.

When designing a patent strategy, it is vital to remember that it is difficult, if not impossible, to predict, when filing patent applications, which applications will mature into valuable patents. Patents that protect fundamental technology may be of little value if no one else seeks to practice the covered inventions. Patents that protect relatively minor technological improvements may be of extreme value if those improvements are necessary to commercialize a product. This was clearly the situation with the Polaroid-Kodak instant photography lawsuit.

Furthermore, the specifics of a well-conceived patent strategy will depend on the nature of the institution. A university that produces intellectual property but does not commercialize any product using that technology does not have to establish a bulwark against another company filing a patent infringement suit. In this example, a patent strategy can afford to focus on specific core technological developments at the expense of patenting the enabling technology, as the university intends to profit from licensing its patents rather than from producing products. Alternatively, a large company with a vast product line has to concern itself with patent infringement lawsuits. In this case the company may need to have patents that cover potential improvements or corrections to short-comings in the products that its competitors produce even if the company itself is not in that particular business. Having such a wide variety of patents enhances licensing value and provides incentive for competitors to settle infringement lawsuits.

As previously discussed, there is a downside to filing a patent application. In exchange for obtaining the right to monopolistically practice the patented advances, the applicants have taught how to solve a problem. Moreover, they have drawn attention to the problem—a problem that may not have been realized by the competition and may have eventually bitten them. In addition, once a problem and a path to solving that problem are known, creative minds in other companies can often discover alternative paths to that same goal. Again, Polaroid had its basic chemistry patents protecting its instant photography business. However, once that technology was known, Kodak was able to develop its own alternative chemistry that did not infringe upon Polaroid's patents. And, as previously stated, after 18 months the USPTO publishes the application, thereby teaching the world your invention, whether or not you eventually obtain the patent. Finally, adding insult to injury, one of your own published patent applications can constitute prior art against subsequent applications you file, making the obtaining of future patents on further advances or even the filing of patent applications aimed at addressing the objections of the examiner highly problematical. Your patents will be more valuable if, prior to filing a patent application, you plan an effective patent strategy.

Patent Engineering and Owning the Problem During the Application Process

With these issues in mind, let us examine how a patent strategy can be created. Owning the problem starts with a seed idea. No technical development exists in a vacuum. You already have the seeds of a strong patent portfolio in the minds of the people designing and building your products. A seed is any idea for a problem and a solution to that problem. Seeds need not be fully completed technical ideas with all the details fleshed out, and usually are not. Seeds may be prototypes, but often arise before a prototype is built. It is never too late to think about owning the problem. Even after a product is released, your people have ideas for the next product. Those ideas may be seeds.

As soon as you have identified a problem and the way you think you are going to solve it, you have a seed. Early analysis of its effects on your proposed technology and patent portfolio is, you will find, a lot less expensive than an analysis later on in the product development cycle that is aimed at trying to correct weaknesses in either. And, more expensive still is the analysis that occurs when your company has to rectify its products or patent portfolio to correct for your product's deficiencies after your competitor has introduced a competitive product or has obtained patents that prevent you from producing or selling your product.

Looking beyond your current products may also help you anticipate the needs and limitations of your competitors. Applying for a patent on technology your competitors are going to need five years after you file is one of the best ways to use your patent dollar. By the time the patent issues, your competitors will be in a position where you can effectively use your patents against them.

Seeds can also come from a surprising place—your competitor's patents. Remember that those patents do not give your competitors a right to practice their patented inventions. It instead gives them the right to stop you from practicing the invention. The risks of infringing patents can be greatly reduced by conducting a "clearance"****** search prior to introducing a product. Not only does this reduce the chance of infring-

****** also called a "freedom-to-use" or "freedom-to-operate" search.

ing upon another company's patents, but, done properly, shows due diligence and can greatly defend against allegations of willful infringement. A clearance search focuses on the claims of presently active patents or, sometimes, pending applications. Clearance searches are discussed in detail in Chapter 10.

A side benefit of conducting a clearance analysis and search is that it clearly reveals your competitors' technology to you. Presumably, your product has advantages over those of your competitor. Have you thoroughly patented those advantages? After conducting a clearance search, you know the competition's technology and the extent of its patent portfolio. This is an ideal time for your company to file patent applications that address the shortcomings of your competitors' products or the holes in your competitors' portfolios. These will often be patents that your competitors will need and for which they will have to pay licensing fees or enter into patent exchange agreements******* with your company. Both can be exceedingly valuable.

Critical Challenge

Remember that a seed includes both an idea for a problem and an idea for its solution. Once you have a seed, the problem and solution should be presented to your patent engineering team. Ideally, this team should comprise engineers who are competent in the technology and patenting, as well as marketing******** and legal personnel. The team determines the "critical challenges" related to the particular field of invention. The team then maps a family of patent applications that cover what your company will do to solve the critical challenges, each principal option for solving the critical challenges, and what your competitor will have to do to solve this problem.

******* The term "cross-licensing agreement" is, perhaps, more commonly used. However, in order to emphasize the pecuniary value of patents and the fact that agreements can also incur the payment of fees or royalties or other forms of valuable consideration, this book tends to use the term "patent exchange agreement", of which a cross-license agreement is a subset of this more general term.

******** Often, marketing people have a complementary view of customer needs and the features of competitive products. As such, they are frequently valuable members of teams set up to identify critical challenges.

"Critical challenges" are problems, limitations, or shortcomings in existing products or services. Specifically, critical challenges are those problems that:

- determine cost, functionality, or profitability; or
- are subject to regulatory requirements; or
- drive customer buying decisions or habits.

The term "critical challenge" can apply to the shortcomings or limitations of existing products. These can be factors that create customer frustration when using a product or drive a customer's decision whether or not to purchase a specific product. Alternatively, the term "critical challenge" can also apply to a perceived need in the marketplace for a new product that addresses customer requirements.

A seed is just one idea for solving a problem. That problem may or may not be a critical challenge, and does not have to be fundamental technology. The seed is just a starting point. Critical challenges are "critical" because they are the challenges that will drive your success as a business.

The seed may be an idea to solve the problem of skidding on the road by pumping the brakes automatically, i.e., antilock braking as we know it today. The critical challenge may be that the friction force of the road against the wheels drops below the friction of the brake pads against the brake shoes during slippery road conditions. What determines the functionality of the braking system is the relationship between these friction forces, and antilock braking is one way—but only one way—of dealing with this critical challenge.

Each critical challenge has multiple possible solutions. For example, the critical challenge of uninterrupted music listening can also be solved by a system for streaming music to a user via a network or AM/FM radio. Another solution to the problem of uninterrupted music listening was the now-defunct Sony Hi-MD MiniDisc format, which could store about eight hours of good-quality audio on a single disk [4]. Owning the problem is locking your competitors out of any way of solving the critical challenge, as much as possible.

The same seed may lead to multiple critical challenges. Considering the seed of multiple albums on one disk, another critical challenge might be that users want to listen to music in a different order than the order in which the artists assembled their songs to make albums. The "shuffle function" on a media player is one way, but only one way, of dealing with this critical challenge. The ability to manually move files in a playlist is another way.

After determining the critical challenges arising from the seed, the patent engineering team also determines, at a basic level, whether or not filing patent applications addressing some or all aspects of the critical challenges seems worthwhile. This is because, in order to file patent applications, you generally need more technical detail than the seed provides. Some seed ideas can be expanded to address critical challenges, but it still may not be worth the time or money to do so. If the team believes the value of any patents obtained on a technology would be less than the cost of acquiring those patents, it may not be worthwhile to prepare patent applications for that technology.

The patent engineering team's initial determination about whether to prepare patent applications is just that—initial. The decision may change as a project progresses. If your competitors release a product that relates to your technology, you might be more likely to file patent applications. Alternatively, if it turns out as you develop the seed that it is too expensive to see through to the end, you might be less likely to file patent applications. To be in the best position to make these determinations, keep an open mind and stay focused on both your competitors and the needs of your customers as you develop your patent strategy.

It is vital to identify the critical challenges arising from, implicit in, or underlying your seed ideas. The particular solution in the seed may be irrelevant to your competitors. However, your competitors will have to deal with the critical challenges if they want to be successful in markets related to the seed. Accordingly, your patents related to the critical challenges will likely be relevant to competitors even if your specific technical solutions are not. As you look for critical challenges, ask yourself in what other ways similar functionality can be achieved without using your design. Your competitors will find those other ways unless you have found and protected the critical challenges.

Remember, your company wants to own as much as possible of the whole of each critical challenge, rather than just a specific solution to that critical challenge. If it is not possible to own any given critical challenge in its entirety, a good fallback is to own a portion of that critical challenge that is sufficient to strongly encourage any competitors to negotiate with your company and to ensure that your company will not be locked out of future technological advances. The oxygen sensors are used in every modern automobile to help reduce emissions and improve fuel efficiency. Being blocked from using them could bankrupt an automobile manufacturer. It is not feasible for a single company to own the entirety of the critical challenges of reducing emissions and improving fuel economy. However, every automobile manufacturer must be able to obtain access to that technology. For small manufacturers, access may be simply buying expensive components from a producer of those components, and electing to pay his prices. For larger manufacturers, it is far more cost effective to have a patent portfolio that ensures directly that the manufacturer has access to that technology.

Owning the critical challenges related to a ubiquitous and/or required component can also block competitors. You only need one claim of one patent ultimately upheld to block your competitors from marketing anything including that claimed technology, no matter how small the technology is.

Therefore, once you have identified the critical challenges worth pursuing, go back to the fundamental understanding of those challenges. Go back to first principles if possible. As much as you can, understand the physical fundamentals and the roles and interconnections of components of the solution before you draft the patent applications. This will help you confirm that you truly understand the critical challenges and their solutions. This will also help you see what you do not yet know, and leave room for future filings as you learn more.

Similarly, once you have identified the critical challenges, dig broadly into related and enabling technologies. No patent strategy that does not adequately identify and file on the enabling technology, i.e. what one actually does in order to commercialize or practice the invention, is complete. Consider the related and enabling technology both as it relates to the critical challenges you have identified and as seeds for new ideas.

For example, the critical challenge of playing songs from an album in an order different from the artist's relates to and depends on user interface technologies permitting the user to control the order in some way. The user interface may be as simple as a button or switch to turn "shuffle" mode on or off, or may be as complicated as a flat-panel touchscreen running a full graphical interface. Either way, if you do not consider how the user will interface with the play order, you leave an opening for your competitors. The Apple iPod was not the first portable media player; however, it was the among first of the major media players to use a capacitive touch sensor to give users the familiar feel of a volume knob in the form factor of a portable device. The capacitive touch wheel contributed to the polished character of the iPod's interface and contributed greatly to its success. Moreover, that touch wheel served as the seed for a great deal of subsequent innovation in touch sensors and graphical interfaces that use those sensors.

Remember, as you review your critical challenges, it is worthwhile to determine the limitations or problems your competitor has with his products that you know how to address. As we discussed, patents on these solutions can be worth a lot of money because your competitor will either need those solutions or at least find them to be quite valuable. It should be remembered that patents are of value if and only if someone else needs them.

Timing

Having determined the critical challenges, the patent engineering team can propose the filing of a family of patent applications. These allow the leveraging of the applications, thereby reducing the time and effort of the technical staff and reducing legal costs. Patents are awarded to the first person to file an application that discloses a novel, non-obvious claim to a particular invention. Time is now a crucial factor in filing and the patent engineering team should carefully balance the requirement of filing early with the ability to obtain more thorough coverage in the future. This tends to place undesirable limitations on both the solutions considered and the way in which the problems are framed.

By incorporating a problem-specific approach into its design process (owning the problem instead of just a particular solution to a problem), a company is more likely to be able to diversify its intellectual property. During design, the end-user problems the product will solve are squarely in front of the designers. It is easy to perceive a variety of solutions in the middle of the brainstorming and/or experimentation phases. After the fact, however, it can be difficult to reconstruct the relationship between a particular alternative (chosen or not) and the user problems it solves. Without this relationship, you can still file a patent application on the solution, but it is difficult to fit that alternative into a coherent patent strategy that will leave you truly owning the problem.

Moreover, decisions made during product development constrain the alternatives that will be considered later. For example, once you decide that your media-player product's user interface will include push buttons rather than a touchscreen, all the touchscreen alternatives disappear from the designers' view. This decision affects choices of form factor, battery technology, accessibility, display resolution, and aspect ratio. Depending on the other constraints of the product, that decision may also affect which peripherals can be included, the requirements placed on the processor, or other details of the design. Filing patent applications during design makes it natural to consider the effects of discarding alternatives and to instead include them in your strategy. After the fact, though, so many possibilities have been eliminated that it is not easy to rebuild a coherent picture of the problem.

Additionally, it will be appreciated that it is at this moment in the development process that all of the elements of patent applications can be most easily and most accurately obtained from the technical team including problem definitions, explanations of components and even design drawings.

Accordingly, problem-centric patent engineering efforts should not stand apart from your ongoing developmental programs. Such efforts should form a complement to your engineering and development efforts as an aid in identifying the problems facing your customers and in characterizing these problems in ways that are not focused on the products that you currently make.

Further, such integration between the product development and the patent strategizing allows work supporting patent applications to be done when it is most convenient. This is a critical feature of this process as it is an important cost containment vehicle that enables a greater number of patent applications to be prepared and filed per dollar of investment. Finally, such tight integration can positively influence the product development itself by encouraging consideration of potential problem solving directions that may not have been on the company's road-map.

Post-Filing Considerations

After filing it is likely that you will have to amend or revise your claims or argue that the prior art cited by the examiner, either by itself or in combination with other prior art, does not render your invention obvious. It is not sufficient that your application differs from the prior art or that the problems being solved by the prior art are different. As discussed earlier in this chapter, it is necessary that no prior art, either singly or in combination with other prior art, can be used to teach the present invention.

U.S. patent law allows an unrestricted number of prior patents to be strung together when an examiner is making a rejection based on obviousness. And remember, this is the case even when the prior art cited are in different fields. Also, you may have to restrict the original independent claim using one or more dependent claims. Applications should be written with these situations in mind. It is far better to conduct a reasonably thorough literature search and argue why the related art does not predict the present invention during the initial application than argue with the examiner or be forced to restrict the claims during prosecution. This will be discussed in more detail in Chapter 7, which deals with prosecuting the patent application.

A theme that runs throughout this book is the concept of filing early and filing often. Filing early is simple to understand and has already been adequately discussed. However, why should you have to file often?

There are several reasons for this. First and perhaps most obvious is technology changes, as was discussed using the example of the automotive O_2 sensor. Evolving technology has to be protected as older patents age and become less relevant and, therefore, less valuable. Moreover, the implementation of the use of an object may change in a non-obvious manner. Perhaps your sales force reports back that customers want different features in a product. Can your engineers incorporate appropriate changes? If so, will those changes be covered by your existing patents or patent applications? When a prior application can be used to allow further patents to be obtained, the process is known as a "continuation" or a "continuation in part". These concepts will also be discussed in more detail in Chapter 7.

It is important to write and file applications with both the prosecution and future filings in mind. These are somewhat contradictory requirements, as the more disclosed in an application, the easier it is to revise claims during the prosecution. Unfortunately, disclosing more than is absolutely necessary in an application can make the prosecution of future applications more difficult. To understand how these contradictory factors are optimized with respect to each other, one needs to understand the structure of a patent application. This will be discussed in the next chapter.

References

1. KSR vs. Teleflex 550 U.S. 398 (2007).
2. 35 USC 261.
3. K. G. Rivette and D. Kline, *Rembrandts in the Attic*, Harvard Business School Press, Boston (2000).
4. http://en.wikipedia.org/wiki/Hi-MD, retrieved 2014/12/21.

5

The Structure of a Patent

It is not just failures of the big-picture strategy that can reduce a patent's value—legal technicalities can render your claims useless against your competitors. Patents that are not carefully planned and drafted may not give the patent owner any effective degree of protection of his intellectual property.

When formulating patent strategies, the structure of patents is even more important to consider. A poorly worded application can impede or prevent one from having the other patent applications in the portfolio allowed, or may compromise the quality of other patents that are ultimately issued. Remember that an invention can only be claimed once. Claim trees comprising the independent and dependent claims for all the conceived applications have to be carefully designed to ensure that the technology is adequately and appropriately protected.

Because of the possibility of diminishing, and even destroying, your patent's value through seemingly insignificant mistakes during the writing of a patent application, writing a patent application is work for an expert, i.e., a qualified, licensed patent practitioner. Giving this job to someone who is unqualified is an expensive, high-risk/low-yield gamble. At best, a patent that was not well written will lack strength in court; at worst, it will not be issued at all. Filing an unsuccessful application costs every bit as much as those that lead to an issued patent, and presents your technology to the public—including your competitors—literally teaching them how to practice your technology while not protecting your intellectual property.

Care must also be exercised when prosecuting the patent application, as all comments and explanations you present to the examiner become part of the permanent record of any patents that are ultimately issued. These can be obtained by anyone against whom the assignee wishes to "assert" the patent (i.e., sue for patent infringement) and can provide an excellent defense if the accused can argue that what the assignee is now stating as the meaning of his patent was not what was stated to the examiner when the patent was allowed.

Hiring a capable patent practitioner minimizes your chances of losing patent value due to subtle mistakes in your initial application. Moreover, comments made when prosecuting one application can undermine the other applications and, even worse, can be used to restrict issued patents that you already own or even be used in a trial to have those patents declared invalid.

Patent Practitioners

If patent practitioners are the ones who should write and prosecute patent applications, why do inventors and assignees need to understand the structure of a patent? A patent practitioner may file applications on a number of different technological areas. It is not feasible for a patent practitioner to be an expert in the technology for which the inventors are trying to obtain a patent. More often than not, the practitioner relies on the expertise and insights of the inventors and assignees during the writing process. Because of this, patent applications are only as good as the information the inventors have given to the practitioner.

For the inventors and assignees to ensure that the practitioner has access to good information, they must be familiar with the kinds of details he will need. In cases where the assignees and inventors are different people, it is especially vital that the inventors understand the benefits of the information they are providing, and are incentivized to provide it. All parties must be familiar with their company's strategy so that the information put forth in the application strikes a balance between what is required to obtain the patent, with that which can be withheld in order to ensure that the ability to file future applications on related technology is not compromised.

Finally, the inventors must declare under penalty of perjury that they believe they are original inventors of the claimed invention. In order to state this in good conscience, inventors must know enough about the structure of a patent to be able to read and understand their own patent applications. Above all, it is the responsibility of the technical team members or the patent engineer* to ensure that the specific applications filed fit properly into the overall patent strategy and intended portfolio and that, as a result, the technology is adequately protected. The patent practitioner, in general, does not have either the business or technical skills to be able to determine the how the pieces all come together. This is especially true if your company relies on outside legal counsel, as opposed to in-house patent attorneys or agents.

Patent Engineering

Successful patent engineering involves incorporating an over-arching sweep of the related technologies, for example, deciding which applications to file, with diligence paid to specific details, for example, not making possibly-damaging statements during prosecution. The first step in engineering a patent portfolio is to identify the critical problems and their solutions.

As discussed in Chapter 4, critical problems, also known as critical challenges, are those that drive the customer's buying decisions or habits. They either address consumer requirements, i.e., they solve the consumer's problem, or are required by regulation in order for you to offer your product for sale. Both ultimately affect profitability. The Apple computer is an example of the former as it allowed a typical consumer to use a computer in his home or office to accomplish tasks such as word processing in a much easier manner than had been previously done with a typewriter. The automotive O_2 sensor is an example of the latter, whereby an automobile manufacturer would not be allowed to sell his products without a means of controlling emissions and enhancing mileage.

A single patent seldom affords adequate protection of intellectual property. Balancing what is disclosed at any time, the number of inventions that are disclosed, and maintaining options for future filings, weighed against

* The role of a patent engineer is discussed in detail in Chapter 11. For the purpose of the present discussion, a patent engineer should have knowledge of both the technical field and patents.

the importance of being the first to file, is vital for establishing and implementing an effective patent strategy. Furthermore, enough must be disclosed to allow revisions to be made to the claims, as might be required during prosecution, without jeopardizing future applications. Patent strategizing is a complex activity. As also discussed earlier in this book, it is not adequate to simply file patent applications on the critical problems. Rather, these challenges should serve as the focus for developing an encompassing and valuable patent portfolio.

Next, some novel technology, although not fundamental, may be necessary to implement the solutions to the critical problems. While a number of patents issued for O_2 sensors cover the device itself, far more encompass how the device will be used. A solution to a critical problem is of minimal value if that solution cannot be implemented. And, very often, your competition may develop alternative solutions to the same critical problems but wind up needing the enabling technology that your company has patented. Your ability to control the licensing of the rights to your technology can allow you to control the market and enhance your revenue.

Finally, it is important for you to understand how your competition is addressing the critical problems. They may have another approach that can have both benefits and limitations that your technology does not have. Obtaining patents in these areas can be exceedingly valuable because your competition needs the solutions covered by those patents. Obtaining those patents is a good way of generating revenues from licensing or, alternatively, licensing agreements that give your company access to your competition's technology.

To review what we have learned so far: A patent, operationally speaking, is a description of a technical solution to a technical problem. The solution must be novel, although it need not be unique. Alternative methods, pieces of equipment, or materials that solve a problem in a manner that have not been disclosed previously and cannot simply be derived by combining the teachings of an arbitrary number of sources including, but not limited to, issued patents, published patent applications, general technical literature, products available or known to the public, etc. are patentable.

A patent is not and should not be confused with any other form of technical publication, including but not limited to scientific or technological papers, and service/instruction manuals. Each of these serves a distinct and separate purpose and, whereas there may be significant overlap in the respective technical contents, their purposes and audiences are different. The purpose of other types of publications is to present information to the intended audience in a manner that teaches. The purpose of a patent is to establish a proprietary position on intellectual property that precludes a competitor from practicing the patented solution without your consent. In exchange for obtaining a monopolistic position, the applicants are required to teach how to practice the purported invention. A patent is written for a purely legal audience with the intent of being able to explain its contents to people as different as a patent examiner, a Supreme Court justice, and a juror. One should not lose sight of that objective.

Both the problems and the solutions play a part in a patent. While multiple problems can be solved by a single inventive solution, only one invention is allowed per patent. If an examiner determines that an application contains inventions that can be practiced independently of each other, he will generally specify which claims are associated with which purported invention and ask the inventors to decide which set of claims they wish to pursue first. The other claims can be subsequently prosecuted in a divisional application, as discussed in Chapter 4. With these factors in mind, let us now turn our attention to the core of this chapter, namely the structure and necessary components of a patent.

Patent Structure

An essential component of a patent is the formal document required to file a patent application in the United States. The requirements and procedures for filing in other countries will be discussed in Chapter 9. In the United States, a patent usually includes:

a. A short—and rarely descriptive—title.
b. An abstract. The abstract is a brief description of the field of the invention and the problem solved.
c. Figures (e.g., charts, graphs, line drawings, or photographs) illustrating the claimed invention.
d. A discussion of the prior art and the problem to be solved. This is in a section called "The Background of the Invention".
e. A brief description of the invention. This is often just a restatement of the first claim.
f. A detailed description of the invention that includes sufficient information so as to allow knowledgeable individuals to follow the description and make and use the invention.
g. Claims. The claims define the invention and constitute those items for which the patent gives your company the right to exclude others from practicing that invention.

There are frequently two additional sections in a patent application. The first, the "Field of the Invention" describes the general area of technology relevant to the invention and assists the USTPO in channeling the application to the correct department. The second, "A Brief Description of the Figures" facilitates the ability of a reader, be that the examiner or someone interested in the patent, to comprehend the patent.

What a Claim Entails

Though the claims comprise the last section of the patent application, they are the most important because they define the patent owner's intellectual property. For this reason, the claims section of the application should be written first, with all of the other supporting sections written afterward. The claims have to capture the entire invention; this means that another person should be able to practice the invention by following every step of the claim(s) precisely.

Often, claims can seem obscure on first reading. In the interest of laying the foundation for a positive outcome in any future legal action involving your patent, make it your goal from the beginning to have your claims be comprehensible to a lay audience. This is not a trivial endeavor.

As an exercise, try writing a claim that describes how to hard-boil an egg. To add to the challenge, every element must be introduced before it is used in relation to another element, and the physics of the matter (the water cannot overflow the pot; there has to be enough for the egg to cook) must be taken into account at every step. The resulting first claim might look like this:

1. A method of cooking an egg, the method comprising:
   a. placing the egg in a container, wherein:
      i. the egg has a minor diameter and a major diameter; and
      ii. the container has a height of at least twice the minor diameter of the egg and a diameter of at least twice the major diameter of the egg and is configured to withstand heating to a temperature of greater than 100 °C;
   b. adding a selected volume of water to the container holding the egg, wherein the selected volume of water fills the container holding the egg to a depth of at least the minor diameter of the egg and at most 75% of the height of the container;

c. applying heat at a selected first power to the container holding the egg and the selected volume of water until the water in the container comes to a boil; and
d. subsequently, applying heat at a selected second power to the container holding the egg and the water so that the water in the container is retained at a simmer for a selected period of time and the egg solidifies, wherein the second power is less than the first power.

In other words, the claim is trying to clearly and unambiguously define the steps necessary to practice the invention.** In order for inventors to give the patent practitioner the level of detail that he needs to construct a strong claim, inventors should understand the claims structure well enough to anticipate what the practitioner will need. The inventor also must be able to communicate the invention to be claimed to the patent practitioner in the manner required by the USPTO. A patent practitioner will insure that proper procedure is followed.

Conversely, nothing that is not required to practice the invention should be included in the claims, as such inclusions serve only to unnecessarily restrict the range of validity of the patent. For example, let us again consider the claim describing the method of hard-boiling an egg. It would be detrimental to add a step "e" to the independent claim that states "remove the egg from the water with a spoon". Such terminology is not required to produce the hard-boiled egg. Moreover, it greatly restricts the claim so that someone who simply pours the water out of the pot would not be infringing upon the claim.

Often, if an application has been rejected based on prior art, the prior art can be overcome by rewriting the independent claim to include a dependent claim. In the egg example, if the examiner found, for example, a patent that describes processing souvenir snake eggs in a manner that follows the specifications of the first claim, that rejection could possibly be overcome by combining the first claim with a second, dependent claim that specifies a chicken egg. This, of course, would only work if the claims in the snake egg disclosure do not say that the process could be used for chicken eggs. It would not matter that the snake egg inventor is producing souvenirs and the chicken egg inventor is making breakfast. The reader is reminded that the owner of a patent enjoys complete rights to exclude others from practicing the patented technology, even if the usage envisioned by the owner is significantly different from another usage.

** The reader is reminded that a patent can cover an apparatus, a material, or a method.

Opportunities to Enhance Your Portfolio

Once the claims for a patent application have been drafted, it is time to ask what other patent applications are envisioned in related areas of endeavor. The easiest way to do this is have whoever is coordinating the application filings*** meet with the members of the team who are working on the project, using that time to determine what other inventions may be ready for patenting, but have not been reported yet. This is also a good time to check in and see what the team is working on that might give birth to new patent opportunities in the near future. Very often, inventors do not realize that they have patentable material; a patent engineer who has knowledge of both technical and legal worlds can direct the conversation in such a way that the inventors can more accurately identify their patentable material. It is up to the coordinator or patent engineer to help the team implement their company's patent strategy, and to ensure that the filings are timely without unduly compromising the filings of future inventions. This is challenging work, which is why having a skilled patent engineer work with the technology team at this time can be a cost efficient way to boost the value of your patent portfolio.

Next, claims should be drafted for the other inventions that are ready for filing, as this will guide the inventors as to what can be disclosed in the applications presently under consideration. If at all possible, attempts should also be made to draft claims for those activities that are not yet ready for patenting because this will enable the formulation of a holistic patent strategy that goes beyond the immediate applications that are to be filed. Although this may seem odd, it is important to file applications with the knowledge and recognition that future applications will follow and the present applications should not prematurely disclose the technology for which patents will be sought in the near future. It should be noted that, just as a patent is limited to a single invention, an invention can be claimed in only a single patent.

Prior Art Searches

Once your claims have been drafted, but before you actually file them, it is extremely beneficial to conduct a prior art search. A careful search enables

*** The coordination should be done by an individual who has technical knowledge of the project, knows what the competitors are doing, and has an understanding of patent law. A patent engineer would be an ideal coordinator.

you to anticipate some, if not many, of the patent examiner's objections to your application. This is extremely important at this time because, based on the search results, the claims may have to be redrafted or even abandoned. It is also possible that the search results may reveal that it is not worthwhile to file the proposed applications, because the most valuable parts of the proposed invention and what remains are not sufficiently significant to warrant the expense of filing and maintenance.

Note that when conducting a prior art or patentability search, any publication can be important, including those that are not claims. It is not sufficient that the present proposed invention has not been claimed by anyone; the important question is whether the proposed invention has already been described to the public. Therefore, searches through patents or patent applications should not be limited to their claims, as any disclosure**** can preclude the ability to get a patent.

Finally, the search results will help the inventors advance the company's patent application, as well as its strategy, by helping them define the greater problem that they have solved and describe why everything that has come before (the prior art) does not solve it. This is crucial if a patent application is to be successfully prosecuted.

While searching may, at first, seem daunting, the internet has made this much easier and more accessible than in previous years. Searches can be conducted through the United States Patent and Trademark Office (patft.uspto.gov). Alternatively, there are numerous private search engines available. Some require that accounts be purchased, whereas others are free. While it is important to control costs, you need to take into consideration that many of the free search engines market their search results, which means that your competitors may know that you are searching a technological area before you are ready to file. If you do end up using free search engines, it is better to use private computers rather than ones that are easily traced to your company. While special-purpose patent search engines and/or services generally keep search results confidential, you should always confirm that before paying for an account.

Although searches can be started in a number of ways, relevant patents known to the technical team can be a good place to start. Entering key words into the patent search engines generally works. Searching on

---

**** The term "disclosure" applies to the disclosing of the information that would allow someone to practice your invention. Disclosures can exist in the form of prior art, which can be combined to allow someone to derive the invention. A disclosure of the invention also exists in the information presented in your patent application.

competitors as assignees or on known inventors at other companies is also effective. Some software allows an entire draft claim to be entered. The results obtained can then be further filtered by entering key words. It is generally worthwhile to use the search engines in a way that, if the search is effective, they will turn up the patents of which you are already aware. If this does not occur, it may be necessary to alter the search pattern. For example, key words used by one company may be very different from those used by another. Performing a key word search with words that do not match will not yield results. Once patents or other documents are found in the search, the search can often be expanded to include citations. The documents you find will usually cite other, earlier documents. Some search engines will show patents or other documents that within themselves cite documents in your search results.

Doing a thorough search will probably not guarantee the examiner does not find prior art that he deems relevant. A thorough search can, however, eliminate much of what would otherwise turn up during prosecution, reducing costs by minimizing the amount of time your legal personnel will need to spend on responding to the examiner's assertions (so-called "office actions"). It also promotes cost efficiency by helping the inventors fine-tune their patent application, particularly the claims, allowing for a stronger, more enforceable patent product.

As important as your inventors' solution is, it is equally important that they clearly define the problem or problems solved so that they can communicate that understanding to the patent practitioner. While the extent to which you discuss the problem in the application is generally the patent practitioner's decision, some discussion is almost always included since a claim describes a technical solution to a technical problem. As such, if the problem is not clearly described, it is more difficult to obtain a patent. Moreover, a clear statement of the problem greatly helps to focus the patent examiner's attention on the issues being discussed. If this is not done, it is very likely that the examiner will cite prior art that is not directly related to the problem, complicating the prosecution of the patent application.

With this in mind, after the claims have been drafted and the prior art search completed, the background of the invention section should be written. This section should include a discussion of the prior art and the problem solved by the present invention. Included in this section should be an explanation as to why the prior art, either by itself or in conjunction with other pieces of prior art, does not give the solution that you are patenting to the problem that you are solving.

Although a patent is limited to a single invention, that is, the claims must describe one and only one solution, there is no limitation regarding the number of problems that the claimed solution addresses. Accordingly, if there are multiple limitations to the known technology that can be addressed by the claims, it may be worthwhile to describe those limitations in the application, either in the background or the details section. This is especially true if much of the application is being used for a family of patent applications being filed, especially if being filed concurrently.

Background Section of a Patent

The background section of the patent application is commonly where the prior art is described. The background (consult your patent practitioner) should describe the problem or problems solved by the invention, as well as how the prior art tried to solve the problem or, quite possibly, ignored the problem or even contributed to the problem.

When discussing the shortcomings of the technology in the prior art, some care should be taken. Specifically, if your company has been working in this area for some time, it probably has a patent portfolio. While the shortcomings of competitors' patents can be discussed in detail, you should always avoid discussing the limitations of your own patent portfolio.

Also, be sure to remember that the information presented in an application is published and available to competitors for whatever purposes they choose, be it prosecuting their own cases, defending against assertions commenced by your company, or using the information in a patent infringement suit against your company whether or not your patent is eventually issued.

Ultimately, the goal of the background section is to lay out the problem or problems solved in sufficient detail and clarity that it is clear the proposed invention is, in fact, novel and non-obvious. A lucid statement of the problem or problems goes far in establishing patentability at the outset of prosecution of the application.

Returning to the example of the hard-boiled egg patent application, suppose your patent search has been completed and you have turned up patents on poached eggs, scrambled eggs, and eggs over easy, but none on hard-boiled eggs. In your application you discuss the unanticipated results, namely that the egg can be cooked in its shell and it retains its shape. In particular, you discuss in your application that it is not obvious that the egg, which nature designed to retain fluids and thus, is relatively impervious, could, in fact, be cooked without rupturing the shell due to the increase in vapor pressure within the egg when the fluids in the uncooked egg are heated. The problem has now been defined in a way that seems to be patentably different from the prior art that you have found. However, a claim merely describing the steps to be performed, but which addresses neither shape nor shell, may not benefit from that difference. This will be our next topic.

Detailed Description of the Invention Including the Figures

The next section that should be written is the "Detailed Description of the Invention". This is the most difficult section to write because it requires careful balancing of what is to be disclosed and what is not to be disclosed.

First and foremost, the detailed description of the invention must contain all information necessary for someone "skilled in the art" to make and use the invention. In other words, anything that is in a claim must be described to an appropriate audience. This holds for all claims—both independent and dependent. The appropriate audience has knowledge of the basics of the field. In our egg example, it is not necessary to explain what a stove is or how natural gas is delivered from a shale field to a burner. However, since the prior art in this example did not describe immersing whole eggs in liquid, a pot of sufficient size to hold both the water and the egg needs to be described. The amount of water, the extent of heating, and any other features that are in the claim must be in the detailed description. The egg itself must also be described since the physical properties of the egg are such that the results—that the egg is converted from a liquid to a solid, the shape of the egg is retained, and the shell has not been destroyed—are, within our hypothetical example, unexpected and thus qualify as novel. Furthermore, the species of egg must be described if, e.g., it is set forth in dependent claims. Suppose a dependent claim specifies that the egg could be a chicken egg. That, too, must be in the detailed description.

Be sure to note that, whereas claims can be revised during the course of prosecution, the rest of the disclosure (i.e., the information contained within the patent application), for the most part, cannot. Suppose the examiner rejects the egg application as allegedly obvious in light of "the poached egg when combined with matzoh ball soup." In the office action, the examiner goes on to explain that placing an egg in boiling water to solidify the egg is known as that is what is done to make a poached egg. The examiner further states that, whereas the poached egg prior art does not disclose major or minor diameters, the matzoh ball reference describes spheroidal, egg-containing matzoh balls, which contain egg and are spheroidal—and therefore have the major and minor diameters cited in the example claim 1, above.

You might respond by amending claim 1 to include cooking the egg in its shell, which is not the case for either the matzoh ball or the poached egg. However, amending the claim accordingly would be permissible if and only if there is explicit information presented in the disclosure that the egg, while in the pot of boiling water, is contained within its shell.

The disclosure would then also have to include a description of an egg, including at least the shell, the membrane between the shell and the liquid portions of the uncooked egg, the yolk, and the white. Again, the goal of the application is to allow someone, upon reading the patent, to practice the invention.

Do not assume that anything is "patently obvious". Every aspect that relates to practicing the invention must be described. This example is simply used to illustrate the detail that is required. The prosecution of a patent application, including office actions and responding to office actions, will be discussed in more detail in Chapter 7. For now, let us continue discussing what should be included and what should not be included in a properly written disclosure.

It should be noted that, when writing a patent disclosure, the writer can define the terms used. That said, those terms should be defined in a way that is unambiguous, but not needlessly restrictive. For example, one can define an "egg" as a natural egg that is substantially free from externally introduced materials, defining "externally introduced" as any material that would not normally be included in the formation of an egg by a similar animal in the wild. This could, for example, keep the examiner from incorporating the matzoh balls into his rejection, as matzoh meal, oil, salt, and pepper added to the egg to make the matzoh balls would certainly fall within the category of being "externally introduced."

That by itself, however, is not unambiguous since antibiotics fed to farm-raised birds can show up in their eggs. Does this mean that you can avoid infringing the patent simply by using antibiotic-laden eggs? In the same vein, aluminum pots are known to introduce aluminum ions into boiling water; these are then infused into the food being prepared in that pot. Would eggs cooked in an aluminum pot and now containing aluminum ions still count as "substantially free of externally introduced materials?" How about adding table salt to the water? Would that avoid patent infringement? While terminology like this can be used to avoid unanticipated related art, it also may reduce the instances in which the patent claims may apply, thus reducing the patent's eventual value.

On a side note, the example method claim above only covers the actual hard-boiling of the egg. In order to obtain a thorough patent portfolio, your company may find it beneficial to file patent applications on specific containers for holding eggs, egg supports for use in the container, container lids, egg timers, or other devices that may be useful during the hard-boiling process. This could be done cost-effectively, as these alternatives could all be described in a single detailed description that is incorporated into each patent application filed, saving you the cost of rewriting common sections.

So far, the disclosure of this patent includes all eggs—that, in and of itself, presents difficulty. Claims broad enough to cover lizard eggs and bird eggs can be rejected over prior art describing either alone. The shells of reptile eggs are leathery, not hard, and will deform when resting on a surface which can present difficulties in clearly defining the minor diameter. Because of this, you might be better off restricting the application to bird eggs, excluding reptile and fish eggs. Even if the application is necessarily restricted to bird eggs, the detailed description should still include enough information to cover all your competitors' foreseeable options—even those lizard eggs you chose to exclude.

The disclosure can also discuss specific ways of practicing the invention. One such way would require that the eggs have a hard, rather than leathery, shell. Another example would be that the eggs are avian, e.g., chicken, quail, duck, or goose eggs. This gives sufficient disclosure to allow you to include dependent claims on those features.

The advantage of describing multiple options in the application is that it allows you to choose during prosecution to restrict your claims to bird eggs only if the examiner makes a rejection involving lizard eggs. Whatever choice you make, all of the necessary details should be stated in the detailed description. You may not get as broad a patent as initially desired, but it should protect most of your business interests.

The same considerations that apply to the eggs may also apply to other components of your solution. For example, when cooking, a stove and/or pot are not the only viable options. Hard-boiling an egg requires a container to hold water and a heat source. The container must be able to hold both water and the egg and be able to withstand heating. Your competitor might use a wooden bowl and an immersion heater!

When contemplating the options, however, it is important to identify their drawbacks. While immersion heaters do exist and would probably be suitable for use in a wooden bowl, it is both more difficult and less efficient to hard-boil an egg in this way. A detailed description that intended to cover all the options might also describe using an alternate heat source, like an electric resistance heater, induction heater, or a flame. It could also cover container materials.

Your customers might prefer that the container did not emit toxic materials into the water, thereby precluding the use of a lead pot. Ordinary glass might shatter upon exposure to heat but a tempered glass, such as Pyrex, might be suitable. Ceramic pots would be suitable, however, they would be less convenient to use than metal ones. Their use can be described as "a less preferred method of practicing the invention" in the detailed description section of the application. Likewise, the use of an aluminum pot can also be described as being less desirable than a steel pot because the aluminum ions dissolved in the water can leach into the egg, imparting an unpleasant flavor. This detail allows you to broadly claim the pot in the independent claim, but then specify the preferred steel pot in a dependent claim.

If any dependent claims relate to the properties of the water, that water should also be described. Moreover, the liquid might not necessarily be water—boiling oil might be usable. The salt or mineral content of the water might affect results and therefore be useful in a dependent claim.

Likewise, dependent claims might relate to how the egg would be placed into the pot of boiling water. One dependent claim might state that the egg should be gently lowered into the water. The egg can be lowered by holding the egg with portions of one's hand. However, it is preferable to lower the egg using an egg cradling device such as a spoon or ladle that can support the egg while being immersed into the water. Also suitable would be a basket or cloth mesh that can support the egg prior to and during immersion. As one generally would not want to leave the egg lowering device in the water, it should be stated that the device is preferably separable (it could be left in contact with the egg during the entire cooking process if so desired) after the egg has been immersed. As before, the use of a device that can be detached from the egg after the egg had been lowered into the water can be included as a dependent claim. It should not be included in the independent claim as its inclusion would restrict the coverage of that claim needlessly.

While this may seem a bit more detail than would normally be required by anyone having any common sense, the fact is that without this detail, the feature of immersing the egg could be rejected over a reference that cited throwing the egg into a container from across a room, or dropping the egg into the container from a great height. Again, the detailed description of the invention must fully describe how someone would practice the invention.

It is also worthwhile to describe how one would measure anything for which the specification states measurements. The example claim 1 above describes the size of the container relative to the major and minor diameters of the egg and the amount of water in the container. The major and minor diameters can be measured using a conventional outsider caliper commonly found among cabinet makers instruments, by spanning the egg until the greatest diameter is found and measuring that diameter with a ruler. The height of the water can be measured by resting the container containing the water on a level surface so that the water is approximately still and immersing the ruler into the water until it contacts the bottom of the deepest part of the container (the container can be shaped like a wok rather than a saucepan) and determining the height on the ruler to which the water reaches.

A single method of measurement should be stated in the patent application because differing measurement techniques can result in different results for the same object. For example, it is conceivable to estimate the major diameter of the egg by wrapping a string around the egg along its major and minor axes and determining the major diameter by subtracting the contribution to the circumference due to the minor diameter. Would such a method work? Probably. Would it give the same result as the caliper method? Probably not. The method of measurement should be unambiguous so that infringement can be clearly determined.

Most patent applications include a section entitled "Figures" that illustrate the invention. Figures can include line drawings, charts, graphs, or

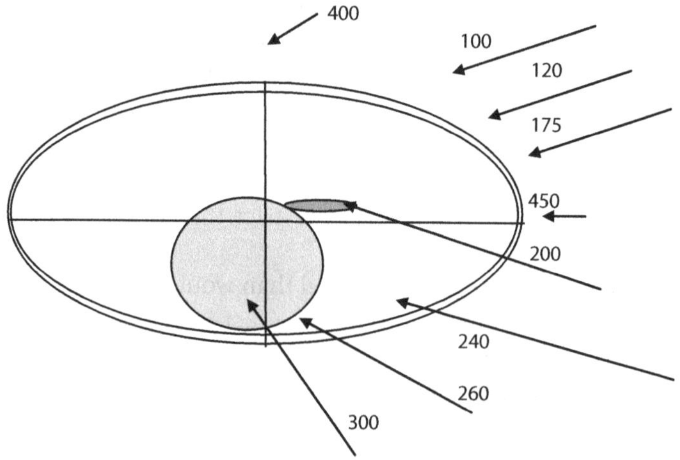

Figure 5.1 An illustration of a figure used in a patent application.

photographs. Figure 5.1 shows an example figure that might be helpful for the hard-boiled egg application. The purpose of the figures, like that of the detailed description, is to ensure that every aspect of the invention can be unambiguously understood and practiced by someone based on the information in the patent. The figures augment the written description. For this purpose every component of the figure should be illustrated and numbered. The numbers are then referenced in the text. For example, the text describing Figure 5.1 could read as follows:

> Figure 5.1 shows an egg 100 having a major diameter 450 and a minor diameter 400. The egg 100 comprises a shell 120 that provides mechanical support and protection for the interior components of the egg. Attached to the interior surface of the shell 120 is a membrane 175 that contains the liquid albumen 240. Within the albumen 240 is a yolk 300 surrounded by a membrane 260 that contains the fluid material of the yolk. Attached to the exterior surface of the membrane 260 and contained totally within the albumen 240 is a germinal disk 200 that, if fertilized, would give rise, after proper incubation, to an animal such as a chicken.

For the hard-boiled egg application, additional figures would likely be included, such as figures showing the container containing water, the heat source, and the egg being immersed into the water. The general rule is that any feature claimed should be illustrated in at least one figure. Figures can also include flow charts, as might be appropriate for an application that claims a method of doing something. Each step in the flowchart is numbered and discussed in the detailed description of the invention.

It may seem a bit much to have to include all this detail. But for a technology more complicated than hard-boiling an egg, could a reader familiar with the general technology of that patent but unfamiliar with the specific invention, practice the invention if the detail were not included? Furthermore, patent law has specific requirements for the kinds of detail that are required.

Benefits of Common Disclosures

As previously noted, the text that is common to a family of applications can be written to cover those applications. Multiple applications can be filed using that text, with small invention-specific modifications in both the background and the detailed description to ensure that the problem and the inventive solution to the problem covered by a specific application are adequately addressed. Writing such common text often saves time for both the inventors and the practitioners. This translates into higher productivity for the technical team and lower legal costs. If carefully written, portions of the common text and figures may even be suitable for future patent applications, thereby saving additional time and money.

What should not be discussed in a patent application or family of patent applications is any technology that may be patentable in the future, but is not yet ripe for filing. For example, hard-boiling an egg generally results in the formation of a bluish green annulus around the yoke. While this does not contribute to the flavor of the hard-boiled egg, it is not overly appetizing either. The formation of this layer can be avoided by turning off the source of heat when, or immediately prior to, immersing the egg and allowing the egg to cook in the heat retained by the hot, but not boiling, water.

Suppose your inventors discover this after an application has already been filed on hard-boiling. If the already-filed application mentions cooking the egg in hot water, rather than boiling water, or discloses turning off the source of heat prior to having completely cooked the egg, the examiner may reject the application on the basis that the prior art (your own application) discloses cooking the egg in hot water.

This is true regardless of whether you recognized any particular advantage (e.g., avoiding annulus formation) at the time you described the way to obtain that advantage (e.g., cooking in hot, not boiling, water).

Disclosing more than what is going to be claimed or directly supports the application is generally a mistake. There are, however, exceptions. One such exception would be to defend one's technology against incursions by "non-practicing entities" (NPEs), sometimes referred to as "patent trolls" or "patent assertion entities" (PAEs).

An NPE is a company that obtains patents on its inventions but does not manufacture any of its patented technology (This generally does not include universities and/or other not-for-profits). NPEs make money by filing lawsuits against alleged infringers of its patents, hoping to extract licensing fees. As defenses in patent lawsuits are very expensive, typically ranging in the millions of dollars, it is often financially advantageous for a defending company to settle such lawsuits on relatively cheap terms offered by the NPE, even if the NPE's arguments are weak.

Companies with good patent portfolios can often settle or totally avoid lawsuits brought about by other companies by agreeing to patent cross-licensing agreements whereby each agrees to grant a license to the other for use of patented technology. This allows both companies to practice each other's inventions, within well-defined limits, thereby avoiding lawsuits. However, since NPEs do not manufacture, they generally have no need for licenses to the patents of others, effectively destroying any possibility of cross-licensing. Because of this, threatening a patent troll with a counter suit is about as effective as shouting into the wind.

A way to reduce your company's exposure to NPEs is to include descriptions in your patent applications that will prevent an NPE from obtaining patents that might be relevant to your products. While it is impossible to eliminate the risk of NPE lawsuits, a company is less likely to be victimized if its patent portfolio protects all aspects of its products. This includes the enabling technology, in addition to the fundamental advances. Unfortunately, developing such a portfolio can be very expensive and, even then, there is no guarantee that it would be successful in blocking NPEs. However, it is necessary to at least try to do so, as the consequence of not doing so can be quite costly. This is another area where a conscientious effort to develop a thorough patent strategy can pay big dividends, even if patents are not filed for every conceivable invention.

Once it has been decided what applications will be filed according to your patent strategy, either presently or in the future, appropriate disclosures can be written. Descriptions of those inventions that are deemed to not be of sufficient value to warrant their own patent applications can still be described in the detailed description of the invention section. This would act as prior art, thereby precluding another company from patenting those inventions. Moreover, your company can still file an application claiming the previously unclaimed subject matter if circumstances within a reasonable time dictate that full patent protection would be advisable. This will be discussed in more detail in Chapter 7.

Note that while the detailed description and figures often describe why an invention works —they are not required to. It is only necessary to include the information that enables a competent person to practice the invention. For the example of the hard-boiled egg patent application, the inventor only needed to describe how to hard-boil the egg; there is no need for him to include a discussion of why the protein chemistry causes the yolk and white to solidify. Consult your patent practitioner regarding the appropriate level of detail for each individual application, bearing in mind that the inventor very likely will have to explain both the problem and its solution to the patent practitioner so that the practitioner can properly advise the inventor as to what needs to be included in the application.

To review, while the patent practitioner is the authority on how the application should be prepared, ultimately, the contents of the claims and applications are determined by business and technology factors. Thus, the inventors are responsible for clearly and thoroughly describing the invention and the prior art to the practitioner. Managers should apprise the practitioner of likely infringers of the invention claimed and should explain the business rationale for filing the application. This will put the practitioner in the best position to recommend appropriate claims and what level of detail is appropriate for the application.

The components of a patent application are fairly straightforward. The claims describe the invention, the background sets the stage, and the detailed description and figures teach the reader how to make and use the claimed invention. The title, brief description of the invention, and abstract are usually derived from or related to the claims in some way. A section entitled "Field of the Invention" is a short paragraph that helps the patent office route the application to an examiner trained in the relevant subject area. The "Brief Description of the Figures" section is derived from the detailed description and includes short captions of each figure. Now that you know the components of a patent application and some of the requirements your practitioner must satisfy, you will be able to more effectively communicate with your practitioner to develop your patent portfolio.

A Closer Look at Prior Art Searching

Your patents will be stronger if you search the prior art literature prior to filing. Prior to the advent of the internet, literature searches were tedious and had to be done either through a library that had access to the patent office or through a company that possessed an ongoing compilation of patents. Needless to say, the ability of inventors to perform background searches was generally somewhat limited, time consuming, and often expensive. Access to the internet has changed that and, today, patent search engines abound. These include the United States Patent and Trademark Office (USPTO) (http://patft.uspto.gov) website for U.S. patents and patent abstracts and the European Patent Office (https://www.epo.org/index.html) or http://worldwide.espacenet.com/ and World Intellectual Property Organization (http://www.wipo.int/patentscope/en/) databases. There are also the fee based search sites such as Lexis (http://www.lexisnexis.com), Thompson Innovation (http://info.thomsoninnovation.com) and Innography (http://app.innography.com/. In addition, there are free search engines such as Google Patents (http://www.google.com/advanced_patent_search) and DuckDuckGo (https://www.duckduckgo.com).

Be sure to read the terms of service of any search service carefully. Remember that some services retain rights to mine or sell data about what you are searching for. That information might make it into your competitor's hands and tip them off about the direction you are moving.

Always keep in mind that a description anywhere in a patent or patent application or other document, whether or not allowed, issued, or expired, is prior art. A patentability or prior art search differs in this respect from a clearance search, (covered in Chapter 10). Whereas a clearance search is limited to the claims of active patents, patentability searches must include the entire disclosure within the prior art, whether or not that particular material was claimed.

Searches can be started in a number of ways. For example, most search engines permit key word searches. These can be effective. However, many companies use their own vernacular that may differ from that used by competitors to describe aspects of a technology. If key words are used, it is beneficial to see if the search turns up patents that are known to exist belonging to competitors. If that does not happen, the list of key words should be expanded. Often employees working for competitors on similar technology are known. Searching on their names can be quite productive. Patents held by competitors are often good sources for much information, especially key words used in the vernacular of the competitor, and, by themselves, can constitute valuable components of a search.

Once patents are found, the list of citations can lead to other patents. Some search engines allow forward citation searches, i.e., searching for patents or patent applications that were subsequently published that cite the referenced patent. This can allow the searcher to obtain more recent references.

Some search engines allow what is called a "semantic search"; that is, searching on a phrase or sentence rather than on key words. A simple but effective way of utilizing a search engine that incorporates semantic search capabilities is to insert the entire first claim into the semantic search. The results obtained can then be narrowed to the most relevant art by searching the findings using a key word search.

It is not necessary that every piece of prior art be discussed in a patent application in the hope of anticipating all possible arguments posed by the examiner. That probably will not happen and is not necessary. What is necessary is that you review the prior art and decide what is most relevant to your application. Those are pieces of art that you should discuss in the background of the invention.

It is possible that the claims will have to be revised in light of what turns up in the prior art search. Should this occur, it is important that the disclosure, preferably in the detailed description of the invention section, explicitly states what is in the revised claims. It should be remembered that, whereas the claims can be revised during prosecution, the rest of the patent application generally cannot. The disclosure has to be complete and correct prior to filing the application.

Once the search has been completed, it is worthwhile to reassess the entire patent strategy being put forth. Is it necessary to revise the claims and disclosures in the other applications in light of the search results? Moreover, have the search results revealed holes or problems in your competitors' technology that present opportunities for you to enhance the value of your patent portfolio? This is an excellent time to make whatever adjustments to the strategy that should be made.

Be sure that the search results are also reviewed by both your technical and legal experts. This is all-too-often an area where the language differences between engineers and attorneys are extremely problematic. The attorneys will be looking at the prior art from the legal vantage point of how it can be used to make the present invention obvious, thereby rendering the invention nonpatentable. Engineers tend to look at prior art as being either the same as the present invention or different. The attorney's assessment could be incorrect as subtle differences can differentiate the old technology from the present invention. Technical team members' patentability analyses are often incorrect because subtle legal differences can make the present advancement patentable or, alternatively, prior art may make the present advancement legally obvious or not novel, even if the problems solved are different.

That being said, written documentation of an assessment of the prior art should be avoided to whatever extent is possible by the engineers and written comments should be limited to statements such as "let's take a look at this patent". Intracompany correspondence is subject to discovery by your opposition's attorneys should you seek to assert your patents. You do not want to give your competitor grounds to have a court rule that your patent is invalid based on written comments from your own technical experts.

It should also be emphasized that for a patent to be allowed and ultimately issued, the solution to the problem must be novel and non-obvious to one of ordinary skill in the art. If the search reveals prior art that is close, make sure, in the background of the invention section, to discuss the shortcomings of that art (assuming that they are not your own patents) and why that art, either by itself or in combination with other art, does not solve the problem at hand. Carefully defining the problem in the background section and clearly specifying how you solved that problem in the detailed description of the invention are key elements in obtaining patent coverage.

If a patent application is well written and the search thorough, there is an excellent chance that the applicant will be able to traverse the objections raised by the examiner. An applicant will not win every battle and obtain every patent for which he applies. A success rate of about 75% is very good, i.e., of all the filed applications, 75% ultimately issue as patents. Success rates that are significantly lower may indicate that the applicant is not searching well or formulating the problem or invention carefully. Success rates that are significantly higher may indicate you have an opportunity to broaden the claims you are filing and seek to lock your competitor out of more options.

6

Inventions and Inventorship: Challenges and Complications

Each of us has a concept of an inventor. It may be a vision of Thomas Edison looking over his light bulb, or Samuel Popeil holding up his Pocket Fisherman [1]. The pictures in our minds often range from a team of scientists and engineers to the lone dreamer tinkering away in his garage, trying to come up with a product that will make him rich. Just as most people have various concepts of inventors, the concept of an invention also differs, sometimes within a single individual.

A person may view an invention as a complicated but significant technological advancement or as a clever, but possibly useless, product from an in-flight catalog. Sometimes people assign moral value to an invention, judging it as either good or evil, or possibly both. John C. Garand's invention of the semiautomatic M1 rifle helped win World War II, likely saving numerous American lives. However, as an instrument of war, the rifle has brought death to countless others.

What is a Patent?

Many people have the mistaken impression that an issued patent is like a government-issued award recognizing some kind of significant technological advance. This impression is often fed by advertisements that make outrageous claims that generally run along these lines—"This product is so amazing and/or advanced that the United States government has recognized it by awarding it a patent." This perception is quite common, especially among those who have not worked with patents before.

While it is true that a patent is a government-issued document regarding a new technological solution, this does not mean that the solution is either amazing or advanced—merely that it is new and non-obvious. In this this chapter we will clarify what constitutes an invention, who an inventor actually is, why patents are issued, and what they represent.

What is an Invention?

Let us first discuss what constitutes an invention. Many people might envision the cell phone as an invention of great significance. In fact, it is not a single invention. In a search of the USPTO database for the terms "cellular" and "telephone", as used in the abstracts of issued patents, 3,150 individual patents that had been issued as of April 8, 2014 were found.

This means that, legally speaking, the cell phone is not a single invention but, rather, a combination of many inventions—possibly thousands. Now, are all of these patents used in, or are they of great significance to, the cell phone? Probably not. Many of these inventions are of marginal significance or may not be used at all. Others are very likely to be incremental improvements, or represent advances in some of the existing enabling technology. Still others may involve uses of cell phones rather than the cell phone itself, or components related to a cellular phone. For example, US 8,923,524 describes an "ultra-compact headset" for use with a phone. What you may think of as an "invention" is likely a whole collection of patents.

It is important to note that the value of a patent, as a legal document, is determined by how much money someone else is willing to pay to have rights to use the patented technology. This is often difficult to determine at the time around the initial filing of the application. Thus, a patent that covers the solution to a critical problem (e.g. the chemical process used to produce instant silver halide photographs) may wind up being of nominal value, whereas a patent covering more mundane enabling technology may have a much greater value.

Terms such as "invention," "patent," and "inventor" are clearly defined by patent law in ways that do not usually match common conception. As we have discussed in previous chapters, a patent is, legally speaking, a description of a technical solution to a technical problem. Both the problem and its solution are necessary components of a patent. The term "invention" is simply shorthand that means "the subject matter claimed in a patent or patent application."*

When considering a patent application, the patent office does not pass judgment on the solution's usefulness or commercial value. On its website, Bloomberg Businessweek has compiled a list entitled "The Most Ridiculous Patents [2]." One patent that made the list was entitled "Pet Display Clothing [3]." The patent describes a vest having clear tubes in which a rodent can run around, with a closeable portal to allow the pet to enter the tubes. Is this invention clever? It would certainly appear to be. Is it useful? Well, for those who have a deep love and appreciation for the constant companionship of our rodent friends, the answer would be a resounding yes. It is true that we have not seen such a device for sale in any stores, but that does not mean that it is not useful—only that it is not actively marketed.

It is clear that not all inventions result from teams of scientists and engineers with PhDs working in well-funded industrial laboratories. The inventions described in many patents may not be earthshaking. They may or may not result in the owner of the patent reaping great financial benefits. It is doubtful whether the owners of the pet display-wear patent became wealthy as a direct result of their patent. In contrast, according to the USPTO, Ronald Popeil holds thirty-one patents covering a variety of inventions including, but not limited to, a food cutting apparatus [4], a rotisserie [5], and a baldness cosmetic [6]. Although we cannot personally attest to Ron Popeil's current financial status, his infomercials are famous and in 2005 he reportedly sold his company to a holding firm for $56 million [7].

Similarly, as previously discussed in Chapter 3, Kodak was forced out of the instant photography business and had to pay Polaroid $900 million because Polaroid owned seven relatively simple enabling patents. The more

---

* Regarding the relationship between claims and inventions, U.S. patent law says "The specification shall conclude with one or more claims particularly pointing out and distinctly claiming the subject matter which the inventor or a joint inventor regards as the invention" (35 USC 112(b)). Under "inventions patentable," 35 USC 101, the law says "Whoever invents or discovers any new and useful process, machine, manufacture, or composition of matter, or any new and useful improvement thereof, may obtain a patent therefor, subject to the conditions and requirements of this title."

complex chemistry patents possessed by both Polaroid and Kodak were not found to be relevant to the patent infringement lawsuit. Simplicity or complexity are not criteria used by the Patent Office in deciding the patentability of an application, nor should they necessarily be the deciding factor used by an organization when determining whether a patent application covering a specific invention should be filed.

With this discussion in mind, it is worthwhile to now ask just what the USPTO considers an invention and what criteria would they use to decide whether or not to issue a patent. For the pet display clothing patent application, the patent office determined that the claims defined an invention and, accordingly, allowed the patent. A claim defines an allowable invention in a patent if it defines subject matter that is 1) novel, 2) useful, and 3) non-obvious. Let us explore what each of these terms mean according to the patent law.

Claims and Novelty

A claim is new, i.e., it has "novelty," if it describes something that has never appeared before in any product, publication, or other disclosure of information to the public. Disclosures can include patents, published applications, unpublished previously-filed applications, and other types of references. Please remember that the more you know about the prior art, the more effectively you will be able to identify problems you can own.

The requirement of novelty can have several pitfalls. If a company publicly demonstrates a product containing a purported invention, that is a disclosure. This can greatly complicate what can be presented at trade shows prior to filing the appropriate patent applications.

Similarly, disclosing or showing technology or products to consultants or potential outside collaborators can constitute a disclosure. According to United States patent law, once an item has been disclosed in any manner, the inventor has one year from the date of disclosure in which to file all pertinent patent applications. However, there is a danger inherent in taking advantage of this time window. Specifically, someone else such as a competitor or patent troll may have been working on similar technology and may have, independently, solved some problems that are critical to you. If that company files first, they, rather than you, may be awarded the patent. The United States, like most of the world today, awards patents to the first to file, not the first to invent. The introduction of your product may spur your competition to rapidly file patent applications on technology related to that product. Your company can wind up having to pay licensing fees in order to practice its own technology.

In addition, because a patent for a given invention is issued to the first party to file a patent application, it is possible that your company can lose its competitive patent position by premature disclosures. Moreover, many other countries do not have a one-year grace period. If a public disclosure were to occur prior to filing the appropriate patent applications, what was demonstrated or disclosed may no longer be patentable in those countries. This situation can severely compromise the value of your patent portfolio.

Companies often attempt to circumvent the novelty considerations by having potential customers, collaborators, or consultants first sign a nondisclosure agreement prior to their obtaining any proprietary information. Although this is a step in the right direction, there are still risks to one's ability for meeting the novelty requirements. Specifically, a nondisclosure agreement does not prevent the recipient of that information from, either deliberately or inadvertently, disclosing proprietary information. Any disclosure may negatively affect your patent rights, whether or not the disclosure was in violation of a nondisclosure agreement. True, parties who violate nondisclosure agreements can be sued for damages, but what can be collected after years of costly litigation might not restore the pecuniary loss suffered by your company if you cannot obtain a patent. Moreover, if the proprietary information is not clearly stated in writing to the recipient, the recipient can argue that he had received no such information to the best of his knowledge and did not willfully disclose any confidential material, reducing even the ability to seek damages.

There is yet another risk aside from that due to a premature disclosure. If you hire a consultant or contract with a supplier, that party probably has some expertise or capability that your company either lacks or for which the added value for your company to perform that task itself is insufficient. For example, let us assume that a company such as a contractual engineering firm was hired to augment the technical capability of your company in developing and/or producing a specific subsystem for a product that your company is planning to commercialize. The contractual company/supplier** will develop the technology that allows your company to achieve its goal. Unless you have arranged otherwise in advance, that company will own whatever patent rights may vest in what they develop.

** If a supplier is developing specific technology for your use in your products, it is considered a contractual company. However, as the term is used in this book, if a supplier is simply selling off-the-shelf items to your company for use in your products, it is not considered a contractual company.

In that situation, the supplier may file patent applications on their advancements that your company plans to use. The supplier will then own the rights to the technology that it developed on your behalf. The supplier will be free to license or sell that technology to your competitors. Moreover, even if your contract with that company allows your company to maintain exclusive rights to that technology, your company can be forced to buy that subsystem from the contractual company, rather than producing it yourself or bidding it out to other companies. Alternatively, your company may face having to pay extravagant licensing fees to use the technology for which your company contracted to develop in the first place. Finally, the contractual company will learn what it is that your company is developing and file a slew of patent applications that can block your company from commercializing your own technology. After all, you did hire that company because it had expertise and capabilities and they can take advantage of the fact that, in the United States, the patent is awarded to the first to file. How does a company avoid these problems?

Protecting Your Intellectual Property When Dealing with Contractual Companies

There are several aspects that need to be addressed in order to develop proper patent protection when dealing with contractual companies. First, having nondisclosure agreements and contracts that give your company exclusive rights to those advances made on your behalf is a necessary starting point. However, equally important is that your company should develop a patent strategy that would allow it to own as much of the problem as possible before engaging a contractual company.

Prior to exchanging any technical information with the contractual company, the technical team should, as a group, describe and list all features that will give the proposed product marketable advantages. This is, in essence, a holistic description of all aspects of the product, as best known by your technical experts. The immediate goal is to file all pertinent patent applications prior to any informational exchanges occurring. This is extremely important because, if the applications are filed prior to such exchanges, the contractual company cannot secure patents on the subject matter in those applications. In other words, your company, not the supplier, will own the fundamental or basic technology to be used in the product. It is extremely important that all known, seemingly novel, features of the proposed product be clearly identified at this time as errors in doing so now can leave gaping holes in your company's protection of its intellectual property.

Once the purported patentable features of the proposed project have been identified, it is time to conduct a thorough patent search. This is important because it will result in the refining of the proposed claims for the entire portfolio that emanates from these activities. Once the search has been completed and the claims revised, if necessary, to increase the probability of their being novel, it is time to write the disclosures.

As this strategy relates to a particular project, it is highly probable that a common description and drawings can be prepared, thus saving time and money on filing the individual applications. (It may also be possible to file a single provisional application containing the common disclosure and all the desired claims.) Once the disclosures have been written and filed, discussions with the consultant or contractual company can begin, as there is no way that any information you have can be patented out from under you.

This procedure, however, does not, in itself, give your company sufficient leeway to negotiate fees or even seek other suppliers. Moreover, it must be recognized that, in all likelihood, the consultant or contractual company was chosen because of the expectation that they would bring their expertise to the table to enhance your proposed product. It is likely that their employees, perhaps in conjunction with yours or perhaps independently, will be filing patent applications on the technology that they invent. This can box in your company with respect to choosing suppliers or paying licensing fees. How does a company address this issue?

Unless a contractual company is hired to just serve as a supplier of some material or subsystem with no input whatsoever from your company about the intended use of their product, it is likely that they were expected to serve, to some extent, as a partner in developing that technology. That seems reasonable because, had they not had that expertise, they would not have been hired in the first place. More specifically, they have expertise that is either weak or lacking in your company. It is not unusual these days for companies to have to enter into joint technology development agreements.

With this in mind, how does your company maintain its ability to practice its own technology? To protect your technology when engaging a contractual company, your company should consider implementing the following two steps as part of your overall patent strategy.

The first step aims to prevent the contractual company from obtaining patents. This is accomplished by disclosing as much technology and as many ideas as can be conceived by your project team in the area that the contractual company will be developing, prior to exchanging any information with the contractual company. The goal is to remove the novelty from that technology to the extent that obtaining patents becomes difficult for the contractual company.

The second step requires that your engineering team analyze the solution proposed by the contractual company and then to design and patent alternative methods of achieving the same result. Care must be exercised to ensure that no information related to the alternative embodiments be communicated from anyone in the contractual company. The ideas must come strictly from your company's employees in order to avoid having the contractual company's employees named as inventors, with the contractual company retaining rights to any allowed patents.

Both steps partially address protecting your technology, but they do so in complementary ways. The first requires that as much material that might be considered enabling technology be divulged in the applications being filed. The second requires that as little enabling technology (or alternative methods, apparatus, or materials) as possible be divulged until your company is ready to patent its concepts. The first step is implemented before the contractual company has proposed any solutions, whereas the second step occurs afterwards.

In summary, novelty is the first requirement for a solution to be patentable. Novelty can be negated by any information available to the public, including that released by your company. While nondisclosure agreements can avoid issues around novelty, they do not preclude the occurrence of such problems. It is strongly recommended that an appropriate patent strategy be designed, a patent practitioner consulted, and patent applications filed before disclosing any possibly-patentable information to anyone outside your company if at all possible.

Utility

The second criterion for something to be patentable is that the claim has to be useful or "have utility" in legal parlance. Roughly speaking, the claim should describe technical subject matter. A patent cannot be granted for the artwork on the front of a greeting card, or for the text of a novel.*** Similarly, patents are difficult to obtain for ways of conducting

*** There is a type of patent known as a design patent which is designated with a capital "D" in front of the number. This limits the ability of a company to copy the design of an object. Ornamental objects such as jewelry, furniture, and beverage bottles are often issued design patents, as are computer fonts when displayed on a computer screen. The operative term for the issuance of a design patent is that it must be related to an object of utility. In some ways a design patent is the technical analog of a copyright or trademark that is designed to limit the ability of another company to copy a distinctive shape. As the focus of this book is utility patents, we will not further discuss these aspects of patent and trademark law.

business using computers [8]. The utility criterion is usually not an issue for mechanical, hard electrical, or chemical inventions. However, the reader should be cognizant of the so-called "do nothing box". This device consists of a box with a toggle switch mounted externally to its side. Upon activation of the switch by a user, a door is pushed open by a member that then proceeds to turn the switch off and withdraw back into the box, with the door closing behind the member. It is doubtful that this device would be patentable as its utility is questionable. However, utility may be an issue in any technology, particularly software and biotechnology [9].

Obviousness and Ordinary Skill in the Art

The third, and most-often problematic, criterion is non-obviousness. Remember that, legally, a claim is obvious if "the differences between the claimed invention and the prior art are such that the claimed invention as a whole would have been obvious... to a person having ordinary skill in the art to which the claimed invention pertains" [10]. This definition raises two questions: First, to whom is the invention non-obvious, and second, what constitutes obviousness? Let us first address the question as to whom an invention should be non-obvious.

The concept of obviousness rests on what distinguishes ordinary from extraordinary skill in the art. What constitutes a person being one of ordinary skill in the art, rather than of extraordinary skill? A member of a team of PhDs with years of experience in a field is generally considered to have extraordinary skill in the art. Alternatively, a casual user of a piece of equipment, say a coin operated printer at a commercial establishment, would generally be considered to lack ordinary skill in the art unless the invention relates to facilitating his use of the equipment.

Consider the following hypothetical example in which a vending machine that has operated by inserting dimes, nickels, and quarters is upgraded, due to inflation, to include modern dollar coins. The inclusion of such an upgrade would be considered obvious to someone who routinely uses the machine and, thus, would appear to be obvious. However, if the machine needed some modifications that would allow it to accept the dollar coins but reject counterfeit coins whereby that method differed from that previously used with other coin denominations, due to mass or composition of the dollar coins, the consumer would no longer be considered as one possessing ordinary skill, as such an internal modification would not be obvious to him. However, if the modification to the vending machine merely included changing the angle of the ramp that transports the coins so that the correct speed could be established to allow the trajectory of the coin to cause it to fall into a slot in a specific location, service personnel already familiar with the internal components of the machine might be considered to have ordinary skill in the art.

Ordinary Skill in the Art: An Actual Example

As an actual example of what constitutes one of ordinary skill in the art, let us consider a project in which the author of this book was involved. Specifically, he was a member of a team of scientists engaged in a project related to the formation of scum on a photoreceptor used in an electrophotographic printer. In that context, the term "scum," refers to a hazy deposit on a photoreceptor used in an electrophotographic printer. This deposit blocked light from impinging on the photoreceptor, thereby degrading its performance. The scum further caused paper dust to adhere to the photoreceptor, which further degraded its performance, thereby making a service call for replacement necessary.

Upon detailed analysis, it was found that new, unused cleaning rollers (similar to paint rollers) deposited a waxy finishing agent, used in the manufacture of the rollers' fibers, from the roller onto new, unused photoreceptors; however, used rollers did not cause the same problem.

By isolating the key problem—the newness of the roller—the team was able to identify a solution. The problem could be solved by removing the finishing agent prior to using the roller. A patent application was subsequently filed and initially rejected. The examiner cited an earlier patent reference for a paint roller and went on to say that, even though the patent did not discuss cleaning the roller after use, it was obvious that the painter would have done so.

Our response to the office action was, first of all, that the reference cited by the examiner did not disclose cleaning the roller at all. Second, it was not obvious that the paint roller would have been cleaned after use, as the painter may have simply decided that an inexpensive roller would not be worth the time or money to clean. Third, the patent application indicated that the roller disclosed was cleaned prior to use, which is the opposite of when a paint roller would have been cleaned, if, in fact, it was cleaned. The patent was ultimately allowed [11].

In this example, a painter, who is not presumed to have detailed knowledgeable or to be accomplished in the area of electrophotography, was deemed by the examiner to be someone of ordinary skill in the art. The facts that detailed scientific analysis was needed to understand the nature of the problem and elaborate testing was required to prove the validity of the method and functionality of removing the finishing agent were not factors initially considered by the examiner.

The examiner originally considered the painter to be one of ordinary skill in the art of cleaning rollers. Whether or not the roller was used for painting or as a cleaning roller in an electrophotographic printer was immaterial. It was only because the problem of scum was spelled out in the background of the invention and the necessity of cleaning the roller prior to its use in an electrophotographic printer was discussed in the detailed description of the invention that we were successful in arguing that the painter was not someone of ordinary skill in the art and that the cleaning of the roller before its initial use was not obvious.

Obviousness: An Actual Example

A discussion of to whom an invention must be non-obvious raises the question of what exactly what is meant by the term "non-obvious". In the United States patent examiners can pick and choose bits and pieces from different prior disclosures to reject your claims as obvious. The disclosures do not even have to be in the same field as the invention, as was the case in the electrophotographic cleaning roller previously discussed. There is no limit on the number of references that an examiner can string together to reject an application as obvious in light of the prior art. As in the case of the electrophotographic cleaning roller, the prior art need not even be in the same field as the invention. In the previous example, the examiner cited a painting roller as prior art even though its purpose, mode of use, and method of maintenance were irrelevant to its perceived application in a printer. How does one handle this seemingly counter-intuitive standard? Perhaps the best way to explain is by an actual example.

The author, together with a team of scientists, worked with a printing company investigating a new method of transferring small toner particles from a photoreceptor to a receiver. The receiver had a paper base and a thin thermoplastic overcoat. The receiver was heated prior to contacting the toner-bearing photoreceptor so as to soften the thermoplastic. Upon pressing the thermoplastic to the toner-bearing photoreceptor, the toner would transfer to the receiver.

The problem the team was tackling was that the thermoplastic, which covered the entire receiver, became a hot melt adhesive when heated. After all, it was supposed to cause the toner, which is also a thermoplastic, to adhere to the receiver. The unintended result was that the receiver strongly adhered to the photoreceptor and could not be separated without damaging both. The customer, who wanted good prints, and the merchant, who wanted to provide good prints without damaging his equipment, would both have been disappointed.

To address this problem, we incorporated a release agent into the thermoplastic that coated the receiver. This was exactly the surface to which we wanted to get complete toner transfer. Doing so solved the problem of the receiver adhering to the photoreceptor while permitting all the toner to transfer. We filed a patent application which was rejected on the grounds of obviousness. The examiner, in his office action, went on to explain that it is obvious to use a release agent to prevent two contacting materials from adhering to each other.

Our patent practitioner responded to the examiner, stating "that no one in his right mind would make the receiver less sticky so that toner would stick to it better". The examiner allowed the patent application [12].

The key feature of this patent is that, while the use of release agents to prevent adhesion was well known, using a release agent to improve the toner transfer process was not. That the toner would adhere to the thermoplastic whereas the photoreceptor would not was, in fact, unanticipated. In effect, the claim defined a whole that was greater than the sum of the parts from the references. This gets right back to defining the problem being solved in sufficient detail in the background section of the application.

Had we simply defined the problem as separating the receiver from the photoreceptor, arguing for patentability would have been difficult. Similarly, in the cleaning roller patent described previously, the background section posed the problem as scum formation on the photoreceptor. We prevailed because the background section clearly stated that the problem solved was the formation of scum on the photoreceptor. We were not simply attempting to patent a method of cleaning fiber rollers.

The lesson here is that the right description of the problem solved, coupled with a well-reasoned discussion as to why the prior art did not solve the problem can be quite helpful in having a patent ultimately issued. However, it is important to remember that there is a fine balance between filing a prosecutable application and disclosing too much information. Consult your patent practitioner regarding the proper balance to be presented in your specific situation.

Only One Invention per Patent

It should be remembered throughout the discussion in this chapter that a patent can only include claims to a single invention. This is particularly important to remember when formulating a patent strategy, especially when having to implement that strategy and file applications prior to disclosing patentable information. While sometimes, even within a single project, distinct inventions are readily distinguishable from one another, this is not always the case.

The key question to be asked is whether or not the claims can be practiced independently of each other. For example, a device for doing something (an apparatus claim) and the way that the device is used (a method claim) can often be practiced separately, as the method claim can often be practiced using a different piece of equipment. Accordingly, method and apparatus claims are often considered separate inventions in the U.S. Should the examiner decide that claims can be practiced independently of each other, the inventor may be required to split the application into separate applications, to be prosecuted independently. These applications are called "divisionals" and will be discussed more fully in a later chapter.

Asserting Your Patent

Patent applications should be written with the idea of asserting the issued patent against an infringer. If it takes more than a single entity such as a single company to infringe on a claim, it is generally better to rewrite the claim to avoid this complication. In other words, it is important that, when asserting a patent, a single individual or company can be shown to be infringing the claim. Let us be more specific with a hypothetical example.

Suppose a patent claim describes a method of producing a novel toner for use in an electrophotographic printer. Further, the claim also requires that the toner be used to print a document onto paper. The manufacturer of the toner, who is not printing any documents, would not be infringing the claim. The printer shop owner, who is actually producing the documents but who is not manufacturing the toner would also not be infringing the claim. Therefore, although the claim is clearly being infringed, no single entity can be identified as infringing upon it. Under such circumstances, it would be difficult for the owner of the patent to recover damages for its infringement.

It is far better to write claims so that any infringement would most likely involve a single entity doing the infringing. Moreover, consideration should be given, should this not be the case in the first draft of a claim, whether or not the claim can be broken into multiple inventions. It is strongly suggested that, when formulating a patent strategy, serious attention be paid to whether or not multiple patent applications will be required to avoid this possibility.

Inventors and Inventorship

Let us now discuss the concept of inventorship or just who is and who is not an inventor named in a patent application. Patent law has its own concept of "inventor," that may differ from the conception held by a lay individual. Just as "invention" is shorthand for "claimed subject matter," "inventor" is shorthand for "technical contributor to the claimed subject matter." Failure to list the correct individuals as inventors has serious legal consequences. Further, either including someone who is not an inventor or omitting someone who is can result in the patent being found to be invalid when asserting against your competitors. Inventorship is a serious issue and, unfortunately, often involves emotional responses of coworkers who have worked closely together and with diligence on a project. Let us discuss exactly what this means.

An inventor must make an inventionable contribution to at least one claim. That is, to be an inventor, a person must contribute something to a claim that could not simply have been looked up in a reference book. An inventor need not make an inventionable contribution to every claim or even to more than one claim. However, there must be at least one claim in which an individual must have made an inventionable contribution in order to be considered an inventor. Inventorship is independent of job title, as an engineer, scientist, technician, manager, sales person, or any other employee who contributes to a claim is an inventor. Being a supervisor of an inventor does not make the supervisor an inventor.

Inventorship decisions often invoke strong emotional responses from individuals who have put in long, hard hours working on a project. The supervisor must be equipped to handle those responses. It is often advantageous to have all contributors discuss their specific contributions to the proposed claims with your legal expert, leaving it to the practitioner to determine exactly who is an inventor. Moreover, as a patent goes through prosecution and claims are revised, the list of individuals listed as inventors may change, with some being omitted and others added. While recognition of everyone's efforts is desirable, listing someone as an inventor just because of such efforts should not be done as proper inventorship is a serious legal issue.

Specifically, the inventors own property rights in the patent application and the allowed patent. Incorrect inventorship means the correct people don't own those rights. A non-listed inventor can hold up patent litigation or license the technology to your competitors under your patent. Given its importance, let us further examine what constitutes inventorship.

In 1905 Albert Einstein published three scientific papers that revolutionized physics while working in the Swiss patent office. One of these, on the photoelectric effect, resulted in his winning the Nobel Prize in 1921. This work eventual led to the formulation of quantum mechanics—one of the leading advances in understanding atomic interactions in the 20th century. However, creating an understanding of the laws of nature or advancing science is not patentable. An invention must be a solution to a practical problem. Indeed, the patent applications on the photocell, which is a device that functions by using the photoelectric effect discovered by Einstein, were filed by Walter Brattain in 1948 and issued in 1951 [13]. It was the device that solved a practical problem, rather than the law of nature, that received the patents. That Einstein was actually working in a patent office when he derived his theories was totally irrelevant in the patent process.

Another notable example of patentability and inventorship is the transistor. This device revolutionized electronics and transformed that industry from vacuum tubes to semiconductors. It gave rise to many new industries and made possible today's digital electronic industry and the technological advances from which we all benefit. For their work in semiconductors and the discovery of the transistor, John Bardeen, Walter Brattain, and William Shockley shared the 1956 Nobel Prize in Physics.

Although most of us probably think of the transistor as being a single invention, in actuality it comprises multiple inventions that are covered by numerous patents. Probably the most notable patent covering this device was issued to Walter Brattain [14] in 1953 and is just entitled "Semiconductor Translator". This patent shows the conventional schematic and performance graphs of a transistor. Other patents include U.S. Patent #2,617,865, issued to Brattain and John Bardeen in 1952, covering a semiconductor amplifier, Bardeen and Brattain (U.S. Patent #2,589,658, issued in 1952) also covering a semiconductor amplifier, Bardeen and Brattain (U.S. Patent #2,524,035, issued in 1950) and Brattain and Robert Gibney (U.S. Patent #2,524,034, issued in 1950), both disclosing a three-electrode circuit element utilizing semiconductive materials. Additional patents on this device include Gerald Pearson and William Shockley, entitled "Semiconductor Amplifier (U.S. Patent #2,502,479, issued in 1950), Walter Shockley, entitled "Semiconductor Amplifier (U.S. Patent #2,502,488, issued in 1950), Walter Shockley, entitled "Semiconductor Signal Translating Device Amplifier (U.S. Patent #2,654,059, issued in 1953), and Walter Shockley and Morgan Sparks, entitled "Semiconductor

Translating Device Having Controlled Gain (U.S. Patent #2,623,105, issued in 1952). This list is not meant to be all-inclusive, but, rather, illustrative.

It is clear that what many lay and even highly skilled technical people often view as a single invention, the transistor, is legally a collection of distinct inventions. Moreover, whereas the scientific community views Bardeen, Brattain, and Shockley as the three inventors of the transistor, in fact, legally there were other individuals involved and Shockley, who was an inventor listed on several of his own patents or with other coworkers, was not a co-inventor with Brattain or Bardeen on any patents. It is quite clear that the legal definition of an inventor and an invention differs greatly from that in common usage. Let us explore this concept by addressing the issue of who is an inventor under various hypothetical scenarios.

Let us first consider a patent application having twenty claims, including one independent and nineteen dependent claims, and two potential inventors—scientist A and technician B. Of the twenty claims, scientist A, by himself, made all the inventionable contributions to nineteen claims and technician B and scientist A both made inventionable contributions to the twentieth claim. In this example both scientist A and technician B are properly listed as inventors. It does not matter that technician B's inventionable contributions only affected part of a single claim. That is sufficient and he must be listed as an inventor.

Now let us assume that the examiner determines that the twentieth claim could be practiced separately from the other claims and must be filed as a separate patent application. Accordingly, the patent application is subject to a divisional. Only scientist A would be listed as an inventor for the application covering the first nineteen claims, whereas both scientist A and technician B would both be listed as inventors for the second case covering the twentieth claim. If further claims are added to either application, additional inventors may have to be added.

In another hypothetical situation, suppose individual A describes a novel left handed widget that overcomes certain shortcomings of previous widgets. Unfortunately, individual A has not been able to actually build the left handed widget, but a coworker, individual B gets the description from individual A and proceeds to build it (reduce to practice in the legal vernacular). Individual A is the sole inventor even though individual B was the first to actually build and reduce the invention to practice. It is generally not necessary for an inventor to actually build a device or demonstrate a method. Individual B could be classified as a skilled pair of hands who follows the instructions and actually reduces the invention to practice. That, by itself, does not constitute inventorship.

However, if individual B finds, unexpectedly, that a certain set of non-obvious conditions is necessary to practice some aspect of the invention, or if individual B finds some non-obvious improvement, and those conditions or improvements are claimed, then individual B would be an inventor of the relevant claims. Again, the improvement discovered by individual B must relate back to a claim of this patent application to be considered an inventor on this application. If it could be practiced independently of the present invention, it would require as separate patent application naming individual B as the inventor.

Let us now consider another example of inventorship. Suppose Brattain had lived in an earlier era and discovered the photocell in 1904, prior to Einstein's discovery of the photoelectric effect. Let us further assume that, Brattain had no understanding of how or why his photocell worked, but simply knew how to build and use it and the fact that, under the described conditions, it did work. Now, let us further assume that Einstein gained knowledge of the existence of Brattain's photocell and was able to develop his theory of the photoelectric effect to explain Brattain's discovery. Would Brattain, who in this example, is presumed to not understand how the photocell operates, be an inventor? Would Einstein be a co-inventor of the Brattain's photocell?

Regarding Brattain, patent law does not require that an inventor understand how his invention works. Although it is frequently beneficial to include some discussion of the theory behind an invention in order to make the case that the invention is not just the sum of a number of unrelated parts in prior disclosures, it is not necessary to do so. Rather, it is only necessary that the inventor describe how to build or practice his invention in sufficient detail that someone of ordinary skill in the art could, upon reading the patent and, perhaps doing some minor experimentation to optimize the invention under specific circumstances, practice the invention.

Regarding Einstein, just as it is not necessary to explain how an invention works, explaining how that invention works does not make the individual who makes that explanation an inventor. Unless Einstein used the photoelectric effect theory to allow additional, non-obvious claims to be included in the patent application, he would not be an inventor.

Addressing Inventorship Issues

Issues of inventorship are frequently very emotional for those who have worked on a problem and who may or may not legally be inventors. These issues need to be addressed with care. Inventorship issues range from individuals who do not believe that they have done anything inventive to individuals who are not inventors insisting that they are and that the named inventors should not be on the patent application at all. Let us see how to handle these issues.

First, let us consider the case where inventors do valuable and creative work that the employing company wishes to patent. Unfortunately, the inventors do not believe that they invented anything or that there is anything inventive about their work. Often, they can cite prior art owned by competitors as the reason for their beliefs. Just as often, it is modesty that prevents their being able to accept the fact that they are, in fact, inventors. Frequently, engineers working in an area are the last to appreciate their inventions simply because, in the present context, invention is a legal—not a technical—concept. The legal consequences of not accepting or recognizing one's inventorship can be serious.

Should members of this team be called to the witness stand during a suit when your company is trying to assert its patent(s) against a competitor, they could be strong witnesses for the opposition. If they argue that, based on the prior art, there was nothing inventive about their discoveries, or state that they do not believe they were inventors, then such statements could result in the patent(s) being declared invalid or even losing the entire lawsuit.

Prior to filing patent applications, every effort should be made to convince the team members, by helping them to understand, that their discoveries do, in fact, constitute inventions over the prior art. Alternatively, the team members may be correct and they might convince you that either the claims need to be rewritten or that, in fact, there is little value in a patent that may be issued because of the prior art.

A concerted effort should be made to resolve such disagreements prior to filing. It is far better to have everyone working together towards the common, understandable goal of protecting the company's intellectual property. Careful and detailed discussions can usually resolve these discrepancies. When facing this situation, the author has enjoyed considerable success in convincing the engineers that they had patentable inventions by asking them why they did not introduce this product in the previous year. This generally led to a discussion of the problems and limitations in the existing technology and how the engineers had to overcome them. If there is clearly an invention, but it is not possible to convince the inventors of such, it may be necessary, although legally more complicated, for the assignee to file without the inventors' signatures. This situation is unusual for active employees, but does occur when an employee dies or has serious, debilitating health issues, or has left the company.

Finally, according to patent law, individuals must be named as inventors if they have made inventionable contributions to even a single claim. If the claim is a minor aspect of the invention, it is possible to omit naming these individuals by omitting the claim from the application. All-in-all, the best scenario is for members of the technical team and the legal advisor to discuss these issues with the employees and try to convince them that this is a worthwhile patent in which they are inventors.

Perhaps not as serious as the above situation, but still problematical, are the individuals who view the writing and patenting process as painful. This constitutes the second group of inventors. They would rather be spending their time advancing the technology. Financial and other incentives frequently do not work with such individuals, who feel pressured, and rightfully so in today's competitive world, to advance the technology. They, too, often fail to realize that what they have accomplished is patentable.

The concerns of such individuals in this second group should be addressed in two ways. First, that they indeed have inventions must be carefully explained. Usually, after an explanation, these individuals will cooperate in preparing patent applications. Second, the time and burden associated with the preparation, the filing, and the prosecution of the applications need to be minimized in order to make the process palatable to these individuals. This can often be accomplished by employing a patent engineer (discussed in depth in Chapter 11), who will interface with the technical team members and the patent practitioners.

Patent engineers can help collect material for the application and help the inventors to focus on their inventions. They can also conduct the prior art searches and present those findings to the patent practitioner. Finally, they can help establish the patent strategy so that the assignee ultimately owns the problem rather than just specific solutions to the problem.

A third group of "inventors" comprises those individuals, working in the specific technological area, who incorrectly believe that they should be listed as inventors on various patent applications. Within this group are several subgroups. Because the motivation for the individuals in each subgroup is varied, how each is approached with respect to addressing issues of inventorship is different. If these situations are not managed well, the assignee may wind up with compromised patents and a very hostile work environment with poor employee morale.

The first subgroup includes those "inventors" who have a real respect for the value of an application and want to make sure that it is done correctly, complete with their advances. They merely want do the right thing and believe that they made inventive contributions. This is often the easiest group to handle. One simply needs to assess their contributions and determine whether or not those contributions comprise inventionable matter. Upon explaining that assessment, individuals in this group will most likely accept the inventorship decision.

The second and third subgroups include those individuals who are hungry for recognition. Addressing issues of inventorship for both will be discussed below. The second subgroup comprises individuals who believe that they are the inventors who should be listed on an application and believe that the other people who are listed as inventors should not be. They may, in fact, be inventors, but do not want any others to be listed. The third subgroup is more problematic as their actions can result in belligerency. Members of this group are often working on the specific or a similar project and may or may not have made inventive contributions to the claims in the patent application under consideration.

When responding to individuals in either of these subgroups, it is often worthwhile to have them meet with both a technical manager and a patent practitioner. Depending on the group dynamics, the meetings can include the individuals alone or the technical team as a whole. It must be emphasized that inventorship is a legal issue, not an emotional one. It is not based on whether or not someone worked on a project or made valuable contributions. The supposed inventors should present their records of what they did that directly contributed to one or more claims in an inventionable manner. The decision of whether or not to list them should be left to the patent practitioner. The legal experts are being paid to make those decisions and to take the heat. As an additional benefit, they are often outside the membership of the team working on the project so their decision will generally not generate the bitterness that can result if the decision is made by either a team member or a manager.

A fourth group of inventors comprises those individuals who are hungry for recognition and are willing to submit invention reports even in areas to which they are not assigned and about which they may not have in-depth knowledge. This group differs from the third group in that they are submitting patent applications wherein the technology is often beyond their expertise and that they are not working with the teams that are actively pursuing that technology. Their submissions can either be in areas in which their employer has a strategic interest or not. In the latter case, it is relatively easy to decline to pursue patents for such submissions. However, in the instance where the company does have strategic interests, especially if it has other teams of employees working in that area, the problem can be more pernicious.

Specifically, an "outsider" (an individual within the company working outside a specific technological area) submitting invention disclosures in the hope of filing patent applications can create antagonism in the groups working in that technological area. Moreover, such disclosures are often very weak and may have incorrect information. Unfortunately, the disclosures cannot be dismissed out of hand because they may have material that is claimable and would, therefore, legally mandate that that individual be listed as an inventor. The problem can rapidly worsen if the members of the team working on that technology or the individual submitting invention disclosures push to have others removed as inventors.

The issue can be addressed by having a technically knowledgeable individual such as a patent engineer assess the submission and decide, perhaps with the project team members, whether or not the submitted idea has merit. If it is decided that the idea is not worth filing an application, it can be dismissed, recognizing that, should the technology turn in such a direction as to warrant patenting that invention, the original submitter may still be legally an inventor. If the idea has sufficient merit, especially if it is along the lines of research being pursued by the technical team, it may make sense to have the submitting individual meet with the team members to discuss his idea. The key here is to try to interface the individual with the team members so that valuable advances are patented and a strategy to own the problem is developed without creating unnecessary hostilities or wasting time and money pursuing weak ideas.

Overall, it should always be remembered that the terms "invention," "inventor," and "patent" have legal meanings and that those are the definitions that we must use in this field. If there are any questions about these, as related to individuals or technical advances, a licensed patent practitioner should be consulted.

References

1. S. J. Popeil, U.S. Patent #4,027,419 (1977).
2. http://images.businessweek.com/ss/09/04/0408_ridiculous_patents/4.htm
3. B. Belisle, U. S. Patent #5,901,666 (1999).
4. R. Popeil and A. Backus, U. S. Patent #4,807,862 (1989).
5. R. Popeil, A. Backus, and K. Popeil, U. S. Patent #7,138,609.
6. K. Pond, R. Popeil, and A. Backus, U.S. Patent #6,436,380 (2002).
7. http://www.bloomberg.com/apps/news?pid=newsarchive&sid=at4OT937iybc&refer=home. Referenced 1/5/2015

8. See, for example, Alice Corporation Pty. Ltd. v. Cls Bank International *et al.* 134 S. Ct. 2347 (2014).
9. See, e.g., Mayo Collaborative Services, dba Mayo Medical Laboratories, *et al.*, v. Prometheus Laboratories, Inc. 132 S. Ct. 1289 (2012).
10. 35 USC 103.
11. T. H. Morse, J. Locke, R. C. Bowen, J. C. Maher, and D. S. Rimai, "Photoconductor Cleaning Brush for Elimination of Photoconductor Scum", U.S. Patent #5,772,779 (1998).
12. W. A. Light, L. J. Sorriero, and D. S. Rimai, U.S. Patent #4,968,578 (1990).
13. W. H. Brattain, U.S. Patents Nos. 2,537,255, 2,537,256, and 2,537,257 (1951).
14. W. H. Brattain, U.S. Patent 2,663,829 (1953).

7

Patent Engineering and Patent Prosecution

The decision to pursue patent protection for your company's intellectual property has been made and a solid patent strategy has been implemented. The patentability search has been conducted, claims describing the invention drafted, a disclosure describing the problem, how others tried to solve the problem, and your company's novel solutions to the problem have been written. You are now at the point that you want to know how to proceed, what to anticipate, and how much all this will cost. In this chapter we will describe the process from submitting a patent application to the issuance of a patent in the United States. We will also briefly discuss the filing of international patent applications in this chapter. We will delve into the costs of filing patent applications domestically and maintaining the issued patents in Chapter 8. In Chapter 9 we will discuss international filings and whether or not they are necessary, selecting countries in which to file, international prosecution, and the costs associated with foreign filings in more depth.

The process for obtaining a patent is summarized in a figure [1] presented at United States Patent and Trademark Office website [2]. This figure shows the path of prosecution of a typical patent application. The reader is referred to that figure for a basic overview of the patent process. We will discuss in some depth many of the steps outlined by the USPTO, as they apply to both prosecuting individual patents and implementing patent strategies.

Types of Patents in the United States

There are three types of patents issued in the United States. Though deciding which type of application to file is not ordinarily the first step in the patenting process, let us consider them now. The first and most commonly issued type is the utility patent, which is granted to protect a useful process, manufactured article or apparatus, or a composition of matter such as a novel chemical. If you are seeking to obtain patent protection on a novel solution to a technical problem, you will be filing an application to obtain a utility patent. Design patents (designated with a capital "D" in the patent number) which protect ornamental features (such as Snap-on Tools patent D654,341 [3] issued in 2012, describing an ornamental design on a handle with a striking end) and plant patents which are issued for new varieties of asexually produced plants comprise the other two types of patents. Unless otherwise specified, we will focus the discussions in this book on utility patents as those are the ones with potentially the greatest value. You may wish to consult your patent practitioner to determine which types of patent applications are most appropriate to file as you seek to develop a patent portfolio that allows your company to own the problem.

Patentability

The first step in the process for obtaining a patent is to determine the patentability of your invention. Prior to engaging the services of an attorney, several issues should be addressed. Perhaps foremost among these issues is to ensure that the proposed invention actually is an invention and is likely eligible for patenting. There are a number of items listed by the patent office, such as perpetual motion machines, that are not patentable. Combining known technologies into a novel, and even highly marketable, product does not make the combination of those technologies patentable. Rather, there has to be either an unanticipated benefit of combining the technologies so that the whole does something more than simply acting as the sum of the individual parts or there has to be a problem with combining the technologies that was solved by the inventor, thereby enabling the individual components to be combined.

An equally important issue is to determine whether or not your invention has already been disclosed or patented. In general, this determination comes out of the prior art search. However, when implementing a strategy aimed at generating a patent portfolio, it is distinctly possible that the invention is covered by a patent that you had previously obtained or is disclosed in another patent for which you have applied. Moreover, a prior disclosure of the invention, even if not claimed in a prior application or patent, can preclude your ability to obtain the presently desired patent. If the application is one that you will be filing in the future, be cautioned as to what you divulge in your present applications about that particular invention, as you do not want your own applications to constitute prior art.

Reviewing the Prior Art Search Results

Determining patentability requires a thorough review of the prior art search to ensure that no one else disclosed the proposed invention first. As we have previously discussed the two factors that determine whether or not the solution to a problem is patentable are novelty and non-obviousness. In order to be an invention, the proposed technology must be novel; that is, it cannot be previously known. If those findings reveal similar technology that is reported to solve the same problem, there is no invention. However, a similar technology that is used for a different purpose, that also has the ability to solve the present problem inherent in that technology, is not patentable because the inventor of the prior technology is entitled to the full use of his invention, even if he did not appreciate some of its aspects.

Let us consider, as a hypothetical example, the invention of a wire mesh contained in a frame that can be inserted into an opening in a wall to prevent the entry of bugs into your home—a window screen. The inventor described the problem as such and has claims on the wire mesh contained within the frame to give it rigidity and support.

Now let us suppose that your company has been contracted to design an apparatus to filter stones and other particulate debris from water. The engineers design a device that comprises a wire mesh supported by a frame that can be placed over a container and through which the water containing the particulates is poured so that clear water can be captured in the container. The device does not constitute an invention as its ability to filter the water is inherent in the original invention, even if the inventor did not appreciate its capability.

The criterion of non-obviousness is somewhat more tenuous. Non-obviousness simply means that one should not be able to take known items and combine them so that each is functioning as it would be expected to function. As an example, suppose that your company, instead of only trying to patent the wire mesh within a frame, attempted to patent an apparatus comprising a wire mesh within a frame and a container suitable for containing water, wherein the wire mesh within the frame is superimposed upon an opening in the container, so that water flows through the mesh into the container. This would not be patentable because of obviousness. The examiner would simply argue that the wire mesh within the frame is known.

Although the inventor of the window screen did not disclose its use to filter water, nor did he disclose the use of a container to capture the water, a well comprises a container that is lowered into water and captures the water. The window screen is placed over an opening in a wall to exclude the entrance of bugs. It would be obvious to place the screen over the container used to capture the water in order to exclude the capture of particulates.

Addressing Prior Art in Your Applications

So, continuing with the hypothetical example, how do you obtain any sort of meaningful patent coverage on the filtering technology invented by engineers in your company? While the filtration of the water is essential, it was also found that, after a period of time, the mesh became blocked with particulate debris, rendering it incapable of performing further filtration. To solve this problem, your engineers devised a frame so that the mesh is held at an angle between about thirty degrees and sixty degrees from the horizontal, with the frame and the mesh extending over the container into which the water is poured by an amount sufficient to allow the particulate debris to be washed from the mesh without entering the container. The angles were chosen as a smaller angle would not allow the water to wash the particulate debris from the screen, whereas a larger angle would cause too much water to cascade over the container.

If the patent application defines the problem as above, it should be allowable. Basically, the inventor of the window screen could not have anticipated the problem of the mesh clogging as bugs would just fly away if blocked by the screen. The container, itself, although a component of the invention and, accordingly, listed in the claim, would not inherently solve the problem because the problem is now stated to address the blocking of the mesh by the particulate debris. Using the water to self-clean the mesh was not taught in the prior art, nor was the way that this was accomplished (by placing the mesh at an angle with respect to the container while having the water wash over the mesh during the transfer process).

The key lesson here is that it is extremely important to properly define the problem solved. This involves integrating the results of the prior art search into the disclosure and a clear description as to why existing technology, even if not used to directly solve the problem, would not provide a solution, either by itself (e.g. the wire mesh window screen) or in combination with other technology (e.g. the well bucket). It is not sufficient to have only solved a problem, which, nominally, in this instance was providing filtered water (without clogging the filtering device). Although claims can be modified during the prosecution, the disclosure cannot.

The foregoing discussion serves to illustrate the divide between building technology (engineering) and obtaining valuable patent coverage (legal). Although it would have been desirable to obtain patent coverage on the use of the mesh to filter water, in conjunction with the container, that was not going to happen. Preventing the mesh from clogging appears to be patentable, in this hypothetical example, and would allow your company to have a serious competitive edge over the products produced by your competitors, as those products would either clog or involve complicated and costly methods of cleaning the mesh.

Should You File Internationally?

After reviewing and addressing the prior art, one should decide whether or not to file the patent application internationally. While different countries have somewhat different patentability requirements, this decision should be based mainly on business or economic considerations. As previously mentioned, a discussion of these considerations, along with the process of prosecuting patent applications internationally and the associated costs are presented in Chapter 9. It should be noted that it is highly probable that multiple patent applications will be filed simultaneously or sequentially as a result of formulating a patent strategy that owns the problem.

One may decide that only a portion of the applications should be filed internationally or that different applications should be filed in different countries, even if the applications have common or similar disclosures. However, it should be remembered that, once an application is submitted, it may constitute prior art. This is especially true in the United States 30 months after the priority date, which is generally the date of submission of the application* to the patent office, or 1 year after publication of the application, whichever comes first.

Upon publication, of course, everything in the application is prior art to anyone, including the listed inventors. For example, apparatus and method applications that describe a piece of equipment to make something and the method of using that equipment, respectively, should be filed simultaneously so that one application does not directly read on the other. However, after 30 months from the date of submission or 1 year from the date of publication, everything in the application is considered prior art that can be combined with other prior art and pose problems for the applicant during prosecution as he attempts to circumvent obviousness rejections (Prior to those periods, the information in an application may or may not be prior art, depending on circumstances).

Whether or not one decides to file a patent application internationally and, if so, in which specific countries to file, it is assumed that it is desirable to file the application in the United States. It is time to hire an attorney or patent agent to prepare and file an application.

Hiring a Patent Practitioner and Reviewing Your Patent Strategy

Patents are legal documents and the strength of the patents and the value of the resulting patent portfolio are direct results of both the technical input going into describing the invention and ensuring that the legal documents protecting that intellectual property are as strong as reasonably possible. Moreover, in addition to ensuring the legal strength of the resulting patents, a patent practitioner will ensure that the numerous formalities will be met when submitting patent applications. Details such as how to submit an application, grammar, formalism in the figures, and a myriad of other factors must be properly addressed by a patent practitioner.

It is rare that a technical expert who is capable of inventing the patentable technology would also have the legal expertise to write, file, and prosecute a good patent application. Under a worst case scenario, a group of patent applications may not be allowed, that is no patents are granted, and the information contained in the applications is published for all competition

* There are legal subtleties that may result in the priority date and the period before a document is considered to be prior art being different. The reader should consult a patent practitioner for specific details.

to see. The reader is urged to hire and use a patent practitioner whenever filing or prosecuting patent applications.

With this in mind, it is now time to perform two tasks:

1. hire the patent practitioner who will provide the legal expertise that is needed; and
2. review the entire patent strategy including what applications will be filed and determine whether these applications have to be filed concurrently or whether they can or should be filed sequentially.

The review can be conducted with the patent attorney if your company is willing and able to pay his fees for this service and if he is willing and able to assist in this review. Remember that attorneys are generally legal, rather than technical, experts. If the attorney has knowledge in the area of interest, it would certainly make sense to use his skills. Otherwise, the review can be conducted with management, a patent engineer, and the technical team members participating. Once filing has begun, it may be late to consider additional filings. Here, too, the patent practitioner can advise you if it is decided that further filings are desired.

Provisional Applications

Another question that needs to be addressed at this time is whether to file provisional patent applications or the actual (non-provisional) application. In general it is better to file non-provisional applications. However, there are occasions when time does not permit this. For example, if a product is being disclosed within just a few days, it may not be possible to formulate an appropriate patent strategy and write all the applications, complete with claims.

Under such circumstances, a provisional application, which may lack the claims, may be filed. The provisional application must include all the disclosure that would be necessary to subsequently file the non-provisional applications and be able to support the claims. In addition, a single provisional application can ultimately give rise to numerous non-provisional applications. There is no need to have as many provisional applications as final applications. Remember that a patent application is limited to one invention per application, as defined in the claims. As a provisional application may not have claims, it does not define any particular invention, but merely describes the problem solved and its solution.

There are several downsides to filing provisional applications. The first is that additional expenses will be incurred, including application fees and legal costs. The actual applications have to be filed within a year of the filing of the provisional or else the ability to file the applications will be lost. Provisional applications are often written in haste and may not contain the complete or correct disclosure to be filed. As such, they can constitute a disclosure that can pose impediments to the actual or subsequent applications. However, under certain circumstances, they can be of value, especially when time is very short.

Once the attorney has made whatever revisions he deems necessary to meet procedural requirements and obtain the best patent protection that he can, the applications are filed. And now you wait. And wait, and wait for a response from the patent office. The response is known as an office action. Eighteen months after filing an application, the application is published. In some instances, a patent application may sail through the patent office in less time than it takes for the application to be published. This is unusual. More often than not, the publication of the application will occur long before the first office action happens.

Office Actions

Eventually, the applicant will receive the office action from the patent office. The response can be broadly classified according to one of three categories. One possible response is that the examiner has searched the literature, found nothing that reads on the claims within the application, and has allowed the patent application. A second possible response is that the examiner has found what he terms "related art" that, either by itself or in combination with other pieces of related art, render the proposed invention unpatentable due to either being obvious or lacking novelty. The third type of response is that the examiner has found procedural issues with the application that must be addressed prior to a search being conducted.

Each of these office actions requires that the applicant take suitable actions within a prescribed period of time if the patent application is to move forward. The applicant will receive notice of the actions taken by the patent office. In addition, the file can be tracked at the patent office website (www.uspto.gov) under the Patent Application and Information Retrieval (PAIR) section. PAIR provides application information to your patent practitioner before publication and to the general public after publication. Let us first discuss the actions that should be taken in the event of an office action allowance.

An allowance may be part of a first office action or an office action following remarks from the applicant responding to a previous office action. Once the notice of allowance has been issued, the applicant will have to pay the issuance fees, which we will discuss in a later chapter. Before the patent actually issues, the applicant may file additional applications using either the disclosure as presently written (referred to as a continuation or divisional) or the disclosure augmented with additional information (termed a continuation-in-part).

Although it is worthwhile to examine every allowed patent for such opportunities, it is especially important to do so when receiving a first office action allowance, as such an allowance is indicative that the examiner has found nothing that reads on the claims as presented and broader coverage may be possible. Such additional applications are treated as new patents so modifications to the disclosure are possible.

The danger in filing continuations or continuations-in-part is that it may become necessary to argue with the patent office to get the patents allowed. The applicant should remember that the information that is presented to the patent office during prosecution becomes part of the file history that is available to defense attorneys should the owner of the patent choose to assert the patent against an infringing company. Everything that has been argued between the applicant and the examiner become part of the file history. A first office action allowance has minimal information in that history. Filing continuations or continuations-in-part can result in the generation of substantial file histories that can be used to limit the scope or even the legitimacy of an allowed patent.

Alternatively, and commonly occurring, the examiner may decide to reject a patent application. In his rejection, he will cite the reasons. These may include formal deficiencies. More commonly, rejections are based on analysis of searches for prior art relevant to the claims in the application.

It should be noted that, although the applicant has conducted a novelty or patentability search prior to his filing his application and, presumably has cited and discussed his findings in his disclosure, it is just not possible to fully anticipate what literature the examiner will cite or what arguments the examiner will make. One simply has to be reasonably thorough when formulating a patent strategy and writing the disclosures. Applicants are not going to have all applications allowed unless the applications are so narrowly restricted or in such an area of extremely limited interest as to be often of minimal interest or value.

An examiner may find a patent that directly reads on the proposed claims in the application. The applicant, assuming that he agrees with the examiner, can propose revised claims or decide that any claims that he may be able to obtain would be of such limited value that it is not worthwhile to further prosecute this application. If he chooses the latter path, the applicant simply does not respond to the office action.

After a prescribed period of time, the application is considered to be abandoned. It should be noted that abandoned applications are published and constitute prior disclosures should one choose to pursue alternative patents in this field in the future. In some instances, the examiner may state that he is rejecting the independent claim but would allow certain dependent claims if they are rewritten to make them freestanding independent claims.

Should the patent application be resubmitted to the patent office with a set of revised claims that require additional searching, it is likely that the examiner will reject the application with what is termed a "final rejection." However, "final" does not mean final, as most of us understand the term. Rather, it means that the applicant has to file a "request for continued examination" or RCE and pay the RCE filing fee to allow prosecution of the application to proceed.

Alternatively, an examiner may find that, in his opinion, pieces of prior art can be combined in such a way that renders a proposed invention obvious. It should be noted that the prior art used does not need to be within the field of the proposed invention, or even within the same field as each piece of proposed art. Moreover, there is no limit to the number of pieces of proposed related art that can be combined.

As in the case of a single piece of related art, the applicant can decide that the claims are obvious if the cited art is combined in the manner suggested by the examiner. The applicant can then alter the claims or decide not to pursue the application any further. Alternatively, the applicant can argue that the related art does not anticipate the proposed invention or render it obvious. This can be accomplished by showing that the primary citation does not describe everything in a claim. It is also possible to show that there is no logical reason to combine the individual pieces of cited art. This can be especially fruitful when the literature cited is from disparate fields and there is no history of combining them.

Of particular value is when the art cited by the examiner teaches away from the proposed invention, i.e. the art claims that some other effect would occur or that the proposed invention would not occur. This is certainly a strong argument for the invention to be non-obvious.

It should be noted that it is not sufficient for the applicant to merely argue that the inventors listed in the cited art were solving a different problem. If the solution to the present problem is inherent in the literature, the proposed invention is obvious and a patent will not be allowed. It has to be argued that the cited art does not teach, either as individual pieces or in combination with other pieces of cited art, and that the art will not result in the proposed invention. Alternatively, it can be argued that there is no reason to combine the cited art, as proposed by the examiner. Even better would be the case where the existing prior art teaches that combining the features of the prior art will not work, or in patent parlance, "teaches away from the invention".

The examiner can either accept or reject the arguments made by the applicant. Even if he accepts those arguments, he can raise new arguments based on either the same or additional art. It should also be remembered that, as the arguments are being made, a searchable file history is being created. The reader is cautioned to be careful about what is being argued. Even if the examiner rejects the particular arguments, but eventually a patent is issued, the rejected arguments are still part of the file history and can be used in court.

It often comes to pass that the limitations of written communications can result in difficulties getting patent applications allowed. This can result from the examiner not fully understanding the invention or the applicant not comprehending to exactly what the examiner is objecting. Sometimes a conversation can overcome the barriers. The process of discussing the application is referred to as interviewing the examiner and can be conducted either by telephone or in person. Interviews with the examiner will become part of the file history. If all else fails and the applicant has solid arguments as to why the examiner is in error and a patent on the technology is of sufficient value, the applicant can appeal the examiner's rejection.

Working through an office action can result in the examiner not allowing a patent but not rejecting the application either. This is usually because of procedural problems with the application. Perhaps the most common of these is when the examiner determines that the claims represent multiple inventions that can be practiced independently. The office action will include a "restriction requirement" requiring that the applicant select which claims to initially prosecute, allowing the rest of the claims to be subsequently prosecuted. This is called a divisional and a single application can give rise to multiple divisionals. It should be noted that the examiner has not commented, at this time, on the patentability of any of the proposed claims.

The possibility of obtaining a restriction requirement and the need to file divisional applications, which will add legal costs as well as application fees, should serve as a reminder that there is only one invention allowed for each application. This fact should be borne in mind when designing and executing a patent strategy. It is especially important that the patentable aspects of the proposed inventions be suitably covered by appropriate patent applications to protect the technology without subjecting a necessary patent application to what would be necessary disclosure for the successful prosecution of one case, but a premature disclosure for another application. Formulate your strategy before filing to maximize your ability to own the problem!

Another common rejection of an application occurs when the claims are not explicitly supported by the disclosure. Patents are very specific legal documents and every aspect of each claim must be described in the disclosure. It is not sufficient, for example, to describe a process of requiring a pressure of between 40 and 50 KPa and then trying to claim a pressure range of 43 to 46 KPa if the latter range is not explicitly stated in the disclosure. In order to guard against this occurrence, many patent practitioners will copy the actual claims into the disclosure, expanding the language around the copied claims with sufficient explanation to support those claims.

This chapter is not intended to be a treatise on how to prosecute a patent application. Detailed knowledge of patent law and procedure is required to do so. It is certainly beyond the scope of this book to provide the depth of knowledge that would be necessary to conduct a successful prosecution. Rather, this chapter is intended to provide the technical reader with the knowledge of what prosecution of a patent application entails. Successful prosecution generally requires close cooperation between the legal and technical experts, with the technical experts grasping the specific arguments made by the examiner. Moreover, the prosecution should be conducted with the intent of eventually asserting the patents obtained against alleged infringers. In other words, it is advantageous if the claims can be readily understood by an ordinary citizen without special training. This is not always possible, but keeping in mind that it may, at some time, be necessary to be able to explain the meaning of the claim to 12 ordinary people would definitely make for a stronger patent. Good teamwork between the legal and technical experts is needed during prosecution.

Abandoning an Application

Let us close this chapter by discussing when the prosecution of a patent application should cease. It is a fact that, no matter how well you have defined the problem being addressed in the application, discussed its solution, and conducted your prior art search, not every patent for which you have applied will be allowed. You should be able to get allowances for about three fourths of your applications. There are cautionary notes about having too many or too few patent applications allowed. If your track record is less than half, you are doing something wrong in addition to wasting a lot of time and money.

Generally, low success rates come from not properly conducting the background search, thereby allowing the examiner to find relevant prior art that was not properly discussed in your application. However, there are numerous other reasons that can give rise to low success rates. It is suggested that you closely read the examiner's reasons for rejection in his office actions. You may want to go over these with your legal expert, as they may contain subtleties that require the interpretation of one schooled in patent law to decipher. Suffice-it to say, appropriate corrective action should enable you to boost your success ratio markedly.

The author of this book has enjoyed a high success ratio, utilizing well developed patent strategies, despite those applications having been filed in the field of electrophotography—a field that is approximately 80 years old and has been of significant commercial value (that is, there are many competing companies investing vast sums of money in R&D over many years and filing innumerable patent applications). The problems and solutions have to be properly defined and a thorough background search has to be conducted if you are going to have success. Owning the problem, rather than just owning a specific solution to a specific problem, is crucial in order to protect one's intellectual property and the ability of one's company to control the marketplace and be the market leader.

There should also be concern if your success ratio is too high—exceeding perhaps 90%. It is possible that you have hit a gold mine in new technology and that you should continue on the path that you are pursuing. However, you may be writing your claims too tightly, in effect limiting your patent far more than it needs to be. Alternatively, you may be filing in the white space of little interest and less commercial value. In either of these cases, the patent portfolio that you are constructing will be costly and of little commercial value.

Let us now consider the case of someone who does not have any other patents and has come up with an idea that he seeks to patent. He writes his description and obtains competent legal counsel, who then files the patent application. The applicant then waits until he receives notice of an office action—a non-final rejection. The applicant responds to the rejection, in some instances revising or restricting claims, and in other instances by arguing with the examiner.

Once again, the examiner rejects the application, in this instance, giving a final rejection. The applicant, once again, responds to the office action, requests an RCE, pays the RCE fees, and waits. He is ultimately rewarded by yet another rejection. The applicant set up an appointment to speak with the examiner, in patent parlance, interviewing the examiner, to try to explain his invention and more fully understand the basis for the examiner's rejections. He then files another RCE.

Again, after waiting, another rejection arrives. The applicant is getting nowhere. He can appeal the rejection, but that costs a lot of money. He can continue down the path of requesting RCEs, but, not only does that cost money, but, with each RCE, the applicant is most likely narrowing his claims and setting up an ever increasing paper trail that will be used to attack his patent, should he ever receive one and decide to assert it against an alleged infringer.

There comes a time when an applicant views the costs and time involved in attempting to obtain a patent and contemplates the ever decreasing coverage and decides that what could be gained from any patent that might be obtained simply does not warrant the effort involved. At that point he simply stops responding to the office actions and, eventually, the patent office lists the application as "abandoned—failure to respond to an office action".

The decision to abandon an application is more complex when the application is part of a patent portfolio. The portfolio may include patents presently owned by your company as well as other present or future patent applications. In addition to all the issues involved in prosecuting a single patent application, there are additional ones when there is an entire patent portfolio. Specifically, the paper trail established can be used to limit or even nullify existing patents or applications. Remember that every bit of correspondence between you and the examiner becomes public record. This record can be used by opposing counsel in a lawsuit to argue against your patent. Even worse, you may be called to the witness stand by the opposing counsel and asked to elaborate on the comments you made during a prosecution.

If an examiner cites, as prior art, patents belonging to another company, you can strongly attack the meaning of the cited art and explain how that art, either by itself or in conjunction with other art, does not teach your present invention. When the prior art cited comprise patents that belong to your company, it may be better to try to restrict the claims in the application.

The implications of a decision as to whether or not to abandon an application extend beyond the value of the application under consideration. Obviously, the failure to cover certain aspects of your technology by not obtaining a patent is not good. However, one also has to consider the effects of pursuing prosecution or abandoning it in light of its effect on the value of the portfolio. It should be remembered that failing to successfully prosecute an application is not catastrophic if it is only a part of the portfolio. Moreover, there is a balance between engaging in arguments with the examiner as to why a patent should be allowed, and the resulting limitations such arguments place on both that specific application, if ultimately allowed, and the extent and validity of related applications, as part of your overarching portfolio. It should also be remembered that, if you fail to get an individual patent but still have most of your applications allowed, you will still control the problem. Moreover, as the rejected application has become prior art, the information contained therein effectively blocks competitors from obtaining patent coverage on that particular problem solved. A rejected patent application may not be a total loss.

One final consideration to be taken into account is whether or not the so-called "disruptive technology", that is, revolutionary changes that have occurred very rapidly, have antiquated the technology that you are trying to patent. This is more likely to occur in our rapidly changing world than ever before. Examples include floppy disks giving rise to thumb drives and CDs giving way to DVDs. It generally takes several years to successfully prosecute a patent application. During that time, it is possible that the significant advances on which your company filed patent applications no longer are viable in the marketplace. If this were to occur, it would be worthwhile to examine the applications that you have filed and see if they still reflect useful technology or whether they have become obsolete and worthless and should be abandoned. In any event, it would be time to start owning a new problem.

References

1. http://www.uspto.gov/patents/process/index.jsp
2. http://www.uspto.gov/
3. B. R. Hantke, M. E. DeVecchis, and D. M. Eggert, U. S. Patent D654,341 (2012).

8

Controlling the Costs of Generating and Maintaining a Patent Portfolio through Patent Engineering

Nothing worthwhile is free, an idea that certainly holds true for generating and maintaining patent portfolios. Cultivating a good patent portfolio can be expensive; however, the cost of not having a solid patent portfolio can far exceed the costs of having one. Moreover, by properly designing a patent strategy that focuses on owning the problem, rather than simply generating a random collection of unrelated patents, the total costs of producing a patent portfolio can be substantially reduced. In this chapter we discuss what having a solid patent portfolio actually costs in the United States. Foreign filings, as well as their related costs, will be discussed in the next chapter, as well as the many ways that significant savings can be achieved while generating a strong, international patent portfolio for your company.

Costs can be divided into three broad categories. The first consists of the legal costs incurred by engaging a patent practitioner. The second category comprises the time that your technical staff spends on generating and prosecuting patent applications. The third relates to the fees that are charged by the United States Patent and Trademark Office.

Legal Costs

Let us begin by first discussing legal costs. Typical attorney fees vary widely, but as of this writing \$350–\$450 per hour is not uncommon. Patent agents charge less—around \$250–\$350 per hour. Some law firms also bill separately for their patent paralegals, at \$100–\$200 per hour. Patent paralegals are an essential part of a legal staff and you are paying for their services as part of the attorney's rate if you are not paying directly.

If an attorney spends one eight-hour day discussing an invention with the inventors and a second eight-hour day writing the application, and assuming that no revisions are required once the draft is reviewed by the engineers who are working on the technology, the legal fees for a single case could already be \$5,600, assuming an hourly rate of \$350. If there are multiple, disparate applications, the fees simply get multiplied by the number of applications. Again, this assumes that no revisions to the case are required. It further assumes that the attorneys do not have to conduct a prior art search because the inventors have adequately done so. This is especially important because it reduces the chances of having to redesign the patent portfolio after the attorneys have started to draft the applications in order to adjust for the findings turned up by the prior art search.

Revisions to an application are generally necessary but, unfortunately, often not done. This is usually because the engineers developing the technology have neither the time nor the inclination to wade through the legal verbiage in patent applications. As a result, the filed applications and the resulting patents often contain errors such as describing the invention inaccurately, resulting in erroneous or improper claims. In the end, the patent protection afforded your company for all the expense incurred may be far more limited than is desirable or obtainable.

The good news is that the legal fees can be substantially reduced while the quality of the patent portfolio is greatly improved simply by practicing the ideas advanced in this book. First, by writing a thorough technical disclosure that includes a description of the problem, the way the problem was solved, and the analysis of the prior art search results, and working closely with the patent practitioner to draft the claims, the engineering team can accurately describe the problem, how others have attempted to solve the problem, the novelty of the invention, and a description of the invention, as described by the claims. Doing this will greatly reduce the time that the patent practitioner needs to spend on the patent application while reducing the chance of miscommunication or misunderstanding between the engineering and legal team members. This directly translates into substantially reduced legal fees, as the patent practitioner will be able to write a more accurate and complete application that will require fewer changes between writing and filing. This can also reduce misunderstandings between the technical and legal experts that can lead to poorly worded or even erroneous statements in the application. Such statements can create problems during prosecution as the examiner searches for prior art and the application misguides his search or even winds up resulting in the application going to the wrong department in the patent office.

The use of common disclosures, such as can be generated when a patent strategy is implemented that strives towards allowing the owner of the eventually issued patents to exercise significant control over the technology, can also greatly reduce legal fees. In effect, the patent practitioner reviews a single disclosure with sections that describe the various aspects of the specific problems being solved and the claims focused on the solutions to those problems. The bulk of the disclosure is similar, if not virtually identical, for each patent application filed and needs to be reviewed and revised by the patent practitioner only once. The use of a common disclosure would also reduce costs associated with items such as the drawing of the figures used in the applications.*

The prosecution of a case will add to the legal costs, in direct proportion to the time needed to craft a response to each office action. Fortunately, legal costs incurred during the prosecution of patent applications can also often be reduced. If the technical members of the project team can examine the art cited by the examiner, for example, and, in a tightly focused manner, address his concerns or identify technical features in the patent application that circumvent the cited art, a patent practitioner, upon

---

* Although the inventors would be expected to provide reasonable sketches of the required figures, the ultimate design and formatting of all such figures must comply with the requirements of the patent office. Accordingly, attorneys often contract with draftsmen who have detailed knowledge of the requirements imposed by the patent office to draw the figures submitted in an application.

receiving the input from the members of the technical team, need only ensure the appropriateness of the response (a legal issue regarding the specific response needed by the examiner). This may further reduce the time spent by legal representation. In addition, if multiple applications using a common disclosure have been filed, it is likely that the office actions by the examiners assigned to the cases (the applications may be assigned to different examiners) are likely to be similar and involve similar art. This would allow for a consistent response.

Indirect Costs

The second category of expense in filing and prosecuting patent applications includes the indirect costs associated with diverting members of the technical team from their primary responsibility of designing products. Engineers are not inexpensive and diverting their time away from assigned projects can be costly. Worse, generating even a single patent application often requires the attention of all the inventors named in the application. Even worse yet is that the time spent on preparing and prosecuting patent applications can result in delays in introducing products. It is clear that time is a factor that has to be closely managed. Is it possible to do everything that is necessary to design a patent strategy and to file and prosecute the resulting applications without unduly impacting the time spent on this activity by the project team members? The answer is yes and may involve the use of a patent engineer.

The role and value of a patent engineer are discussed in detail in Chapter 11. However, as one role of a patent engineer is to reduce costs of obtaining patents while increasing the value of those granted, it is beneficial to partially anticipate that discussion within the present context. A patent engineer is an individual who has in-depth knowledge of the technology being developed for use in the present project. His knowledge in this area is generally sufficient so that he either has or could make significant technical contributions to the project. In addition, a patent engineer must have a solid working knowledge of patent law although he need not be formally trained as a patent agent or attorney.

The role of a patent engineer in an industrial setting includes determining the specific inventions pertinent to the project. This includes discussions with the project team members to determine what inventions have occurred and discussing those inventions with the inventors to determine at least the independent claims. Once this has been done, the patent engineer can propose claim language to the patent practitioner, conduct the literature search, and develop a patent strategy that would broaden the protection that the patent portfolio would afford the company. These activities would free up the engineering team to work on the project, rather than on patent activities and would greatly reduce legal costs. Once these activities have been completed, the information could be forwarded to the patent practitioner for completion of the application, final review with the inventors, and filing.

The patent engineer would also be in an ideal position to assist with formulating responses to office actions. Again, such responses would include both project team member's and practitioner's time, but legal time can be reduced and the response focused by engaging the patent engineer. It is clear that a patent engineer can greatly enhance patenting efficiency while containing generation and prosecution costs. Perhaps it is more appropriate to ask what would be the costs to your company if your market advantage were undercut because you chose not to protect the technology that your company spent so much to develop.

Fees Charged by the Patent Office

The third category of costs comprise those fees charged by the United States Patent and Trademark Office. In contrast to the legal and engineering costs, mandatory fees charged by the United States Patent and Trademark Office are not subject to economies of scale or scope and cannot be simply reduced. However, the applicant can make certain decisions or choose certain courses of action that can add to the mandatory costs. These are discussed later in this chapter and offer the applicant the opportunity to considerably control those costs. The current fee structure is published by the USPTO at their website (http://www.uspto.gov/learning-and-resources/fees-and-payment/uspto-fee-schedule#Patent%20Fees.) There are individual charges for everything imaginable and perhaps a few items that would escape one's imagination. However, even here, judicious choices can help contain these expenses. Let us discuss this topic more specifically. We will begin by considering what fees are unavoidable.

As of 2015, the basic filing fee for a utility patent that is filed electronically is $280. There is a utility search fee of $600, a utility examination fee of $720, and a utility patent issue fee of $960. These add up to $2,560. If everything goes reasonably well, that is what your company will pay the government for a utility patent.

After a patent is issued, there are additional fees. For example, there are three sets of maintenance or renewal fees.** If a patent is not maintained, it becomes public domain. The first maintenance fee is due at three and a half years after issuance and is $1,600. The second, due at seven and a half years is $3,600. The third, due at eleven and a half years, is $7,400. That's right. A patent is valid for twenty years from the date of filing, but only if you pay the government to maintain it.

The decision as to whether or not to pay an upcoming maintenance fee is based on business concerns. The value of a patent is not whether or not it protects a fundamentally new technology, but whether or not another company needs the specific patented technology. Often, it is the relatively minor advances that are critical to market a product rather than the fundamental technology on which the product is based.

Questions that should be raised when deciding whether or not to pay the maintenance fees are whether the world has moved away from a technology, such as Beta Max losing to VHS and VHS becoming obsolete because of the advent of recordable DVDs. In addition it should also be considered whether or not equally viable methods of accomplishing a task exist.

Yet another question is whether or not another company, either an existing and well-established or a start-up, would be interested in practicing the technology. Finally, determine if the claims extend beyond the specific products being produced by your company so that they have applications to seemingly unrelated areas of endeavor. All of these questions are manifestations of the underlying question—will another company have to pay your company money through licensing fees or, in some instances, due to legal damages being assessed due to infringement, because it needs to practice your invention?

It should be remembered that it typically takes a few years between the time a patent application is filed and the time it is issued. If we assume a two-year application processing time, it means the first renewal is due five and a half years after the application was first filed. This can still be too soon to fully assess the value of a patent at the time of first renewal, so the applicant is advised that paying the first maintenance fee should inherently be added to the cost of the application. By the time the third and most costly maintenance fee is due (11½ years after issuance), it is often feasible to determine whether or not the patented technology has become

** The reader is reminded that fees are imposed by the USPTO on a periodic basis. Failure to pay an upcoming maintenance fee will result in your losing your exclusive rights to practice your invention.

antiquated. The second maintenance fee (due 7½ years after issuance) is often the most difficult to assess. It should be apparent that, if another company is paying licensing fees to you for the use of the patent, the patent should be maintained. Similarly, if there are inquiries about licensing the technology or if your company is asserting the patent, the maintenance fees should be paid.

For the sake of estimating costs, it should be assumed that the first and second maintenance fees will be paid (total: $5,200). Thus far, together with the cost of $2,560 discussed earlier, the cost of a single utility patent is at least $7,760. Obviously, multiple patents simply result in that cost being multiplied by the number of patents under consideration. There is no economy of scale.

Avoidable Costs

Thus far the discussion has focused on costs that will be charged. In addition there are costs that will likely, but not necessarily, be incurred. For example, if, in response to a first office action rejection of an application, the applicant responds by revising at least some of the claims, it is likely that a new search by the examiner will be required. As a result, it is very likely that a so-called "final rejection" will be given. However, the term "final" does not mean the end of the application. Rather, upon filing a Request for Continued Examination, or RCE, the patent office will continue to examine the patent application. For a first RCE, the cost is $1,200. Should additional RCEs be filed, each subsequent one adds $1,700 to the bill. It is likely that, during the prosecution of a patent application, at least one RCE will be filed.

Appeals can rapidly add significant costs to the prosecution of a patent application. Costs include filing fees, legal expenses, and, of course, the time and effort spent by the members of the project team. It is often (but not always) more cost effective to exercise alternative options, including interviewing the examiner, before appealing. As perhaps an overly simplistic statement, a company is generally better off filing multiple patent applications that comprise an effective strategy protecting proprietary technology than it is appealing applications that are not essential. A company should recognize that, despite all the care, effort, and searching that it conducted prior to the filing of an application, it is unlikely that all of its applications will be granted. This is true even if a company is very conservative and narrow in its filings. As discussed before, an approach that is too narrow and/or conservative is generally not prudent and, not only exposes a company to insufficient patent protection, but cannot even guarantee that the applications that are filed will be ultimately allowed.

Additional fees can occur during the prosecution of an application. For example, let us consider how revising claims can affect fees. As noted, inventorship is a legal concept requiring that, in order to be considered an inventor, an individual must make an inventive contribution to at least one claim in a patent. Let us now suppose that, during prosecution, some claims are rejected by the examiner, during or after the first office action, that happen to be the only claims to which one of the proposed inventors made such a contribution. That person is no longer an inventor and legally must be removed from the list of inventors. Conversely, it is possible that additional claims will be added to the application following the first office action that results in one or more additional inventors being listed. In either event, the list of inventors needs to be corrected. The fee imposed for correcting such a list after the first office action is $600. The penalty for having individuals incorrectly listed as inventors is that the patent can be found to be invalid if challenged.

The next group of fees imposed on an applicant arises from choices that the applicant makes. For example, verbosity can also incur additional fees as any application that exceeds 100 pages is assessed an additional fee of $400 for every fifty pages. An applicant should carefully examine any application that is that long. It should be remembered that the information that is disclosed should directly relate to proposed claims or, at least, information that could lead to alternative claims should the proposed claims be rejected. Meandering discussions not only can add to the cost of an application, but can preclude the ability to get future patent protection as the technology advances.

Too many claims can also add fees to an application. If there are more than three independent claims, a fee of $420 is added to the cost of the application. Similarly, if there are more than twenty claims, an additional fee of $80 for each claim is assessed. Moreover, the inclusion of numerous claims adds to the probability that the examiner will determine that the claims constitute more than one invention and require a divisional.*** It is recommended that the claims be partitioned out as the patent strategy

---

*** The reader is reminded that deciding to prosecute a divisional incurs risks in addition to expenses, as this creates a second file history that can be searched by a defendant against whom you are asserting the first patent. However, judicious use of divisional patents can strengthen your portfolio, depending on the coverage obtained. You are advised to discuss filing divisionals with your patent practitioner.

evolves so that no one case has too many claims. If this is not feasible, it may be worthwhile to include the material in the disclosure so that alternative, more limited claims can be written after the first office action should the original claims be rejected for good reason. In essence, the applicant should strive to procure the broadest claims possible, leaving the information that would support additional, narrow claims within the application so that a fallback position would be available, if necessary.

The use of provisional applications adds costs as a fee of $260 is charged, providing the application does not exceed 100 pages. In the latter case, an additional charge of $400 is assessed for every fifty pages in excess of 100. This is in addition to the fees that would be charged for an actual utility patent application, which would have to be ultimately filed anyway. Limiting the use of provisional applications to situations where they are absolutely necessary, such as when a technology is to be disclosed within a few days and there simply is insufficient time to develop a good set of claims, is a good way of saving money. There are additional risks in filing provisional applications. Normally, the claims are the first section written in a patent application so that the rest of the disclosure can be written to support the claims. With a provisional application, the claims are often omitted so that the applicant does not have this advantage. As a result, the provisional application can divulge too much information that would not be directly relevant to the ultimate application or applications, thereby making future applications more difficult. In addition, there may not be sufficient disclosure to support the claims that one would ultimately wish to file. This may make obtaining the desired patent protection more difficult.

These situations can be avoided, for the most part, by developing the proper patent strategy in advance of filing applications. Although multiple, distinct applications can result in more filing fees, legal costs can be minimized and unnecessary expenses can be avoided.

Finally, there are the fees that result from an applicant's errors. Missing a deadline imposed by the patent office will result in either fees having to be paid or the application being abandoned. For example, if an applicant misses a deadline for a response to an office action, the applicant would have to pay a fee ranging from $200 within the first month to $3,000 if within the fifth month. Certificates of correction to fix errors in a patent that are the applicant's fault entail a fee of $100. Late payment of maintenance fees within six months of each due date results in an additional fee of $160. And processing fees charged to correct the inventorship result in a charge of $130. The author has seen cases where inventors have signed applications indicating everything was correct, but listing their own names erroneously. These are but a few of the errors that occur and for which the applicant gets billed in order to correct.

The list of additional charges is quite long and, for the most part, results from addressing specific legal issues. It is beyond the scope of this book, as it would require extensive legal discourse, to delve into these issues. Charges can be assessed well in excess of $10,000 for some of these issues. Many, if not most, can be avoided if care in developing the patent strategy is exercised. Good planning in advance results, not only in a better patent portfolio, but in obtaining that portfolio at a significantly reduced cost.

9

Patent Engineering in a Global Economy

Thus far in this book we have discussed the first three key steps in the patent engineering process—identifying important problems, mapping a portfolio of patents to "own the problems" and efficiently generating these patent applications. These steps define what patents you want to file. Now that you have decided what to file, you have to decide where to file, and why. As you are about to discover, these decisions can be among the most time consuming and potentially expensive decisions that you will face in the patent engineering process.

No patent will block your competitors around the entire world. While there is an international patent application, there is no international patent. The most any one patent will cover is a group of closely related countries, such as the 38 member countries participating in the European Patent Convention [1]. There is also the African Regional Intellectual Property Organization [2] (ARIPO) consisting of 19 African countries and the Gulf Cooperation Council Patent Office [3] (GCCPO) consisting of 6 Gulf states. A "jurisdiction" is the geographical reach of any particular patent office. It should be noted that patents granted through these organizations are not centrally enforceable. Rather, assertions have to be conducted in the individual countries under the laws of those countries in which the owner of the patents wishes to recover damages. To own the problem effectively, consider patent coverage in countries where you or your competitors make, ship, or sell products, or from which or in which you or your competitors offer services.

The Case for Building an International Portfolio

To the large, prosperous multi-national firm, obtaining and maintaining an international patent portfolio may seem to be the only course of action. However, small cash-strapped companies that are located within major markets such as the United States, the European Union, Japan, South Korea or China might be inclined to ask why they should file outside of their country of origin. To such companies, establishing a successful presence in the domestic market may constitute success.

Such a view is somewhat short-sighted in a global economy. Bringing new innovations to the customer in any major market will not go unnoticed for long. Once noticed, imitators and copyists, even if not direct competitors in the local market, will soon introduce or assimilate any successful business model or product feature into global markets. After a time the innovator may well appear to be the imitator and begin to lose hard fought gains even in the domestic market.

Furthermore, especially for software-related technology, competitors can export to your customers via the internet from a country in which you do not have patents. This may violate your patents in the countries where your customers are, but it may be difficult to trace and block software imports. For example, ready-to-use versions of the LAME mp3 encoder [4] are distributed from Argentina, where there are no patents on the included technology.

Let us further illustrate this point with a hypothetical example. Assume that your company produces a software product that is produced and sold principally in the United States. As such, you have extensively patented and marketed that software in the United States. As your company does not market in, let us say, Country W and there are no known producers of similar software packages in that country, your company did not file for patent protection in that country. Along comes Company F, whose headquarters and production facilities are located in Country W. This company was founded by a couple of entrepreneurs, who recognized the value of your software and decided to market their own version of it, also marketing it extensively in the United States. Perhaps their version has some upgrades or perhaps it can be offered for sale at a lower price than for which your company can sell its version. It is clear, however, that Company F is using the technology that you have protected in the United States with your patents. Let us further assume that Company F has no assets in the United States. Its banking, headquarters, and production facilities are located in Country W. If Company F were exporting to the United States physical versions of its product, that product could be impounded. However, Company F is not doing that. Rather, they are selling licenses over the internet to use their software.

What recourse does your company have for the damages it is suffering as a result of Company F's infringement of your patents? Winning an infringement lawsuit would allow your company to seek to recover monetary damages from the infringing company. However, under the scenario presented, how could such damages be recovered? First, without a physical presence in the United States, pursing a patent assertion can just be an exercise in futility, as the probability of recovering damages is not great and the expenses of attempting to do so are high. Your company can engage the services of an attorney with expertise in the business law of Country W. That may or may not be a fruitful avenue to pursue. Your company can seek to have the United States government intervene with the government of Country W to force Company F to stop infringing. It is doubtful if many individuals would actually believe that such a course of action would be productive.

Your company may decide that the market for the software package is just not worth protecting and abandon it. However, the fact that another company has moved into that area suggests that there is still much revenue to be extracted. Alternatively, your company can reduce its prices and attempt to compete for market share, at the expense of both market share* and profitability.

Finally, your company can reexamine its patent strategy. Specifically, it may be necessary to start filing patent applications in Country W and, if Company F can relocate to yet other countries, in those other countries as well. It may be possible, if the period since disclosure has not exceeded the time allowed from disclosure by the respective patent offices, to file the appropriate applications on the patentable features of your software product.

* It should be remembered that decisions to buy a product from a company are often driven by factors other than simply price. Lowering the price without being able to offer the required features may not allow your company to maintain its market share.

Regardless of whether that is feasible, your company should carefully analyze what improvements or upgrades it will be commercializing in the future and what upgrades Company F would have to introduce to overcome limitations of their product and file the appropriate patent applications in Country W. It might even be worthwhile to generate an extensive patent portfolio in Country W in order to put pressure on Company F.

Additional Factors Driving International Patent Filings

In a global economy, larger firms that may be seeking to license your patents will consider the extent to which your patent portfolio impacts their markets or key markets of their competitors. A firm that sells a product internationally will inherently perceive greater value in licensing a portfolio of patents that are enforceable in countries in which the firm sells 90% of its products than in a portfolio of patents that are enforceable in countries in which the firm sells 10% of its products.

Another factor to be considered is that having an international portfolio can increase the value of your company. During acquisition, potential acquirers of other firms will consider both the number of and the global reach of the patents in the patent portfolio of the firm being acquired in determining the value of the acquisition. In essence filing internationally adds both global reach and a greater number of patents to your portfolio. Moreover, increasing your company's value can also reduce the chance of hostile take-overs, while increasing shareholder value should you decide to sell your company.

Having an international portfolio can protect your place in the international market. Additional pressures on your competitors to pay either licensing fees or damages to your company, or enter into patent exchange agreements with your company, should they need to use your technology, will be increased. And, if your company is practicing the teachings of this book, the need for your patented intellectual property by competitors should be great. Finally, an international patent portfolio will give you an enhanced ability to control the marketplaces where you compete.

Building an International Portfolio and its Risks

It will be appreciated that filing patent applications in multiple jurisdictions can add significant value to your portfolio. However, doing so is one that is not without risk.

In part this is because each jurisdiction has its own rules for granting and enforcing patents and the rights obtained by the owners of those patents. Typically, governments perform this function themselves,** establishing patent granting authorities such as domestic patent offices as agencies to receive, examine and decide whether to accept or reject the patents, as well as courts that try alleged cases of infringement brought by the owner of a patent. China, Japan, South Korea, Russia, India, Brazil, Israel, and the United States*** each use such a national patent granting authority.

While in some cases governments may agree to recognize patent applications granted by a non-governmental patent granting entity such as the European Patent Office, these patents are generally enforced by national courts using domestic legal processes which can vary significantly from jurisdiction to jurisdiction. Any kind of global patent strategy will necessarily require that an individual patent undergo separate examination by more than one patent granting authority.

Each patent granting authority has its own rules, its own way of deciding what is patentable. Further, there is the human dimension in that each patent application will be examined by a different examiner with a different background, a different technical and cultural perspective, and with a different set of priorities. Accordingly, there is no guarantee that patent granting authorities will reach similar conclusions regarding your patent applications.

For example a patent application that is filed before a first patent granting authority and that is allowed without comment by the first patent granting authority may be rejected or be allowed only after years of complex negotiations with a second patent granting authority. In some jurisdictions, the conclusions reached by the second patent granting authority may create complications when an effort is made to enforce the patent granted by the first patent granting authority.

In this regard, international patent prosecution can be likened to playing several different variants of chess at the same time against different opponents. Additionally, given that what you say and what patent granting authorities say in your patent applications are not only public record but also are available online, it is not unlike playing different variants of chess

** As discussed earlier in this chapter, there are several regional authorities that can grant patents on the behalf of multiple countries. However, even there, enforcement is generally country by country.

*** This is an exemplary, rather than an exhaustive, list. Even countries that are members of a regional patent granting authority generally maintain their own patent offices as well.

against multiple opponents all of whom watch your moves and all of your opponent's counter moves in real time and can adjust their own strategies accordingly.

Costs of Building an International Portfolio

Each jurisdiction's patent granting authority charges its own fees to examine patent applications and issue and maintain patents. In addition, there are expenses associated with converting patent applications into the particular forms preferred by individual patent granting authorities and translations that add significant expense to the process of filing the same patent in multiple jurisdictions. For example, China, South Korea, and Japan all require translations of English applications into their respective languages. Finally, in most jurisdictions, each patent granting authority requires that patent professionals have specific credentials, and those are generally jurisdiction-specific. In general, prosecuting your patent application before multiple patent granting authorities will require retaining and compensating a different patent attorney for each jurisdiction.

Building an International Portfolio: Making Choices

The previous discussion points to the realization that one must be judicious and carefully select what applications to file in which of the more than 200 foreign countries in which such applications can be filed. This may seem like a daunting challenge. However, it is not nearly as difficult as it might, at first glance, appear. It is a goal of a good patent strategy to afford great protection of one's intellectual property while containing costs. Towards this objective, there is a relatively straight forward set of questions that one can ask to help winnow down the list of countries in which patents should be sought. Most of these are variants of the same question which can be phrased either as, "Why should I obtain patents in a particular country if my competitors will not care about those particular patents?" or alternatively, "In what countries do I have to have enforceable patent rights for this invention in order to protect my existing market and my plans for growth?"

This market-based analysis is an important one as market protection is the goal of a patent system. Accordingly, a first look at your portfolio may well be to identify key markets for your products both domestically and abroad both now and over the twenty-year span your patent will remain effective. Ask yourself these questions:

a. Does a country contain a sufficiently large market for the patented product?
b. How speculative is the market for your products in that country?
c. When will the market in that country mature if it is not mature now?

Once you have identified your key markets, you have to address the following concerns about how to protect your inventions in these markets:

a. Is a country hostile to issuing or enforcing patents in general, or to those patents that are assigned to a company from another country?
b. Can the courts in a country be relied upon to act in a predictable and fair manner when asked to determine infringement of a patent or when enforcing patents?
c. What are the enforcement options in the country?
d. How much does a patent cost over its lifetime in a selected country? This includes filing fees and associated costs, such as translation expenses, legal expenses, and maintenance/renewal fees.

These questions are a good place to begin your evaluation. That said, you might find that your own process may not be quite that straightforward. Today, many former developing-world countries are becoming industrialized, with South Korea, China, India, Brazil, and many Eastern European countries becoming industrial powerhouses. Even small countries, such as Israel, support strong industrial economies. Such countries may present marketing opportunities for your products and, accordingly, patents in those countries can be valuable components of your international patent portfolio.

The United States is still the dominant industrial and economic power in the rapidly changing world; it has a reliable judicial system, and moderate expenses. As such, many companies patent their technology in the United States even if they have no plans to market or manufacture their products in the United States.

Such patents can be especially problematic for a company that has ignored generating a patent portfolio in other countries. As an example, let us consider a foreign competitor that has patented his competitive technology in the United States but does not otherwise conduct business here. Let us further assume that your company could benefit if you could use some parts of your competitor's patented technology in your products that are only produced or offered for sale in the United States.

You have a problem. Your competitor is free to practice your technology as you do not have patent coverage in the countries of interest to your competitor, whereas he has patents in the United States that preclude your ability to access technology that you need. He is not likely to enter into any sort of patent exchange agreement with your company as there is nothing your company has that he needs. If you want or need his technology, your company will have to pay a substantial licensing fee. Moreover, your company may be blocked from obtaining components from suppliers in foreign countries if those components contain technology that has been patented in the supplier's country or if, in order to export those components to the United States, they must be transported through a country in which there are valid patents.

Manufacturing and Marketing Considerations

With this discussion in mind, let us consider how to formulate an international patent strategy by first addressing the issue of manufacturing. It may seem obvious that it is worthwhile to file patent applications in countries that may produce competitive products. However, such an assumption may or may not be valid. One should consider how much of the product is actually produced by competitors in the targeted countries and whether or not the products are sold principally in that country or mostly exported. In addition, is the entire device produced in the targeted country or merely a critical subsystem whose technology has been patented in the United States?

Before filing patent applications in a country, it is necessary to determine if there is a sufficient market in that particular country for your company's products and, if so, whether or not it is economically worth filing for patents in that country. If a competitor is producing within that country mainly to export its products, there are other options that may be more valuable economically. Specifically, patent applications can be filed in countries that contain the target market. If the target market is the United States, your company presumably has already taken the necessary steps to protect its intellectual property with the intent of owning the problem. If, on the other hand, the market within that particular country is sufficiently large or the competitor produces a significant portion of the products that serve the market internationally, it may be desirable to file patent applications in that country.

It is worth filing patent applications in countries where competitive products are not necessarily produced, but which serve as a large market for your products. Where there is an opportunity, competition will arise. However, under the scenario just presented, the products have to be imported into that country. If this is one of a number of countries that share a similar characteristic such as geographic location, cultures, economic structure, etc. that import but do not manufacture competitive products, it is possible to file an application at a commercial bottleneck. For example, the port of Rotterdam in the Netherlands is a major facility for importation and exportation, serving much of Europe. Even though the Netherlands, by itself, may be only a relatively small market, it is often worthwhile to file in that country as it would preclude the ability of such products to enter into the Netherlands. By filing in the Netherlands, one can accomplish much without incurring the expenses of maintaining patent portfolios in multiple European countries.

Another question that should be addressed prior to filing a patent application is whether or not a country is hostile to either issuing patents or allowing issued patents to be enforced if the assignee is from another country. This is a topic that would need to be discussed with the appropriate legal counsel that specializes in patent law of the targeted country.

It should also be emphasized that, as is the case in the United States, holding a patent or a family of patents in a foreign country does not give the assignee the right to practice the patented technology, nor does it convey the right to offer for sale, make, use, or import the patented technology. This is because there may be other legal considerations such as the existence of prior patents owned by others that would be infringed if the present patented invention were practiced. Also, rules and regulations put forth either by legislation or regulatory agencies or injunctions issued by a court against the product incorporating the specific invention can preclude the use of the patent. A patent merely allows the assignee to block others from practicing the invention without its permission.

Containing Costs and Adjusting Disclosures

Let us now explore how to formulate an international patent strategy that does not cost more than the benefits you obtain. It may not be necessary or even practical, in general, to totally own the problem, as is the goal in the United States. Rather, it should be the goal of an international patent strategy to impede one's competitor from encroaching on the assignee's market. This is accomplished by patenting the key technological advances. Thus, one could choose not to patent the enabling technology. In addition, when formulating an international patent strategy, the assignee should determine what technological advances can be patented that would be needed or desired by a competitor to improve his products in the country of manufacture.

When discussing what information should be included in a disclosure written in the United States, we have stated that information that is not to be claimed should be omitted, as inclusion of such information can impede future patents. In other words, the disclosure should focus tightly on the claims. Given the high cost of foreign patents, it may be useful to include more disclosure than you would in the United States so you have more scope to amend the claims to secure a patent.

It is recognized that the revised claims may not be as encompassing as the original claims and a decision may be made not to pursue a patent, but, alternatively, it may be possible to obtain claims of substantial value if they are supported by the disclosure. This will be discussed in more detail forthwith.

Patent Cooperation Treaty (PCT) and International Searching Authority (ISA)

As previously stated, there is no such thing as an international patent. Rather, a patent application should be filed and prosecuted in each country in which patent protection is desired. This allows the specific claims to be tailored to the legal and business climates in the specific countries and is often more cost effective to do so. Fortunately, the task of filing patent applications in specific targeted counties has been simplified by the Patent Cooperation Treaty, often referred to as PCT. This is an international treaty concluded in 1970 that went into effect in January of 1978. Presently, there are 148 signatories of the treaty. This includes most industrialized countries including the United States. Most notably absent from the signatory nations are Argentina and Taiwan.

PCT allows a single application to be filed, in a single language, with a receiving office. This is often referred to as an international, or PCT, application. The filing of the application establishes a uniform priority date from which prior art will be determined.

Upon submission, the PCT patent application is sent to an International Searching Authority (ISA), which issues a search report and a written opinion of the patentability of the proposed invention. The patentability report includes an evaluation of the novelty, the industrial applicability, and the inventiveness (non-obviousness) of the application.

The ISA search report includes three classes of cited references. The "X" references are those that, by themselves, read, in the opinion of the ISA, directly upon the patent application. The "Y" references are those that, by themselves, do not read on the proposed invention, but taken together, do. The final group consists of "A" references, which are those that are in the same general area but that do not read directly, either by themselves or in conjunction with any other references, on the invention.

It is generally necessary for the applicants to address the issues raised by the ISA for the X and Y references. This frequently requires revising the claims, which is why it is important for the disclosure to be as thorough as possible. Writing an application that allows the inventors to modify their claims and block others from obtaining patents on competitive technology while not disclosing more than is necessary is, obviously, a difficult balancing act that requires careful analysis of your company's patent goals. There is a fine line between disclosing too much information and not disclosing enough. Either can compromise your ability to obtain the patent portfolio that you desire. Ultimately, the patent applications will be published and the applicant will have to select those countries in which he wishes to file. It should be noted that the PCT was not written with the authority to determine what is patentable in a specific country. Patentability is determined solely by the laws of the countries to which the application is ultimately submitted.

The Role of International Patents in Owning the Problem

Let us explore how to devise and implement a strategy for filing patent applications internationally with the intent of obtaining a patent portfolio that aims to own the problem.

As previously discussed in this chapter, there is no such thing as an international patent. Certainly, the Patent Cooperation Treaty (PCT) simplifies the international filing of patent applications. The findings of the International Searching Authority (ISA) may even help the inventors focus their claims. However, the simple facts are that patent applications will have to be filed and prosecuted in each and every country in which the inventors seek to obtain patent protections. As each country's patent granting authority charges its own processing and maintenance fees, and attorneys expert in the laws of those countries would have to be engaged, the expenses incurred with attempting to obtain such coverage can be astronomical. In some countries a fee is actually imposed for each claim in addition to all other fees.

Moreover, despite the findings of the International Searching Authority and the necessity of the inventors to address their objections, it is likely that the patent office in each country in which an application is filed will conduct its own search and analysis. Again, these objections will have to be addressed. All of this creates a long paper trail that can degrade the value of those patents that have already been obtained or of other applications that had been filed. To add insult to injury, some countries tend to view foreign applicants and assignees unfavorably, and some are even reputed to imprison individuals who attempt to assert a patent but lose the lawsuit. With these factors in mind, let us discuss the role of international patents in one's portfolio and how to augment that portfolio with international patents.

Designating Focus and Satellite Countries

Let us begin this discussion by defining the terms "focus country" and "satellite countries". A focus country is the country (or conceivably several countries) that you have chosen in which to file and obtain those patents that are contained within your patent portfolio that is aimed at owning the problem.

Implicit in this discussion thus far is that the United States is the focus country. This is often the case because the United States is the world's largest economy. However, there is no requirement that the United States needs to be that country. For example, if products were made in India and sold predominantly in India, it would make more sense to make India the focus country. If your company produces technology that is suitable only on automobiles using right-handed steering, it might make sense to designate Great Britain, for example, as the focus country.

In contrast to the focus country, satellite countries are those countries in which patent coverage is highly desirable, but in which it is neither cost effective nor practical to obtain the in-depth and broad coverage discussed thus far in this book.

There are several criteria that can be used to decide if it is worthwhile to consider a country as a satellite in developing a patent strategy. A first criterion is whether or not the country under consideration comprises a sufficiently large market for you that is also attractive to your competition. A second criterion to consider is the extent of the manufacturing within a country, irrespective of the size of its market. Israel, for example, might be a suitable satellite country for some businesses because of the extent of its high-tech manufacturing, even though many of its products are exported. A third factor to consider is whether or not competitive products are produced in the country under consideration. A fourth factor to consider is whether a country serves as a hub for international commerce. As previously stated, most goods being imported into or traversing through Europe enter Europe through the port of Rotterdam, thereby making the Netherlands a valuable satellite country even though its manufacturing capability may be limited and the size of its market small.

It is only necessary that a country meet only one of these conditions to make it suitable as a satellite country. Conversely, if none of these conditions are met, it may not be worth the costs and risks to file patent applications in that country.

So, what is the goal of obtaining patents in satellite countries as it relates to a patent strategy that is designed to allow your company to own the problem? The goal of such coverage is to amplify the threat of assertion and the damages that could be awarded that result from successful assertions by being able to file suit in each of several countries instead of just one, as well as to further enable your company to control the market for its products. In other words, the role of internationally held patents is to enable the assignee to seek additional damages from an infringer by suing in multiple countries. This increases, not only the sum of the damages to be collected, but the probability of receiving favorable verdicts, as multiple lawsuits can be filed. It also increases the legal costs incurred by the allegedly infringing companies. The latter may help enhance the chances that the targeted company may seek to pay licensing fees to the assignee, as the consequential expenses of multiple expensive trials in multiple countries that result in extensive damages may be too much for a competitor to accept.

Now that we have discussed the risks and benefits of filing patent applications internationally, as well as those factors that contribute to deciding in which countries to file, let us discuss what should be filed.

The goal of a patent, or a family of patents in a portfolio, is to prevent a competitor from selling his products in your marketplace. Alternatively, patents can be used to force your competition to pay licensing fees or damages should they decide that the market is sufficiently valuable.

To achieve either of these goals, the claims must be written with the intent of asserting. As an example, claims that cover mechanical devices are much simpler to explain in a court than are those covering mathematical algorithms. In addition, the patent applications should contain those claims that are not only enforceable, but which would also result in costly damages to an infringer. The claims chosen should also, if possible but not necessarily, read on the core technology that is central to the patent portfolio in the focus country. However, the reader should also consider, when deciding which applications to file, i.e. what inventions to protect with patent coverage, that there is little reason to establish paper trails during prosecution of a patent application that can be used to challenge your patents during an assertion.

If this chapter were about allocating resources in order to fight a war, the central front would occur in the focus country and secondary fronts that are necessary to weaken the enemy should be opened and fought in the satellite countries. Specifically, secondary fronts are designed to draw off resources from the central front and raise the specter of incurring greater losses. There is an analogy to this in the business world. In many aspects, today's global business environment is analogous to a war. Certainly, people are not being killed. However, your competition is seeking to take your markets away from you and possibly even drive your company out of business. It makes sense to adopt the mindset of having to fight for your company's life in today's highly competitive global economy.

Asserting patents costs a lot of money and takes a lot of time and effort. If a company has to defend itself against assertions in multiple countries, it will incur great legal expenses and will be diverting its international workforce in mounting that defense. Risks of loss increase as the company may lose a lawsuit in any or all of the countries in which it is defending itself. Moreover, as any company has limited resources, it often can only defend against a lawsuit in one country by diverting the resources that it would need to defend against that suit in another country. Throughout all of this is the added risk to the defending company that it can lose multiple lawsuits and incur even greater expenses than if the assertion lawsuit was filed in only one country. This increases the pressure on the defending company to settle the suit, thereby enabling your company to prevail.

References

1. http://www.epo.org/service-support/useful-links/national-offices.html, retrieved 2015/01/10.
2. http://www.aripo.org/
3. http://www.gccpo.org/, http://www.gccpo.org/DefaultEn.aspx
4. http://lame.sourceforge.net/

10

Avoiding an Infringement Lawsuit through Patent Clearances

The introduction of a new product often generates great angst in a company. Many of the reasons for this stress were mentioned previously in Chapter 1. However, there is yet another factor that causes concerns—the fear of a lawsuit.

In today's litigious times, suits arise in multiple ways. There is the product liability lawsuit resulting from the claim that someone suffered some sort of injury, whether real or not, from your product or service. There is the lawsuit filed by a government agency. These could be the result of regulatory actions, such as an alleged failure to meet an emissions or safety standard. Suits against various power companies often fall into the former category while actions commenced against automotive companies are frequently the result of the latter. Then, there are the lawsuits that are politically motivated and are based on novel concepts of law. For example, several years ago, various municipalities filed lawsuits against firearms manufacturers claiming that the sale of the firearms resulted in criminal shootings. And, there are the patent infringement lawsuits.

Attorneys specializing in patent litigation and their clients are hoping to gain financially from your product's revenues. Moreover, they are often hoping, not only to extract large licensing fees and damages from your company for their clients, but also to prove that your company willingly infringed upon their clients' patents, thereby tripling the damages you will owe.

Your company has executed a patent strategy aimed at owning the problem. This can reduce the risk of patent infringement suits originating from companies with whom you either have patent exchange agreements or who need your patented technology, but not eliminate that risk. Often the range of the intellectual property covered by patent exchange or cross-licensing agreements is limited. As such, it is possible for a company to infringe upon the patents owned by another company even with patent exchange agreements in place. Moreover, the company entering into the exchange with your company may own the rights to use patented technology of a third company, but cannot include those patents in any exchange agreements. And, even if a company needs your technology, it may decide that your needs are more pressing to you and therefore more valuable to it than are its own needs to gain access to your technology simply by entering into patent exchange or cross-licensing agreements. It may choose to assert its patents against your company in order to pressure your company to grant it more advantageous terms. And, even in cases where symbiotic agreements exist between two companies in certain specified technological areas, managerial decisions can still place those companies on a collision course.

It should be noted that such exchanges can reduce the value of your portfolio, as other companies now have access to practice your patented technology. In addition the value of your portfolio to a third company can be diminished if another company also has rights to your intellectual property. The factors governing the decision of whether or not a company should enter into an exchange agreement should be carefully weighed prior to making a commitment.

Then there are organizations and entities that do not need your technology, but certainly aspire to sharing your revenues with you. These include not-for-profit organizations such as universities or research institutes. They also include companies whose products do not utilize your technology or do not even compete with your products, but who have patented technology that your company may need, and which may assert their patents against you should they believe that you have infringed upon those patents. Lastly, there are the non-practicing entities (NPEs). As discussed in a previous chapter, NPEs are people or companies that obtain patents but who do not produce any goods or services. They make their money by bringing, then settling, patent infringement lawsuits. As they do not produce anything, they do not need any of your patents because there is no way that they can infringe on them.

Remember, a patent owned by your company does not give your company a right to practice the patented invention, but rather, gives your company the right to exclude others from practicing the invention. However, your company must do more than just own patents to ensure that it can avoid or win what could be very costly patent infringement lawsuits. This can be accomplished by making reasonable efforts to avoid infringing upon the patents owned by others. The risks of infringing patents can be greatly reduced by conducting a clearance search prior to introducing a product.

Difference between Patentability and Clearance Searches

Clearance searches are conducted in order to minimize the chance that a product that is about to be marketed would contain technology that infringes upon a patent that is owned by another company or individual. A clearance search is significantly different from the patentability searches that are conducted prior to filing a patent application. A patentability search is, in some ways, more exhaustive, but in other ways less thorough.

A patentability search focuses on novelty. To be novel, a claimed invention cannot have been disclosed before the priority date of that claim. A disclosure can be in a scientific or technical paper, an actual product, a book, or a patent or patent application. Furthermore, the invention may not be totally described or incorporated within a single document or item. Rather, patentability can be compromised if a series of disclosures can be pieced together to render the proposed invention obvious in the mind of the examiner. Patent professionals such as examiners and patent attorneys tend to search the patent literature in preference to other sources. However, material from any source is suitable as prior art.

It should be noted that, in the case of the patent literature, it is irrelevant whether the patent has been allowed or rejected, as a patent application can still be a prior disclosure. It also does not matter where in a patent or patent application the prior art is found. It can be found in the background, abstract, or drawings. The material does not have to be, but can be, in the claims. It also is irrelevant whether the patent is valid, is current or has transitioned into the realm of public domain, or even if the patent has been found by a court to be invalid. A disclosure is a disclosure irrespective of the source of the disclosure or the country in which the disclosure had been made.

When conducting a search to determine the proposed patentability of an invention, it is generally not necessary, and it may not even be possible, to attempt to do a totally exhaustive search. Rather, the goal of a patentability search is to identify the most-closely related art. This is often limited to no more than perhaps half a dozen citations. The related art may then be incorporated into the proposed patent application, and should certainly be taken into account when writing claims. You should have good arguments as to why a piece of prior art, either by itself or in combination with other prior art, does not either state or have inherent the proposed present invention.

A clearance search is greatly different. What has been disclosed or is used in prior products is irrelevant. Information contained in scientific or technical papers or books is likewise irrelevant. Disclosure of technology in patents that have expired, have been allowed to lapse due to a failure to pay the maintenance fees, or have been declared invalid are also irrelevant. Only the claims of presently active patents count and, accordingly, only those claims need to be searched.

For the purpose of the present discussion, "product" refers to an object, item, or device offered for sale, a material, a process, or an article that has been manufactured. A claim can be infringed upon by a product. A claim cannot infringe upon another claim and a product cannot be infringed. This means that a product that seemingly copies another product that is not protected by current patents is not infringing on that product because only a claim can be infringed. Furthermore, if Company A has a patent and Company B obtains a subsequent patent on an improvement on the product patented by Company A, Company A cannot allege that company B's patent infringes upon Company A's patent. However, Company B may not be able to produce its product if its product infringes upon Company A's patent. As stated previously, a patent does not give the owner of that patent the right to practice the invention claimed therein.

A question that should be considered is whether or not patent applications, in addition to actual active patents, should also be examined when conducting clearance searches. To address this question, the reader should recognize that the so-called "claims" in a patent application are merely proposed claims. The claims that are ultimately allowed, if any, may be vastly different from those proposed in an application.

The assignee of a patent application has no recourse against a company that produces a product that would infringe upon the proposed claims in an application because those claims are not in an actual patent. That being said, there is a fair chance that a patent application will ultimately become

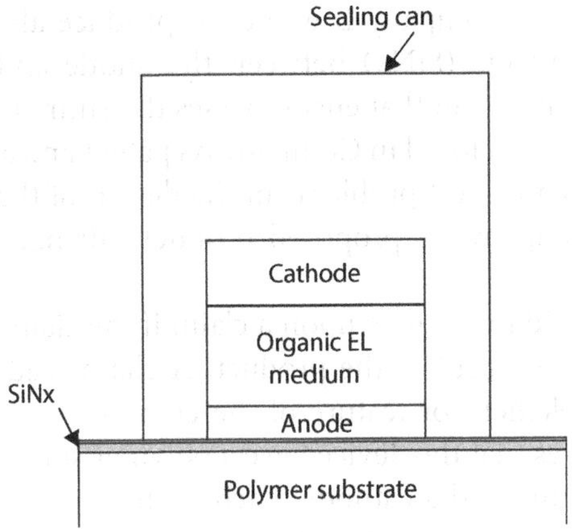

Figure 10.1 A hypothetical product produced by Company B.

a patent with enforceable claims. At that point, the company producing the product would have to either obtain a license to practice the claimed invention or else alter its design immediately to avoid infringing upon the allowed patent.

Considerations Related to Claims

Hypothetical Claim: Version 1

With this discussion in mind, let us consider a hypothetical electroluminescent (EL) product proposed by Company B and a hypothetical patent assigned to Company A. We then ask if Company B's product would infringe on Company A's patent. A design for the device is shown in Figure 10.1 and consists of an EL device comprising a polymer substrate, a SiNx (silicon nitride) film, an anode, an organic EL medium, a cathode, and a sealing can. Let us further assume that the one and only claim in the patent assigned to Company A reads:

> An electroluminescent (EL) device comprising:
> a polymer substrate;
> an organic EL medium;
> an anode positioned between the organic EL medium and the polymer substrate; and
> a cathode positioned in proximity to the surface of the organic EL medium that is opposite the surface that is in proximity to the anode.

The product that Company B wishes to produce also contains a thin layer of silicon nitride (SiNx) between the anode and the organic EL medium and a sealing can that encompasses the entire EL device. The latter features are not disclosed in Company A's patent and appear to be novel and solve some significant problems in the design of the hypothetical EL device. Does Company B's proposed product infringe on Company A's patent?

A product is said to infringe upon a claim if the claim can be "read on" (to use the legal vernacular) the product. A claim reads on a product if each and every element or feature of the claim is found in the product. The patent requires that the device have a polymer substrate, an anode, an organic EL medium, and a cathode. Each of these components is present in Company B's product, and, therefore, the product would infringe upon the claim. The fact that the product also contains a SiNx layer and a sealing can is irrelevant to the issue of infringement.

Company B may be able to obtain patent coverage on the SiNx layer and the sealing can, at which time Company A would not be able to manufacture a product with those improvements. That may encourage Company A to seek a patent exchange agreement with Company B, if the improvements are significant. Presumably, Company B would obtain the rights to practice the invention claimed in the patent assigned to Company A. Alternatively, Company B may decide not to produce the product in competition with Company A, but choose, instead, to license its patent to Company A. Finally, Company B may decide to redesign its product. For example, if Company B decided to use a ceramic substrate instead of a polymer substrate, it would no longer be infringing upon Company A's patent.

Hypothetical Claim: Version 2

Let us now add an additional phrase to the claim in Company A's patent so that it reads:

> An electroluminescent (EL) device comprising:
> a polymer substrate;
> an organic EL medium;
> an anode positioned between the organic EL medium and the polymer substrate;
> a cathode positioned in proximity to the surface of the organic EL medium that is opposite the surface that is in proximity to the anode; and
> an epoxy coating that hermetically seals the cathode.

Because the product being introduced by Company B does not have an epoxy coating, the product does not infringe the patent, as presently written. Every aspect of a claim must be practiced in order for a product be infringing, and, in this particular case, one aspect is not.

The second version of the claim could have been written to include the epoxy coating because it was necessary to seal the device against air for it to function. In this case, Company B may have come up with a novel design that accomplishes the same objective without the epoxy coating.

Alternatively, Company A may have originally included the epoxy coating in a dependent claim. The original independent claim may have been rejected and Company A may have had to combine the dependent claim with the independent one in order to get the patent allowed. If it were the latter case, it would serve as an example of how the proposed claims of a patent application could become much more restrictive claims in an actual allowed patent.

Because a patent is a legal document, there is often the concern as to whether or not the words of a claim mean what would be normally assumed. According to patent law, the words used in a patent have their normal meaning to one of ordinary skill in the art unless defined differently in the specification or during the prosecution of the patent application.* The latter would be available in the file history, which is one reason that it is important to have as clean a file history as possible. Everything in the file history is available to the public.

Broad or generic features in a claim can be supported by specific examples within the disclosure. For instance, if the disclosure supporting the epoxy coating in the EL device listed a specific epoxy used in the fabrication of the device, a claim for an epoxy coating, rather than restricted to the specific epoxy, could still be allowed. As another example, if the EL patent application disclosed a polyester substrate, it would still be valid to claim a polymer substrate because polyester is a polymer.

Limitations on Claims: Means Plus Function

A limitation on a claim occurs when an element of that claim contains so-called "means plus function" language [1]. An example of this is the feature "an epoxy coating that hermetically seals the cathode" as found in the second

* "[T]he ordinary and customary meaning of a claim term is the meaning that the term would have to a person of ordinary skill in the art in question at the time of the invention, i.e., as of the effective filing date of the patent application." *Phillips v. AWH Corp.*, 415 F.3d 1303, 1313, 75 USPQ2d 1321, 1326 (Fed. Cir. 2005) (*en banc*), cited in MPEP 2111.01, III.

version of the above claim. In this example, someone simply applying epoxy such as disconnected droplets or areas of epoxy to attach electrical leads to the cathode would not be infringing on the claim as the function of the epoxy (the means to which the objective is achieved) is to provide a hermetic seal. The use of epoxy for any other purpose, provided the coating of the epoxy does not inherently achieve the claimed result, would not be an infringement.

Doctrine of Equivalents

A claim can be infringed even if the product does not literally practice the claimed invention. This can occur if the differences between the claim and the product are not substantial. This is often referred to as the "doctrine of equivalents". In the case of our hypothetical version 2 claim, if Company B decided to coat the cathode with a varnish instead of epoxy in order to hermetically seal the cathode, Company A's patent might still be considered to have been infringed, even though the product does not exactly practice the claimed invention. Infringement by the doctrine of equivalents is a very gray area and can be problematic and expensive for both companies.

The applicability of the doctrine of equivalents is limited by claim amendments made during prosecution of the patent application [2]. Again, a minimal paper trail during prosecution of an application is desirable and the searching of a file history during a clearance search may be necessary, as will be discussed forthwith.

Willful Infringement

It should be remembered that the purpose of a clearance search is to reduce the probability of your company's being sued for patent infringement and to increase the chances of your company's winning patent infringement lawsuits filed against it. A final goal of a clearance search is to minimize the chance of a patent holder winning a "willful infringement"** suit against your company, as willful infringement can be quite costly—triple damages. It should be realized that inappropriate or unfortunate comments, especially any sort of written documentation including notes written on copies

** Willful infringement can be considered to occur when a company has knowledge of a patent and deliberately or intentionally infringes on that patent. If after the knowledge of the existence of a patent occurs, infringement continues to occur, that is also willful infringement. As this is a legal issue, the reader is encouraged to consult with a patent practitioner for further clarification.

of patents, can undermine your defense considerably, despite the findings and analyses of your legal counsel.

Infringement is a legal, not a technical, issue. The technical staff should avoid comments such as "this patent of Company A claims what we are doing" or "our product infringes on this patent". Similarly, the technical staff should avoid making comments about your patents such as "our patent is invalid in light of this patent". Such judgements can and should be made only by individuals having the legal expertise and requisite qualifications to make them and who have been hired by your company. Moreover, any such comments made by legal counsel retained by your company are generally protected by attorney-client privilege.***

If there are concerns regarding infringing a patent that you wish to discuss with your attorney, you can flag them with comments such as "let's discuss or review this patent". In other words, do not allow your technical staff to voice their inexpert opinions on legal issues. Such mistakes can prove to be very costly.

Conducting a Clearance Search

With this limited background in patent law, let us now examine what needs to be cleared prior to the commercialization of a product and when such clearances should be conducted. The operative word is commercialization. Patent clearances are costly and time consuming. Unless a product is commercialized, there are generally no damages and the probability of a patent infringement lawsuit is small. In other words, exploring various potential product designs in a laboratory does not require clearances.

The three questions that need to be addressed are 1) what should be cleared; 2) in what countries should a clearance search be conducted; and 3) when should a clearance search be done. Let us address these questions in order.

What Should Be Cleared?

The decision as to what needs clearing in a new product depends on several factors. First, it should be asked whether the product is totally new or whether the product simply includes new features that advance an older

*** It should be noted that attorney-client privilege may not include confidentiality between a client and a patent agent unless the patent agent is working for an attorney with whom your company has contracted. Be sure to clarify such confidentiality before entering into discussions with a patent agent.

product. One example is the design of the open end wrenches by Snap-on Tools that have roughened or serrated jaws to improve the gripping of a fastener [3, 4]. Open end wrenches have existed for many, many years and their operation is well known. The roughened or serrated jaws are the novel feature that should be cleared. The fact that Snap-on Tools has obtained patents protecting this technology does not imply that Snap-on Tools can market products with these features. The novel features should be cleared to ensure that they do not infringe on a prior patent.

If it is simply a matter that the product has been produced by the company for some time, but now has novel features, as it would be in this instance in which the novelty is an improvement in the ability of an open end wrench to grip a nut or bolt, it may not be necessary to conduct a clearance search on the entire product. However, the novel features should be cleared to ensure that they do not infringe upon the patents owned by another company. Alternatively, a proposed new product may have features that closely resemble those of competitive products. These may be necessary to allow your product to continue to compete with those of other companies. However, such improvements definitely should be cleared of potential infringements.

When determining if a clearance search should be conducted, it is generally worthwhile to assess the presence of competitors' products in the intended marketplace. Specifically, if the presence of competition is sufficiently small, it may seem that it is not worthwhile to pay for a clearance search and evaluation. However, that may be a mistake. After all, if your company manages to make a large profit on the item, it is likely that competitors who hold patents will seek to enrich themselves at your expense. NPEs may also seek to profit by extracting damages or licensing fees from your company.

If either the entire product is novel or if the product to which the novel features have been added is relatively new to your company, a more comprehensive patent clearance evaluation should be conducted. Products are rarely conceived in a vacuum. Rather, they generally evolve from prior products and, as such, may infringe on others' patents. Accordingly, the question that should be asked is what is relatively novel for your company. The modifier "relatively" refers to products on which the improvements are added that are less than a few years old.**** If a product has been on

**** It is not possible to state specifically how long a product should be in existence before patent clearance becomes unnecessary. Some technologies evolve rapidly and the proposed advancement may rejuvenate a product that otherwise has become obsolete and on which the patents were allowed to expire. Others, such as the O_2 sensor discussed in previous chapters continue to evolve and receive patent coverage long after the initial patents have expired.

the market for 20 or 25 years, any patent with a priority date earlier than the release date of that product would likely have expired and could not be infringed. Consult a patent practitioner for specifics.

In some instances, the novelty may be covered by an indemnity agreement with another company or entity. For example, a company that makes a specific alloy of stainless steel that is highly suitable for production of knives may be willing to indemnify a company that makes knives if the knife company buys its steel. However, it should be ascertained that the pockets of the indemnifying company are sufficiently deep and that the contractual terms are sufficiently protective before assuming that the expenses of a clearance exercise can be foregone because of the indemnification.

In essence, the knife manufacturer, in this example, is relying on the steel company to cover any damages and legal expenses should the particular alloy be found to infringe on patents owned by another company, such as a different knife company that has already known and patented the particular alloy for use in its knives. Also, even if the steel company indemnifies the knife company with respect to the steel, the knife company may still bear liability for patents relating to the shape or construction of the knife, or even ornamental designs etched into the blade or present on the handle.

In summary, clearance searches are generally conducted for novel technology that is going to be commercialized. However, the novel technology must be clearly and accurately described in order for the clearance search to be properly conducted. Vague generalities will undermine the search results. What needs to be searched is exactly what is going to be introduced in the product. The detail that is required to write a claim, as discussed in an earlier chapter of this book, is required to conduct a clearance search. This is because the technology advancement is being compared directly to the claims found in the patent literature.

In Which Countries Should a Clearance Search Be Conducted?

The second question to be addressed is in which countries a novel feature or technology must be cleared. As previously discussed, there is no such thing as an international patent. A patent affords the owner of that patent protection only in the country in which an application had been filed and a patent granted. Even if patents were granted in multiple countries, the claims that had been allowed may differ. However, this does not mean that patents in every country in the world have to be clearance searched. It does not even mean that every country in which related patents are known to exist need necessarily be cleared.

Given that the rights to a patent are limited to within the issuing country, if a product is not being sold in, produced in, or transported through a nation, there is no need to clear that item.***** It is emphasized if any of the three conditions are met, there is the potential for infringing someone's patent. If your product is going to be produced in the United States and sold in Luxembourg, it is likely that the item will be imported into Europe via Rotterdam. Accordingly, a clearance search should be conducted in the United States, Luxembourg, and the Netherlands, as well as any other country in which the product is transported on its way to the market.

It should also be noted that every country's patent laws differ. To effectively determine whether or not a claim held by a competitor in a foreign country reads upon your product, an attorney with expertise in the patent laws of the country in question should be engaged.

When Should a Clearance Search Be Conducted?

The third question to be addressed is when is it appropriate to commence a clearance search. This is perhaps the most difficult of the three questions to answer. If something in the design of a product is covered by someone else's patent, your company may not be able to practice the proposed design. This will be discussed in more detail later in this chapter. However, it is important to note that such an issue may require obtaining patent licenses or redesigning the product to avoid the infringement. Both have serious and expensive consequences. Moreover, product redesigns almost invariably result in product delays, which are costly by themselves and, in an extreme, can destroy the value of the proposed product altogether.

As mentioned, a patent clearance requires that the technology to be used be well-defined and/or described very precisely, as even small variations between the wording of the claims of the patents that might be infringed by the product and the product itself can determine whether or not the claims

***** This is generally true even if patents for the country in question were issued by a regional issuing authority, as discussed in Chapter 9, because assertions would still be conducted in specific countries. The reader is urged to discuss this issue with a patent practitioner.

are infringed. In other words, the technology that will be used in the product has to be precisely determined. This often occurs when a potential product has reached that stage in research and development that it is close to being ready for marketing. By that time any required changes resulting from the clearance search would normally involve massive redesigns of multiple, interacting subsystems. This would also require that the revised product with the corrected designs functions reliably and can be produced at a cost effective price.

Conducting a clearance search prematurely is costly, time consuming, and nonproductive. Moreover, repetitive searches may have to be conducted as the final product design takes shape. Conducting a clearance search later than is absolutely necessary can result in significant delays in product introduction and costly redesigns or licensing fees. Neither scenario is good. There is a delicate balance that is required when deciding when to conduct a clearance search. This is further complicated by the fact that a clearance search and evaluation of any patent literature that is discovered during such a search can take weeks or longer to fully evaluate.

Questions that should be answered when determining when to commence a clearance search on a novel piece of technology include:

a. Is the technology totally defined so that it is unlikely that it will be changed? For a complicated piece of equipment comprising numerous subsystems, this question often focuses just on advances in the specific subsystem being considered. Thus, modifications to a fusing subsystem used in an electrophotographic printer, for example, would have to be cleared, irrespective of changes to the toner formulation or paper handling subsystems.
b. Is the use of this technology, in addition to its design, well defined and unlikely to be changed?
c. Are there reasonable alternatives available instead of using the proposed technology should it be found that the proposed technology may infringe upon a patent?
d. Is it likely that changes in other aspects of the design of the product would force the redesign of this particular technological subsystem? If so, would such alterations be expensive or time-consuming or otherwise impose high levels of risk?
e. Would design changes in other subsystems, whether novel or not, require that this technological device or process be altered? Using the example of the fuser mentioned above in

question 'a', a change in the toner formulation or paper handling may require modifications to the fusing subsystem that would then have to be cleared once more even if previously cleared.

These are some of the factors that go into deciding when to conduct a clearance evaluation. Clearly, it makes no sense to conduct such evaluations if the proposed technology is likely to change, because the claims of any patent of potential interest must read directly on the technology to be practiced. On the other hand, a product that relies on a specific technological improvement with no reasonable alternatives can pose very high risks if its development goes on without knowing that your company can use that technology. Remember, just because your company has a patent or even a family of patents on the technology does not give your company a right to practice that technology.

How to Conduct a Clearance Search

Let us now discuss how to go about conducting a clearance search. Although such searches can be done by the engineers or managers who have been working on the project, and, certainly, they understand the novel technology better than anyone else, it is generally advantageous to contract such searching with an external patent search firm. The outside firm does not have a vested interest in your success. Accordingly, it can objectively evaluate claims and provide a targeted list of patents to be considered.

An accurate and detailed description of the novel technology should be included in the search request. If your company knows of certain patents that may affect the product being developed, also provide those to the patent searching company at the beginning of the search. This may permit the searchers to input key words or terminology from those patents into their search, rather than just relying on your engineers' specific wording.

It is recommended that the patent search company be informed that the purpose of the search is for clearances and that searching should be restricted to the claims of active patents and patent applications. However, they should be explicitly told that they are not to make any comments whatsoever about the relevance of the patents that they discover. Moreover, your employees should not make any comments about the relevancy of any other patents, whether previously known to your company or discovered during the searching. Such information may be subject to the discovery process should a lawsuit against your company be filed and can be quite damaging. Remember, infringement is a legal concept and the determination of whether or not a product may infringe upon a claim in another's patent should be left to a legal expert, with input from your technical staff.

Some Cautionary Notes

Once the search has been completed, the role of the patent search company is done. Unless something comes up that requires additional searching, such as a change in the technology that will be used in the forthcoming product, there is no need for any further discussions with that company. At this point any discussions should be between your employees who are involved with the particular technology in question and the attorney who is representing your company. Any correspondence about the clearance results should only be between the attorney and the necessary employees, with the correspondence headed by words to the effect "Privileged and confidential. Prepared at the request of an attorney." This is to allow the information that is being discussed, which might otherwise be discoverable, to be communicated under attorney-client privilege. Discussions and analyses of potential patent infringements can be quite costly if they are subject to discovery by opposition attorneys.

Because of its importance, the reader is once again cautioned about written opinions of patents by your employees. They should be avoided to all extent possible, even if they are between your employees and your attorney. If a patent, for example, needs to be called to the attention of your attorney, a comment such as "This might be of interest" is sufficient and further written elaboration is neither necessary nor desirable. Avoid establishing a paper trail to all extent possible.

Once potentially problematic patents have been identified by the clearance search team, it is time for the technical experts in your company to sit down with your attorney and discuss their claims, in light of your proposed technology. It is likely that the attorney will find that most are not infringed and can be ignored. But, what happens if it appears that your proposed product may infringe upon the claims of one or more patents? There are several possible courses of action.

When reviewing a patent for infringement, carefully read each of the independent claims and look for those elements in those claims that your product does not have. As previously stated, it is not sufficient that your product has additional elements. That is irrelevant. However, as also previously stated, for a claim to be infringed, every element of the claim must be present in the product. In addition, even if the elements in the product are not exactly as stated in the claims, are those elements in the product sufficiently close to the claim that the doctrine of equivalents might apply? The latter is a gray area that has to be addressed by your attorney.

If the independent claims do not read on your proposed product, the patent can be ignored. However, if the claims do appear to read on your product, it would also be necessary to examine the dependent claims to determine whether or not there would be further infringement should your product, in its present configuration, be commercialized. Because the dependent claims further elaborate the independent claims, they can only be infringed if the independent claims are infringed. However, infringement of the dependent claims strengthens the case of your competitor and can add to the damages incurred.

If Your Product Appears to Infringe

After examination of the claims and the appearance that there may be an infringement, your attorney can search the file history. There may be non-infringement arguments that can be made based on the information contained in that file history. This is the reason that, when prosecuting a patent application, it is desirable to limit discourse with the examiner as much as possible. A brief file history reduces the opportunity for others to evade your patent claims.

It may be possible to design your product around the infringed claims. For example, let us consider the hypothetical claim discussed previously in this chapter that includes the means plus function phrase "an epoxy coating that hermetically seals the cathode" in Company A's product. Should Company B need the epoxy to connect electrical leads, Company B could make the coating discontinuous so that it cannot serve as a hermetic seal and might, therefore, avoid infringement of this claim. However, if the seal is necessary, simply substituting a varnish instead of the epoxy may be ruled the same due to the doctrine of equivalents. To avoid infringement under the doctrine of equivalents, it would be necessary to show that the feature in question performs a different function or performs the same function in a different way. The file history of the patent application may help Company B's attorney decide on the extent of the technology covered by the claim under the doctrine of equivalents.

Another possible course of action would be to question the validity of a patent. If the independent claim or claims can be shown to read upon a single piece of prior art, the patent would lack novelty and be invalid. The prior art need not be a claim from an earlier patent. It can be a description of what is claimed anywhere in a patent, a patent application, a publication, or an earlier product, including on-line disclosures. A product deemed to be prior art can even be that of the owner of the patent if the assignee introduced that product prior to the filing of the patent application. The prior art can have been introduced by anyone in any form. As long as prior art exists, the patent lacks novelty and would be invalid.

Alternatively, a patent might be deemed invalid based on obviousness. This occurs when, instead of being disclosed in a single piece of prior art, several prior references have to be combined that result in the patented claim. However, this is more difficult to prove. Novelty-based invalidity arguments are often preferable to obviousness-based arguments, but both can be useful.

To determine whether prior art exists, a "validity search" is conducted. This is similar to a patentability search, but is based on an issued claim rather than on a technological development. Validity searches may be much more extensive than are clearance searches. They may include interviews with people familiar with the field and who can identify earlier products that would constitute prior disclosures or who are cognizant of literature that would not typically turn up in a patent search. It should be emphasized that the validity of a patent is ultimately determined in a court of law.

Be aware that numbers also have meaning. If you find five or more patents that may block your product, but for which invalidity arguments may be made, think long and hard before deciding to release the product. To the knowledge of the author, no one has ever been able to have five patents declared invalid. One or two might be found to be invalid. Five presents a difficult task.

The final alternative when clearing a novel product, in the event that an infringement is found, is to obtain a license to practice that invention. This can be part of a patent exchange agreement or based on a royalty or fee payment. It is possible that the owner of the patent may not be willing to negotiate a license, at which point one of the other options above would have to be pursued.

Pending patent applications do not have to be incorporated into a clearance search, but it may be a good idea to do so. A patent application cannot be infringed and there is no guarantee that a patent will be eventually issued based on that application or that the claims that are eventually allowed, if any, would have any resemblance to those in the application. However, it does alert you to the fact that something that may affect your product is pending and, if it is issued, can affect whether or not you can continue to market the product, as designed. Remember, if a patent application was filed before you release your product, the patent will be relevant to you even if the patent did not issue until after you released your product. Additional information regarding many pending applications, including the office actions of the examiner, can be found at the United States Patent and Trademark Office (www.uspto.gov) under the section entitled Patent Application Information Retrieval (PAIR).

Clearance Analysis and Memoranda

After completing the clearance search and the review of the results of that search, related to the technology in the proposed product, the attorney will write a legal opinion memorandum that presents both the facts found and the legal analysis that supports his conclusions contained therein. Technical experts may be quoted by the attorney in the memorandum to support the technical facts used in the analysis.

The analysis is only as good as the information presented to the attorney and errors or omissions by your technical experts can prove to be quite costly. If no literal infringements have been found, it is also important to include an analysis based on the doctrine of equivalents.

If the attorney determines that a patent is invalid, i.e. the patent should not have been issued in the first place, he should prepare a detailed analysis, based on factual information, that has led him to that conclusion. If this sounds like you are preparing for a legal defense in case of a patent infringement lawsuit, it should. Part of that defense is that any patent that was infringed was done so inadvertently, based on the analysis by your attorney, and the infringement was not willful.

It should be recognized that a clearance search and the subsequent analysis does not remove all risks of a patent infringement lawsuit or losing a legal action and having resulting damages assessed against your company based on such a lawsuit. It simply is aimed at reducing the risk to an acceptable level. Lawsuits can be filed quite readily and no search or analysis is perfect. There are always risks. However, a clearance analysis reduces those risks substantially.

Distribution of the legal opinion memorandum should be limited to those individuals who have a need to have a copy of that document in order to maintain attorney-client confidentiality. Moreover, anyone receiving a copy should avoid making any written comments on or regarding that document. In addition, employees should avoid making comments about the legal opinion. Presumably, the employees are technical, rather than legal, experts and the document is a legal analysis. Technical information has already been inputted and utilized by the attorney preparing the memorandum and further commentary can only serve to degrade the value of that document. Engineers need to understand that legal analyses are in a different category from the documents the engineers normally encounter, and need to be handled differently.

The writing of the legal opinion memorandum, by itself, is not sufficient to show that the company has acted in good faith to avoid infringing patents. It is equally important that the legal opinion memorandum be communicated to corporate management or the appropriate decision makers and that demonstrable action based on that memorandum be taken. This can be quite simple if the analysis shows that there is no infringement. Alternatively, in the case of potential infringement, the actions taken should be consistent with the recommendations of the attorney, be they redesigning the product or arguing that the infringed patents are not valid. In any event, decisions should be made after decision makers review the memorandum and perhaps even after they discuss the analysis with the attorney. The company must be able to show that it has acted in good faith.

A final benefit of conducting a clearance analysis and search is that it clearly shows your competitors' technology. Presumably, your product has advantages over those of your competitor. Have you thoroughly patented those advantages? You now know the competition's technology and the extent of its patent portfolio. This is an ideal time for your company to file patent applications that address the shortcomings of your competitors' products. These will often be patents that your competitors will need and for which they will have to pay licensing fees or enter into patent exchange agreements with your company. Either can be exceedingly valuable. Moreover, as such patents would encompass alternative approaches undertaken by your competition, it enhances your goals of owning the problem and controlling the marketplace for your products.

References

1. 35 USC 112(f).
2. *Festo Corp. v. Shoketsu Kinzoku Kogyo Kabushiki Co.*, 535 U.S. 722 (2002).
3. D. A. Huebshen, W. T. Pagac, F. Mikec, T. S. Severson, and D. M. Sorbie, U. S. Patent #5,148,726 (1992).
4. W. T. Pagac, F. Mikec, T. S. Severson, and D. M. Sorbie, U. S. Patent #5,117,714 (1992).

11

The Role of the Patent Engineer

It should be apparent by this time that patents can be extremely valuable to your company. Besides protecting your intellectual property that gives you a competitive edge in the marketplace, patents should be considered a valuable product in their own right. In either event, patents are valuable only if another company needs access to the technology claimed in your patents. It is the need to gain access to your intellectual property that generates the demand for your patents. If no one needs the technology contained in your claims, your patents are not just valueless. Rather, as discussed earlier in this book, they are expenses. They cost money to obtain. They cost additional money to maintain. And, they educate your competitors.

On the other hand, patents can prevent competitors from using your technology to gain access to your markets. However, it is up to you to enforce or assert your patents. No one else will do this for you.

Patents are worth money to you if other companies find that their need for your patented technology is so great that they are willing to offer something of value to you. This generally occurs through patent exchange agreements*. They may license your technology and pay you fees. They may buy ownership of your patent, thereby becoming the assignee. Or, they may enter into cross-licensing agreements with your company, thereby giving your company access to their technology.

Patents that disclose and claim a particular solution to a specific problem can be quite valuable [1–3]. However, as discussed in Chapter 3, solution-specific patents are often of far less value than ones that form part of a portfolio that holistically focuses on solving or owning the entire problem. However, as also discussed, problem-specific patent portfolios rarely come about by accident. Rather, they arise by carefully generating and executing a patent strategy designed with the goal of owning the problem in mind.

Alternatively, as discussed in Chapter 10, patents owned by other companies, or worse, non-practicing entities (NPEs) can limit your ability to sell your products. Such organizations may choose to deny you access to technology that you desperately need, forcing you to either pay exorbitant licensing fees or royalties or to have to offer them access to far more of your patents than you would otherwise desire.

As discussed in Chapter 9, we live in a global economy and international patents may be important to your business. Decisions have to be made as in which countries to file. These patent applications can enhance the power and value of your portfolio. However, they also incur risks and expenses that need to be carefully considered.

It is clear that, whether your company is large or small, well-established and profitable or entrepreneurial and new, patents will impact it. The effect can be positive or negative or both. Helping you navigate the intricacies of patents for your technologies should be a patent engineer.

In this chapter, we will review and expand upon the role of a patent engineer within your organization.

What is a Patent Engineer?

Typically an engineer or scientist, patent engineers need to have sufficient in-depth knowledge of your company's technology to allow them to contribute to the technological development of your products. In addition

* The reader is reminded that we generally use the more inclusive term "patent exchange agreement" instead of the more commonly used, but more limited term "cross-licensing agreement", which is a subset of the former term.

they should have sufficient knowledge of patent law and process that they can guide the engineering and management teams in all areas related to patents. Patent engineers should also possess excellent written and oral communications skills.

Patent engineers are probably not patent attorneys. They may be certified as patent agents** and such certification can be of value. However, that is also not necessary. It is, however, necessary that patent engineers understand what constitutes patentability and have sufficient imagination to envision alternative methods to achieve a technological goal.

A patent engineer who possesses a reasonably broad and in-depth knowledge of your competitors' processes, products, and patents and related literature would be a substantial asset in both crafting a patent strategy that includes filing patent applications that give you control of those solutions that would be needed by your competition and in preparing disclosures that would not subsequently be deemed obvious by a patent examiner in light of or inherent to the related art.

More important though is that the patent engineer has the knowledge, skills, and attitude to navigate the legal issues of patentability, enabling your company to develop a valuable and powerful patent portfolio. The patent engineer should blend an expert ability to execute both written and verbal communications necessary to prepare drafts of patent applications with those necessary to interface with engineers, scientists, and managers, on the one hand, and patent attorneys on the other.

Why is it vital that your organization have patent engineers? Notice the use of the plural. If your company has multiple, distinct product lines that do not employ similar technology, then, in view of the requirement that the patent engineer have the in-depth knowledge and understanding of the technology in which he will be working, it may be necessary to have more than just one.

Product lines employing similar technologies may well fall within the knowledge required of a patent engineer. Thus, a company producing tools and hardware may need only one patent engineer, whereas a company that

---

** A patent agent is not a patent attorney. Rather, a patent agent is an individual who has obtained training in patent law and has been certified to file and prosecute patent applications. A patent agent cannot appear before the Patent Circuit Court of Appeals representing clients. Also, some discretion should be exercised as discourse between a client and a patent agent who is not working under an attorney is not subject to attorney-client privilege. However, legal costs are often reduced when using a patent agent instead of a patent attorney.

produces both pharmaceutical and home care products may require more than one patent engineer.

The Patent Engineer in a Corporation

The activities in which a patent engineer can add value depend on the nature of your organization. Challenges faced by a manufacturing company proposing to produce and market products using a novel technology would differ from those of a university seeking to license, but not actually produce, products using its technology. A financial institution that seeks to invest in companies, but that neither develops nor markets technology would have still other needs that are distinct from either a manufacturer or a university.

Some law firms either help clients extend patent portfolios or are involved with patent litigation or both. The latter represents its clients in asserting its patents against infringing companies or by defending them against assertions by other companies. Both of these types of law firms could use patent engineers for a multitude of reasons. These include using patent engineers to help devise appropriate patent strategies or devise tests of the products in question that show or contradict infringement allegations. Furthermore, whereas it is often advantageous for a manufacturer have patent engineers permanently on staff, a financial institution/investment firm or law firm may want to contract with specific individuals who can help guide their activities related to specific patent assertions or patent applications. A university may want to have a small permanent group of patent engineers whose expertise is augmented by adding patent engineers on a contractual basis. Let us examine each case separately, starting with manufacturing organizations.

A manufacturer endeavors to establish a proprietary advantage over its competition by producing products using its novel technology. Accordingly, a patent engineer would be involved in 1) establishing a patent portfolio that protects the intellectual property of the company; 2) collaborations between the company and others in co-development activities; 3) ensuring the company can produce and market its goods and services while reducing the risk of patent infringement; and 4) establishing a patent portfolio of intrinsic and marketable value. Let us explore each of these topics separately.

Relying solely on your engineering, R&D, or management teams is seldom effective in devising and maintaining a strong patent portfolio. As discussed in an earlier chapter, inventors often fail to recognize that they have an invention, and, even when they do, and proceed to submit an invention disclosure, they tend to focus on the solution to the specific problem rather than on owning the problem. The resulting patent application or applications tend to be too narrowly focused and easily circumvented by a competitor.

The engineers are deeply immersed in their assigned projects and under great time pressures to complete them. They seldom have time to put together a coherent patent application, let alone work with the attorneys to produce one. Critical aspects such as conducting related art searches are often not thoroughly performed, leaving the strong probability that the patent application would be rejected by the patent office. Likewise, the management team has its targets that must be achieved within tight time and budget constraints. All too often, the management team looks upon the filing of patent applications as a nuisance that is undesired and unnecessary. They certainly do not want their team members devoting time and effort to filing applications. And, in any case, neither the management nor engineering staff have an adequate working knowledge of patent law to enable them to write disclosures that protect the company's intellectual property while circumventing obviousness rejections from the patent office.

The primary role of a patent engineer is to formulate and execute an advantageous patent strategy. While the technical staff that is dedicated to the project cannot be entirely freed from engagement in the filing of the resulting patent applications, the use of a patent engineer will minimize the time that the staff is distracted from their primary obligations.

The patent engineer would first meet with the technical team members to precisely determine what problems they have solved, are in the process of solving, or intend to solve. From this information, generally in the presence of the staff members, the patent engineer will propose draft claims, or at least an independent claim, for each of the perceived inventions. Developing these claims in the presence of the project staff ensures that the patent engineer understands the problem and that the staff understands the invention or inventions and the wording of the claims thereof. Both aspects are vital.

It is perhaps obvious that the patent engineer needs to understand both the problems and the solutions in order to formulate the patent strategy. However, it is equally important that the technical staff understand what is being filed. Remember, patent applications should be filed with the intent of asserting the issued patents against infringing companies. If an infringement is found, the technical staff must be able to clearly describe the details of their invention, as written in the patents, as well as how it is being infringed.

Once the independent claims are written, the patent engineer can proceed to conduct a prior art search. The search can often start by using references supplied by the project staff. Alternatively or concurrently, the search can be conducted using vernacular searches of the proposed independent claims that are within the capabilities of many modern patent search engines.*** The searching reveals the most relevant prior art and will help the patent engineer both refine the claims, if necessary, and to write the background section of the forthcoming disclosures so as to argue against the presently proposed inventions being either inherent to or obvious in light of prior art.

The patent engineer would next explore alternative methods of accomplishing similar technological goals. This can be done in conjunction with the project team members as well as examining the approaches taken by competitors. Applications can be drafted covering these alternatives with the goal of owning the problem and, in particular, owning those portions of the problem that are needed by your competition. This equips your company with revenue-enhancing patents that are extremely valuable either for licensing purposes or in the event that patent exchange or cross-licensing agreements are necessary.

Perhaps most important in formulating a patent strategy is to make sure that the information presented in an application does not preclude the obtaining of patents on future applications. The patent engineer is responsible to ensure that the filing of individual applications is consistent with a comprehensive plan to secure the most coverage for the least expense of dollars and project-team time.

Tackled next are proposed dependent claims for the specific inventions presented to him by the project team, as well as both independent and dependent claims for those applications that would cover alternative solutions. The project team can review these claims at this time if so desired. However, the specific review of these claims now is less important than having them involved in drafting the initial independent claim or reviewing the entire disclosures after they had been drafted.

After completing the drafts of the claims and the formulation of the patent strategy that will be pursued, the patent engineer can write the appropriate disclosures that will be incorporated into and comprise most of the patent applications. This can include the sketching of figures, tables, and

*** Some search engines allow the searcher to enter a phrase, which can be an independent claim. The search engine proceeds to list a number of relevant patents. The searcher can then enter key words and narrow the search results to those most relevant.

charts, although frequently the members of the project team may have material that is suitable for this use.

The drafts should incorporate all patent applications that will comprise the initial filings. It is beneficial to also include, if and to the extent possible, the drafts of the applications that will be filed subsequently, recognizing that those applications may be incomplete because not all information is available. This will allow the project team members to assess the proposed strategy and also ensure that the disclosures to be filed do not prematurely disclose information that will be claimed in subsequent applications.

Once the patent applications have been drafted by the patent engineer and reviewed by the appropriate members of the project team, it is time to present those applications to the legal expert who will be filing and prosecuting them. The legal expert, who is an attorney or patent agent, will review the applications and make appropriate legal revisions to them, and may suggest revisions to tighten the legal wording of claims, ensure that the claims are supported by the disclosure, and to be certain that proper procedure is followed. One example of the latter relates to the use of the words *a* and *the*. The first time that an article is referred to it has to be prefaced with the indefinite article *a*. Subsequently, as the article has now been defined, it must be referenced with the definite article *the*. This is just a sample of the detail that is involved in properly filing patent applications, but a failure to follow correct procedure, as well as patent law, can rapidly derail the best of proposed patent applications. The cautionary note here is that appropriate legal expertise must be involved in the patent application process.

Broadening Your Patent Portfolio—An Example

As the focus of this book is on generating a patent portfolio that maximizes the value of your company's intellectual property, let us illustrate the process just discussed with a hypothetical example. Let us first consider an example where your company uses technology distinct from that used by your competitors. In this example, companies K and X both produce electrophotographic printers. In both instances, a primary imaging element (a more general term than "photoreceptor")**** is uniformly electrostati-

**** The use of the term "primary imaging member" instead of just saying "photoreceptor" is commonly used to allow any patent that is issued to encompass the more general electrostatographic printing, of which electrophotography is a subset. The use of the broader term would broaden the range of the technology covered by the claims, thereby extending the range of protection afforded by an issued patent.

cally charged. The primary imaging member is then exposed to light, pixel by pixel, using an exposure device, thereby creating an electrostatic latent image. The latent image is converted into a visible image by dusting the electrostatic latent image with toner.

The exposure devices used by companies K and X are totally different. Company K uses an array of LEDs that traverse the entire width of the primary imaging member and, upon being triggered uses a writing algorithm contained in the central processing unit to expose a single pixel when required. The principal advantage of this system is that it does not introduce any distortions to the pixels along the width of the primary imaging member because the light emitted by each LED impinges normally (i.e. at a right angle) onto the primary imaging member.

In contrast, Company X creates the electrostatic latent image by exposing the primary imaging member, pixel by pixel, by using a laser scanner. In this device, a laser is pulsed at a correct time to expose the primary imaging member pixel by pixel. In order for the light to impinge on the correct portion of the primary imaging member, the light is reflected into a rotating polygonal mirror, which then sends the beam to the appropriate region of the primary imaging member.

Both the LED array and laser scanner have their own advantages and disadvantages. It is clear that neither company would use the technology of the other company's exposure technology, but would most likely need technology patented by the other company in its other subsystems, thus creating a need for either a patent exchange agreement between the two companies or one company's being able to extract licensing fees from the other or even prevent the other company from entering into a desired market for proposed products.

Let us now assume that a major deficiency of laser scanner technology is that the laser beam becomes elongated as it impinges the primary imaging member at angles less than 90°. Assuming that the laser is located at the center of the primary imaging member, as the beam is deflected to expose pixels at the extreme edges of the primary imaging member, it becomes elongated much the way a flashlight beam illuminating a wall at an oblique angle is elongated. This creates distortions in the pixels that then give rise to distortions and image degradations in the final, visible print.

Company K decides that it would be advantageous to obtain patent coverage on methods and apparatus that would be important to Company X, even though such intellectual property would not be used in Company K's products. This is important if Company K is to own the problem, or at least enough of the problem so that Company X would have to pay licensing fees or negotiate a patent exchange agreement with Company K.

Accordingly, the patent engineer calls a meeting, inviting engineers specializing in optics, exposure and writing systems, and imaging algorithms. It should be remembered that, in order to obtain a patent, a non-obvious and novel solution to a problem must be proposed. Company K cannot obtain a patent just on the idea that it would be beneficial to correct the distortions created by a laser scanner. One must propose how that would be done.

In the meeting, several ideas are advanced. These include:

1. Changing the writing algorithm in a prescribed manner so that the pixels that are exposed correct for the distortions in the final print.
2. Varying the rotational velocity of the polygonal mirror so that the pixels to be exposed are selected to minimize distortions.
3. Introducing a curve into the primary imaging member so that the laser beam impinges onto it at a right angle.

Time is then spent in the meeting discussing how each of these proposals could be implemented and the impact of the implementation on the functioning of other subsystems. After due discourse, it is decided that proposal 3 would be difficult to implement and it is unlikely that Company X, or any other foreseeable company, irrespective of the actual products being produced by the other companies (that is, it need not be in the same product line or even be a competitor) would actually desire to use such technology.

This is a tough decision because it involves looking out as many as 20 years into the future. However, if there is little, if any, foreseen interest in a solution to a problem, it probably is not worth the expense of obtaining a patent. Company K may simply wish to publish the proposal to preclude a different company from patenting it.

Proposals 1 and 2 appear to have more direct applicability to the products of Company X. Accordingly, Company K has its technical team members design specific equipment and methods that would allow each of these proposals to be implemented.

As a patent is limited to a single invention, the patent engineer writes proposed independent claims for each of these ideas to totally capture the inventions. It should be remembered that each patent is limited to a single invention. In other words, if the technology covered cannot be described by a single overarching claim, the patent engineer may have to use the independent claims to draft multiple applications. Once this has been accomplished, a prior art search on the proposed independent claims can be conducted. The results of this search may give rise to additional inventions that should be patented or require that the independent claims be modified. Once this has been done, appropriate dependent claims can be written, followed by the drafting and filing of the patent applications.

The advantage to Company K of obtaining these patents is two-fold. First, if the analysis leading to these patents was done thoroughly and correctly, the patents specifically address problems that Company X will have to address. This makes its obtaining access to Company K's patents very important and may encourage it to negotiate cross-licensing agreements that gives access by Company K to technology that it needs from Company X without surrendering technology that may be more valuable to Company K. Moreover, as published patent applications are frequently used by corporate intelligence to assess where its competition is heading, these patents can serve to mislead Company X with respect to the future products of Company K.

How the Technical Teams Benefit by Interaction with a Patent Engineer

In contrast to Company K's filing on the technology that might be needed by a competitor, it is more common and desirable to protect the proprietary technologies that give your company an advantage in the marketplace. Ideas for individual inventions may or may not have been submitted by members of the technical staff working on a project. However, these tend to be solution-specific and may serve as a lead-in to a more complete patent portfolio, but will not provide adequate protection in and by themselves. More often than not, however, once a meeting has been convened, the technical team members who have been working on a project for an extensive period of time will emphatically state that they have not invented anything.

Rather than asking what inventions they have, the author of this book has found it more fruitful to ask the technical team whether they would have been able to put the product together a year ago. This prompts a discussion of the problems encountered by the team and how they addressed or how they plan to tackle them next.

This is also a good time to explore alternative solutions to the problems being discussed, because it is likely that the technical team members considered those other options and based on assumptions that may or may not be valid under alternative scenarios, discarded those ideas as less than optimal under the present assumptions. However, assumptions can change rapidly and such ideas are valuable fodder for filing patent applications that may be valuable under other circumstances.

The patent engineer can now conduct prior art searches and propose dependent claims. It is likely that additional meetings with specific team members who have played significant roles in the specific inventions for which a patent application will be filed will be required.

It should be noted that, despite the best of care in conducting searches and describing the problems and solutions to get around the prior art, it is unlikely that all the patent applications will be ultimately allowed. However, if the techniques described herein are followed, a majority of the applications should result in patents that provide your company with an extremely valuable portfolio.

The overarching role of a patent engineer in the generation of patent applications is to serve as the bridge between an attorney, who is a legal expert but who does not have a detailed expertise in the technology in question, and the members of the technical team, who are not legal experts. Employing a patent engineer can free up your technical staff to work on assigned projects and reduce legal expenses while generating a much more valuable and powerful patent portfolio.

Deciding which applications not to file can be as important and cost-effective for a patent engineer as determining what to file. These include proposals for so-called "combination patents" such as those resulting from known technologies that, when combined, result in a novel product but whose components are known and are used to produce known effects. As in the hypothetical example of the eraser and the pencil presented in a previous chapter, using known technology to produce a novel product that does not have any unanticipated benefits is not patentable.

In addition to the combination patents are proposed applications that are simply not ripe for submission. These might require additional research or might even be headed in an incorrect direction. However, the submission of such applications constitutes disclosures and can impede more solid, subsequent patent applications. Again, proper and effective handling of such proposed applications requires a good working knowledge of both the technology and patent law.

The Role of the Patent Engineer in Joint Product Development Projects

Product development requiring interactions with at least one other company has become commonplace. Should your company, for instance, envision a new product that necessitates working jointly with another company or institution in order to develop some of its novel features, or if you require an outside vendor to custom-design a critical component for the proposed project, a patent engineer can implement a proper patent strategy and skillfully craft nondisclosure agreements to ensure the protection of your intellectual property and your ability to use that property.

Let us begin by considering a collaboration with another company to develop some aspect or component for your proposed product. It should first be recognized that the intellectual property developed by the supplier belongs to the supplier. While the contract into which your company has entered with the supplier might stipulate that you have a license to practice any and all inventions arising from the collaboration, such licensing may not allow your company to bid the component out to other potential suppliers. Therefore, you might have to pay whatever your collaborator wants to charge to use the components for whose development you have contracted and, perhaps, for which you have already paid.

The situation can become even messier when, for example, engineers employed by both companies have devised a novel, critical component. The patent would list, as inventors, engineers from both companies and, therefore, both companies may be able to claim rights to the invention. Because the collaborating company also holds patents on its contributions to your critical components, it could conceivably prevent your company from marketing your novel product. Alternatively, your company may have to pay licensing fees to the contractual company to use that technology or your company might have to purchase the component from the contractual company at whatever price that company wants to charge, thereby limiting your company's ability to seek alternative, more cost-effective, suppliers.

This demonstrates how vital it is that your company's intellectual property be protected before any technical discussions with the supplier take place. The patent engineer is key to ensuring that this occurs.

The technical team in your company probably knows a lot more about the components to be supplied than is often realized. They certainly appreciate the specific applications for those components, as well as the problems integrating the components into your product. They may have some ideas already as to how to solve the foreseen problems. They certainly know what the outcome has to be.

The role of the patent engineer is to gather what is known from the technical team, including stretching the concepts presented by that team to address potential problems and alternatives, drafting and researching appropriate claims, following up with preparing the drafts of the applications in attorney-ready format (including figures, charts, and tables where needed) and presenting the drafts to an attorney so that the applications can be filed prior to the commencement of discussions with the supplier. The key words here are "prior to the commencement of discussions". This is very important as there can be no argument as to whom the intellectual property belongs and who the inventors are if the applications are filed prior to the commencement of discussions. Even if further intellectual property results from the collaboration, having some patents gives your company alternatives should the supplier's prices become too high and may, in fact, allow your company to negotiate from a position of strength with the supplier should it need some of your technology.

Is the task of filing the applications prior to discussions with a supplier challenging, especially as the supplier presumably possesses expertise lacking in your company? It certainly is. However, with the participation of a patent engineer, it is achievable and can be extremely valuable.

The role of a patent engineer in joint development projects involving multiple companies is not limited to just obtaining patent coverage. Rather, it involves protecting all intellectual property that is exchanged between your company and your partners. Specifically, proprietary or confidential information must be routinely exchanged between the partnering companies. This information needs to be protected and a patent engineer is both well-equipped and in an excellent position to ensure that this happens.

Nondisclosure Agreements

Complementary to pursuing an appropriate patent strategy is the use of nondisclosure agreements. It should be emphasized that both patents and nondisclosure agreements are vital in order to protect your interests when dealing with external organizations. As both require a detailed understanding of the technology and a working legal knowledge, patent engineers can play a crucial role in both. Let us now discuss various aspects of nondisclosure agreements and how they benefit your company.

Nondisclosure agreements (NDA), also often referred to as proprietary information agreements (PIA), confidentiality agreements (CA), or confidential disclosure agreements (CDA), can be "mutual", "bilateral," or "two-way," meaning that both parties are restricted in their use of the materials provided and identified as confidential. Alternatively, they can restrict the use of the material by only one of the contracting parties, and is referred to as a "one-way" NDA. An NDA is considered to be one-way if only the information transmitted from a first company to a second company must be held in confidence by the second company, whereas the first company is free to do whatever it chooses with information transmitted from the second company to the first. In contrast, a nondisclosure agreement is considered to be two-way if both the first and second companies agree not to disclosure information transmitted by the second or first company, respectively.

It is generally advantageous for your company to seek a one-way nondisclosure agreement with companies with which you seek to co-develop technology or from whom your company will purchase specific components or subsystems that are of a particular design for use in your products. This is because your company can transfer confidential material to the partnering company while maintaining that materials' confidential status.

However, in a one-way nondisclosure agreement, your company would be free to use the information transmitted from the partnering company to your company in any manner that your company deems appropriate. This includes using the information in patent applications, publications, or in trade shows.

If your company entered into a bilateral nondisclosure agreement, it would be prohibited from disclosing that information without the consent of the partnering company. That being said, there are occasions where partnering companies may insist on two-way nondisclosure agreements in order to protect what they consider their intellectual property, especially if they plan to file patent applications or sell that technology or modifications thereof to other companies.

Nondisclosure agreements are contracts and, as such, must be signed and executed by authorized members of both signatory companies in order to be valid. This generally means that the nondisclosure agreements, whether one-way or two-way, have to be signed by a corporate officer or an individual explicitly empowered by corporate management to sign such agreements. Failure to properly execute a nondisclosure agreement may result in the information transferred between companies to be considered as a prior disclosure and may negate the ability to obtain proper patent coverage. In addition, such a failure can also preclude the ability to recover damages should the other company disclose or otherwise use that information.

Nondisclosure agreements should be explicit as to what is considered confidential. The agreement should include a general statement describing the work and the anticipated material that would be confidential. In addition, in order to ensure that there is no confusion, the agreement should state that all confidential material covered by the agreement would be marked as such and it should be explicitly stated, either on the material itself or in an accompanying cover letter, that the material is covered by the nondisclosure agreement.

Finally, the nondisclosure agreement should designate specific contacts, preferably a single specific person, for each company. The contact need not be the individual who signed the agreement, but can be someone who is intimately engaged in the project. In addition, the disclosing company should keep a detailed log of what material was transferred and when that transfer occurred. It is important that the recipient company know that your company plans to treat the nondisclosure agreement seriously. Violations of the nondisclosure agreement should be promptly handled by an attorney.

A patent engineer can handle many of the details of generating nondisclosure agreements and maintaining the required records. The actual drafting of an initial agreement, because it is a contract, should be done by an attorney. Subsequent nondisclosure agreements, if there are no substantive changes (e.g. changes other than the nature of the work or the company with whom the agreement is being executed) could be handled by a patent engineer.

The corporate contact could be a patent engineer, although it may be more expedient to have a project team member serve as the contact. The patent engineer could keep copies of all correspondence between the companies. The goal is to reduce the time spent by the project team members on handling the details of the nondisclosure agreement while ensuring adherence to the terms of the agreement.

Patent Engineers and Patent Prosecution

Patent engineers can also prove invaluable during the prosecution of patent applications. Although some patent applications sail through the patent office as initially submitted (so-called "first office action allowances"), such allowances are the exception rather than the rule. During the course of prosecuting patents, it is common to receive non-final or final rejections, requirements to select certain claims (so-called "divisionals"), etc. The office actions require that the applicant make decisions whether to argue against the assertions of the examiner or to amend claims, or otherwise respond to the office action.

Upon occasion there may be a need to actually speak with (interview) the examiner, or to appeal. Both avenues can be fruitful, but should be exercised with some discretion, for reasons discussed in Chapter 7. Again, the knowledge of both the technology and patentability possessed by a patent engineer would be beneficial to your company when formulating and crafting responses to office actions, interviewing examiners, and participating in the decision-making process and the preparations for appeals.

Finally, there may come a time when, despite all reasonable efforts, it appears that any further pursuit of a patent is simply not worth the money or time and the application should be abandoned. Pursuit of the patent may be an exercise in futility, running up costs without any real expectation that the patent will be granted. Alternatively, the claims the examiner may be willing to allow might be so limited that they are worthless. The decision to abandon further prosecution should be made by the managerial and technical teams, with input from the patent engineer and your patent practitioner.

Patent Engineers and Clearances

As discussed in detail in Chapter 10, it is not sufficient for a company to just maintain a solid patent portfolio on the technology that is used in its products. It is also necessary for a company to minimize the chance that it is infringing upon the patents owned by another company, whether or not that company is an actual competitor. It is even more important that a manufacturer does not willfully infringe upon another's patents as willful infringement can incur triple damages. Patent engineers can play a vital role in ensuring that patent clearances are properly performed.

Patent clearances ask very specific questions, mainly what specific aspects of the technology are novel and does that technology infringe on the claims of any active patents. Searches are only as good as the information presented to the search company. Legal decisions as to whether or not patents are infringed depend on the attorney getting an accurate description of the specific aspects of the technology in question and the related patents that have been revealed by the search company. To these issues are added legal subtleties, discussed in Chapter 10, such as the doctrine of equivalents. There is, perhaps, no other area of patent law where the language divide between technical and legal staff can be both more important and more problematic than in formulating clearance searches and analyzing the results obtained thereof.

It is precisely because of patent engineers' knowledge of the technology and their understanding of patents that allow patent engineers to serve as the ever-so-vital interface between the technical and legal communities. Specifically, being able to read and understand exactly what a claim states and determining whether the proposed product practices the claimed technology is absolutely crucial to properly clearing a new product. Moreover, patent engineers are often in an excellent position to assess what aspects of the product need to be cleared.

In some instances, when time is of extreme importance and a search company cannot return results in a timely manner, the patent list obtained by patent engineers can serve as a nucleus that allows your patent engineers to conduct the clearance search. It should be emphasized, however, that this is not generally the preferred course of action for the reasons presented in Chapter 10.

The patent engineer is also uniquely suited for determining the specific technology being used in the proposed product. Again, the emphasis is on specific. It does not matter what may be used or can be used. The question is whether or not the specific embodiments of the technology read on the wording of specific claims. Unfortunately, project engineers often miss the specific legal descriptions in the claims, opting for more general statements of the technology being used.

Should the clearance search find that there are claims that the technology may read on, patent engineers, working with the product team members, are in a strong position to determine whether or not the proposed technology actually reads on the claims. Please remember, however, that this determination should be made by an attorney who is acting under the advisement and expertise of the patent engineers and with the technical team members. Should it be determined that the technology would infringe on the claims, patent engineers, again working with the product team, can steer the technology so that it avoids infringement, if possible.

There are times that a certain technology is necessary in a product despite the fact that it would appear to infringe upon someone's patent. As discussed in Chapter 10, there are several options to pursue. The first option is to engage in a serious redesign of that product so that it does not infringe.

The second option is to seek a legal opinion as to whether or not the patent in question is valid. Again, this is a legal decision and does pose risks. However, it is an option that may be worth considering. Here, too, a patent engineer's knowledge of the technology, the field in general including what has been done or disclosed by anyone prior to the issuance of the patent, and the specific technology envisioned by your company in the product would be of immense value to the patent attorney when considering patent validity arguments.

The third option available is to seek a patent exchange agreement. If a strong patent strategy has been formulated by your patent engineers and implemented by your company, a patent exchange agreement may be readily obtained. The expertise of patent engineers enables them to determine what your company can offer to the owner of the infringed patent that would be of minimal value to your company, but vital to the owner of the infringed patent.

The fourth and fifth options, namely to pay licensing fees or cancel the project, are managerial decisions that should be made with input from both the patent engineers and technical team members.

The Role of the Patent Engineer in Patent Renewals

Decisions as to whether or not to renew patents are often complicated and can have expensive ramifications. Alternatively, failing to renew certain patents can also be costly, especially as the exclusivity they provided by preventing your competitors from using the patented technology will be lost and may ultimately limit your company's ability to commercialize its products. With their technical knowledge of both your products and those of your competitors, as well as an understanding of where technology is heading, patent engineers can be of immense value when reviewing a portfolio to determine which of your patents should be renewed. As discussed in Chapter 8 regarding the United States and Chapter 9 regarding international patents, renewals are common throughout the world and, unless renewal fees are paid, your patents will become public domain and you will succeed only in teaching your competition about the previously protected intellectual property.

In the United States, as previously discussed, patents have to be renewed at periods of 3½, 7½, and 11½ years after issuance, with the renewal fees escalating with each renewal. Paying renewal fees on every patent you own could be a waste of money. Conversely, not paying them can result in a significant loss for your company. If the technology protected by a patent is being used by your company in a valuable product, it should be renewed, as other companies might be interested in copying that product. Certainly, if the patent is bringing in licensing fees or is part of a cross-licensing or other patent exchange agreement, it should be renewed. If a patent is being actively cited in patents held or applications filed by other companies, it may signify interest in that technology and probably should be renewed. And, if a patent is the subject of litigation, especially if your company is asserting it, it should probably be renewed.

Alternatively, if present or future technology has moved away from that being claimed in a patent, it might be worth abandoning it. And, if there is no interest expressed by other companies in that patent, it may not be worth paying the renewal fees.

The factors allowing for an informed decision of whether or not to renew a patent may be unclear at the time of the first renewal. This is often because the technology is novel and its full commercial value has not yet been realized by your competition. Patent engineers often have the knowledge of how the technology may evolve and may be able to provide desired input when reaching this decision. Fortunately, the fees for the first renewal are rather modest and, absent clear indications to the contrary, they are generally worth paying.

By the time the third and most costly renewal is due, it should be fairly clear as to whether or not a patent is sufficiently valuable as to warrant the expense of renewing. Here, too, patent engineers can use their knowledge of the competition to help guide your company.

Renewing for the second time is often the most difficult decision of the three. Here, the technology is just maturing and its full commercial value and that of its protecting patents may be difficult to determine. At the same time, the renewal fees are substantially higher than those incurred at the first renewal, but not as high as those experienced at the time of the third renewal. A patent engineer's input into the likely value of your patents at the time of the second renewal can be particularly beneficial.

Because product lines commonly evolve over a period of years, if not longer, it is beneficial to have patent engineers who have gained long-term expertise in relevant areas. Alternatively, if a company is exploring the possibility of entering a novel market, it may want to simply contract with patent engineers having experience in the new areas of endeavor.

Patent Engineers and Assertions

Patent engineers also play important roles in enforcing or asserting patents. Assertion requires that the owner of a patent or patents prove that someone is producing goods or services that read on one or more claims of those patents. As in the case of a clearance discussed in Chapter 10, in order for a claim to be infringed, the infringing product must read on every element of that claim. It is up to the owner of the patent to prove infringement.

Infringement is a legal issue and will require legal expertise to pursue. That being said, company A, seeking to prove that company B is infringing its patents, must first identify the patents it believes are being infringed. This mandates a preliminary knowledge of the workings of the product or products in question. Those products must then be carefully examined to determine whether or not they are infringing the patents of company A and, if so, precisely which patents are being infringed.

Demonstrating that a product infringes on a patent often requires a detailed analysis of that product. This frequently includes conducting specific tests, experiments, or analyses of the product in questions. Often, a family of products produced by a company may be subject to this type of scrutiny. Attorneys often prepare "claim charts" that detail the claims of your patents that you suspect are being infringed against the actual technology being practiced by the alleged infringer. The claim charts break down the asserted claims into its component phrases in one column and the results of the study on that product in a second column to show that each aspect of the claim is being practiced by the product. These activities require a combination of both technically and legally skilled people and, fundamental to this, is that the technical individuals participating in this activity understand the precise meaning and requirements of the claims of the patents, as well as the operation of the allegedly infringing products. Patent engineers are ideally suited for this role. They can design and conduct or supervise the tests to determine whether or not a claim is being infringed, as well as assist your attorneys in the preparation of claim charts.

As discussed earlier in this book, demonstrating that at least five patents are being infringed greatly reduces the probability of company B being able to escape damages by having the patents declared invalid. While invalidity arguments may be successful with one or two patents, to the knowledge of the author of this book, no defending company has ever been successful in having five patents declared invalid. Polaroid asserted nine patents in its suit against Kodak. Kodak alleged that these patents, representing obvious devices for producing instant photographs, were invalid. Indeed, the court ruled that two of the patents were, in fact, invalid on those grounds. That left the other seven, which Kodak was found to have infringed. This is yet another reason why a company would strive to protect its intellectual property with multiple patents generated from a strategy focused on owning the problem rather than a single patent aimed at protecting a particular solution to a problem.

Patent Engineers and Universities

Universities, law firms, and investment firms can also benefit from the services of patent engineers. In general, none of these organizations manufacture products. It is recognized that universities sometimes form technology parks or own subsidiary companies in order to produce products or services using its intellectual property.

It is further recognized that each of these types of companies can and do produce products upon occasion and may wish to obtain patent protection covering the intellectual property used in those products. In those instances, the previous discussion related to the role of patent engineers in manufacturing would be relevant. However, it is also recognized that such product production is generally not the focus of these organizations. Accordingly, a discussion of the unique opportunities pertinent to universities, law firms, and investment firms will now be undertaken. Let us first consider the role of patents and patent engineers in universities.

First, let us recognize that a university is a business with a variety of products and customers. Customers include students seeking knowledge and/or degrees, employers seeking to hire graduates, alumni who donate money or attend admission-charging university events, and agencies and companies funding university research. Products include results from research, educated students, employees at various companies, alumni who pay to attend sporting events, and intellectual property.

Yet, in the face of rapidly-escalating costs, universities often give away their intellectual property for free. Faculty members are encouraged to publish their results and obtain grants in order to obtain tenure or promotions. While the value of obtaining patents may be recognized at universities, most faculty members, even in the engineering and scientific disciplines, have little training in recognizing patentable intellectual property and generally do not pursue such options. As an example of this, how many times do researchers at universities devise novel methods and equipment to measure something and then fully disclose this information in a publication that focuses on the results obtained?

Universities often have dedicated staff empowered to evaluate technology and file patent applications. Unfortunately, these offices are often pressured to focus on the costs of obtaining patents rather than the value of obtaining a coherent patent portfolio that focuses on potential income from the licensing of patents. Faculty members, pressured to publish, tend to write their papers, which are immediately sent to appropriate journals or presented at conferences or seminars. Moreover, universities encourage open communications and dissemination of novel information—the very disseminations that constitute legal disclosures and start the clock ticking on the time frame in which patent applications can be filed. Finally, in contrast to industries where relatively large teams of employees work on a limited number of projects, university research often consists of small teams working on a wide diversity of projects.

Paradoxically, given the free-exchange-of-ideas culture of universities, research and disclosures conducted by faculty in one department may be unknown to members of another department, even if there is legally significant overlap.

Universities have, in general, several characteristics that simplify patent issues and the role of the patent engineer. As universities primary mission is not manufacturing, concerns about patent infringement or actually being able to practice its technology without infringing on patents owned by others is often not relevant. Accordingly, clearances and patent exchange agreements tend to have minimal importance. However, universities need money and licensing fees can make significant contributions to university coffers.

Universities are often concerned with the expense of patenting. Faculty members are all-too-often insufficiently knowledgeable about patents and are being pressured to rapidly publish. As a result, decisions in universities regarding what technology to patent and how extensive that patent coverage should be are frequently being made by individuals or offices that often are not sufficiently versant about the novel technology. This creates a situation where universities are failing to capitalize on their intellectual property. It is also recognized that research grants may pose constraints on the ownership of patents resulting from the funded research. In addition, universities often fail to educate their students, especially those enrolled in the science or engineering curricula, about patents. This is especially troubling as many of these students will ultimately be employed in industry, where knowledge of patents is important.

The situation at universities begs for the addition of patent engineers to the university staff. Although a patent engineer may be employed by a single department, it would often be more effective if patent engineers were university, rather than departmental, employees, focused on specific areas of technology, and working across the boundaries imposed by departments or schools within a university.

Accordingly, a patent engineer who specializes in photon detection can enhance patent opportunities in electrical engineering departments where solar cells are being designed, physics departments where highly efficient photon detection systems are developed to detect particles in high energy experimental physics, and the chemistry and chemical engineering departments where novel advanced materials aimed at enhancing quantum efficiency are being developed.

Patent engineers can make great contributions to both the financial and educational opportunities afforded to universities. Their visible presence and interactions with students and faculty can serve to educate members of the academic community as to the opportunities and requirements of pursuing patents.

Patent engineers can examine technological advances made by researchers in the various academic departments, ensuring that synergistic developments are treated in an appropriate fashion to obtain proper patent coverage. Because of their technical expertise, patent engineers can draft patent applications that would give broader coverage to the university's intellectual property than is presently done. Again, the issue here is that lawyers are legal experts, not technical experts, and are rarely in a position to visualize the entire technological advances or to formulate a patent strategy that aims at owning the problem. By drafting applications, a patent engineer would alleviate placing additional pressures on graduate students and faculty members, thereby freeing them up to continue to pursue their other activities, and, at the same time, introducing the students to patents. Moreover, a patent engineer can expedite the filing of applications so that publication or presentation of results is not significantly affected.

The patent engineer would also be responsible for developing a commercially valuable patent strategy. All too often, patent applications filed by universities focus on the fundamental advancement rather than what is of commercial value. Again, we call to the readers' attention that, in the Polaroid patent infringement lawsuit against Kodak, it was not the fundamental chemistry patents that were ultimately of financial value. Each company had its own, unique chemical process for producing instant photographs. Rather, it was seven patents that described and claimed relatively simple enabling technology that proved to be valuable. Finally, the patent engineer would be responsible for identifying businesses that may have an interest in licensing university-owned patents.

Implementation of a Patent Strategy at a University

In order for a university to obtain a patent portfolio of significant economic value, as opposed to one of only reputational value, the patent engineer should devise a strategy based on the marketability of the patent portfolio centered on the inventive technology. At this time the patent engineer should draft claims that summarize the invention and conduct a patentability search on those claims, revising them as necessary. The patent engineer should also propose a preliminary list of inventors, subject to ultimate revision by the attorney filing the patent applications after the claims have been finalized by that attorney. This is because inventorship is a legal issue and requires that each named inventor make inventionable contributions to at least one claim. As a result, the inventors named on a patent application may differ from those listed as authors on the scientific papers that will be published or presented.

Should alternative methods of accomplishing the goal of the present invention be found, the patent engineer should explicitly indicate the advantages of the present invention, which could include technical, environmental, legal, or cost benefits, over those presented by competing technology. The goal of this exercise is to determine whether or not pursuing these patents is a suitable investment for the university.

The patent engineer can now prepare a review of the proposed patent strategy, to be presented to the university's patent office, as well as appropriate faculty members. This should include the drafts of the proposed claims (subject to revision upon review by an attorney), as well as the proposed marketability of the invention. Potentially interested companies can be highlighted in the review. The goal of the review is to present, not only the patent strategy, but the economic benefits and costs to the university in implementing that strategy.

Should the university choose not to proceed with a patent application, the faculty member can use the patent engineer's report to decide whether to file and pay the fees personally or with grant monies, depending on the approval of the university.

The Role of a Patent Engineer in a Law Firm

The role of patent engineers in law firms practicing patent law differs from those employed by either companies that produce marketable products or universities. Law firms generate revenue by representing clients in the filing and prosecution of patent applications and in the assertion of patents against infringing companies after the patent has issued. Conversely, law firms also defend alleged infringers in assertion cases. Patent engineers having expertise in the field of the invention can be of great value in both the generation and prosecution of applications and in the litigation. Because of the specific field of expertise requirement, it may often be most beneficial for a law firm to hire a patent engineer with the appropriate technical skills on a contractual basis.

The role of a patent engineer in the assertion of patents is similar to that of his counterpart in a company; namely, to identify potentially infringed patents and to show that the technology employed in the products of that company do, in fact, read on the claims of the patents. As such, if the asserting company already has a suitable patent engineer, it may not be necessary to duplicate his role within the law firm. Conversely, when defending an alleged infringer, a law firm may benefit from the expertise of a patent engineer to help design and orchestrate tests to show that the products in question do not practice the claims. In either scenario, the patent engineer, under the guidance of the attorneys, would work closely with the technical teams from the respective companies to build a case for infringement or in preparing a defense against such allegations.

Let us now focus on another role of a patent engineer in a law firm: enhancing its business in the area of generating and prosecuting patent applications for clients. To do so, we must first set the stage and describe a familiar scenario of law firms advising clients on obtaining a patent. Clients approach patent law firms with the intention of obtaining a patent on an item that the clients perceive as novel. The attorney working for the firm will discuss the device and proceed to write a patent application on that technology. The clients will review the application, may or may not understand the legal description of the invention or the claims, sign an affidavit stating that they have read and understood the application (whether or not they have or do is moot), and the attorney files the application with the patent office and awaits the resulting office actions.

Upon receipt of the office actions, the attorney may or may not contact the clients, depending on whether the response required is strictly legal formalism or if a more detailed, technical response is necessary. All too often, the client does not understand the specific objections raised by the examiner (assuming that the response was not a first office action allowance) and has difficulties helping the attorney draft a response. Throughout all of this, the attorney, who is a legal expert, probably has not spent the time to develop the technical expertise in the area.

The above scenario certainly has numerous shortcomings. The clients' interests are not well served, as they are likely not to get the patent coverage that they desire or for which they pay. Moreover, the firm has not gotten the billable hours that it could have. This can be changed with the judicious use of a patent engineer.

We propose a method for law firms to interact with clients to enhance the value of the patents obtained. This method would be cost effective for the clients as it allows for the use of common disclosures while increasing the billable hours for the law firm.

Upon submission of an invention disclosure by a client to a law firm, the law firm engages a patent engineer. The patent engineer would discuss the proposed invention with the client and conduct, possibly during that discussion, a preliminary patent search that would reveal the most relevant prior art.

The patent engineer would then propose and discuss enhancements and/or alternatives to the proposed invention focused on ensuring that the client would own the problem rather than simply a specific solution to a problem. A family of patent applications, based on a common disclosure with whatever modifications are necessary, would then be proposed.

The key element here is that the clients should walk away from this meeting with a good understanding of what is inventionable and how to go about generating a family of patents to protect their intellectual property. The law firm has, in effect, guided the inventors instead of simply filing an application based on the proposed description of an alleged invention by the clients. The patent engineer can propose a series of draft claims for consideration by the attorney and write the actual disclosure or disclosures to support the claims. These can be discussed with the clients so that the clients more fully understand the invention, which is a legal, rather than technical, concept.

The patent engineer can be of additional value during the prosecution of the patent applications. Having a solid knowledge of the technology and a working knowledge of patent law and the technical literature, the patent engineer would be able to assist in preparing responses to office actions and with interviewing the examiners, if necessary. Obviously, the expertise would be of value in preparing appeals, if necessary. The patent engineer would also be able to help decide and prepare continuations or continuations-in-part, as appropriate, and would also be able to assist the clients in deciding to what extent the patent applications under consideration to be filed would be worth the expense.

In essence, a patent engineer would enable a law firm to guide clients in developing their patent portfolio as well as improving the quality thereof.

The Patent Engineer and Investment Firms

The final type of business to be addressed that can benefit from the services of patent engineers are investment firms. There are numerous types of investment firms, ranging from banks that loan money to established or start-up companies to firms such as Bain Capital that actually purchase and manage companies. Firms such as Manning and Napier invest their own and clients' money in publically traded companies. Other investment firms manage the assets of bankrupt companies or engage in leveraged take-overs.

Investment firms have numerous interests in patents. These interests include the determination of the monetary value of a company's patent portfolio, the ability to increase the value of a company by enhancing that portfolio, and the ability of a company to compete in, and possibly control, the market. Patent engineers can provide valuable analysis and assistance in enhancing the value of client or subsidiary companies.

While investment firms generally can analyze the present value of patents owned by a company, technology trends that may affect the patents in the future often require the input from a technical expert in the area.

Similarly, it is often advantageous for the investment firm to examine the patent holdings of a company, compare them to those of its competitors, and produce a strategy that would significantly enhance the value of the company's patent portfolio. This generally requires the technical analysis and the generation of an understanding of the breadth and depth of the patents held by the company in question as well as those of competitors, and is best performed by a patent engineer. Once that analysis has been completed, the patent engineer can draft appropriate claims and disclosures for patent applications, as well as participate in the prosecution of those applications that, once allowed, would enhance the value of the patent portfolio.

Controlling the Marketplace

The world has changed and how we adjust to it must also change if we are to survive and prosper. Technological innovations, at one time a slow and evolutionary process, occur at faster and faster rates. Manufactured goods, produced primarily in Europe during colonial times by artisans working under the auspices of the guilds that existed under the economic philosophy of the mercantile system [4] gave rise to the teachings of Adam Smith, who advocated for an economic process that is now known as capitalism.*****

Goods, once produced in small, independent shops, are now produced in large factories that came about during the industrial revolution. Blessed with natural resources and protected from the devastation of war by two oceans, the United States became the industrial powerhouse of the world during the late 19th through the mid-20th centuries [5]. The last third of the 20th century saw the industrial monopoly of the United States eroded by global industrialization. The latter has presented challenges in the form

***** It is interesting to note that *The Wealth of Nations* was published in 1776, the same year as the adoption of the *Declaration of Independence*.

of increased global competition and accelerated advancements, as well as opportunities presented by new potential markets.

Accompanying the changes in how goods and services are produced and sold are massive and ongoing changes in patent laws. All these changes combine to make the role of patents in your business more significant than ever before. It is no longer sufficient to assume that a single patent will adequately protect your paradigm-altering innovation. Patent portfolios need to be much more extensive and focused on owning a problem rather than just a specific solution to that problem, as alternative solutions can be readily designed and implemented.

This is especially true as technological advances make interactions between products in disparate industries more common. At one time a fuel pump and carburetor delivered fuel to a cylinder in an internal combustion engine, where a spark generated by an ignition coil and distributor ignited it. Today, this is all controlled by computers using technology that arose from the space program. This is the same technology that has also given rise to home computers and cell phones and interactions abound. In a recent article in an automotive trade journal [6], the author Dan Marinucci sites the presence of a cell phone on the front passenger seat of a car triggering a diagnostic trouble code. The signal from the cell phone was apparently interacting with the electronic control signals of the car. Indeed, technological advances in one discipline can often both present opportunities and problems in seemingly unrelated businesses.

Modern patent portfolios must be designed with such interactions in mind. Your patent portfolio, if properly built, can be used, not just to block competitors, but can also be a valuable source of income, through licensing, from both competitors and seemingly unrelated industries.

In addition, care must also be exercised to reduce the risk of infringing on patents held by others. This can often be accomplished by conducting clearance searches prior to introducing your product. Being able to avoid infringement lawsuits filed by your competition is an essential part of your strategy. Owning patents covering solutions that your competitors need is an important component of that strategy.

While very important to your business, your technical staff is generally not sufficiently versant in patents. Conversely, patent practitioners are quite knowledgeable with respect to patents, but are probably not so regarding your technology. To build a strong patent portfolio both groups must communicate effectively with one another. The patent engineer possesses the technical skills and knowledge about patent law which can facilitate that communication.

There is no doubt that patents affect your business. The effect can be positive. They can protect your vital market by giving you exclusivity. They can allow you to enter into agreements with other companies that enable you to access their technology. They can create a significant source of revenues through licensing or sales of the patents. Alternatively, unless due care is taken, patents owned by others can limit or even destroy your business.

However, as discussed throughout this book, having patents focused on specific solutions to the technological problems that you encountered during the design of your innovative product is not sufficient to protect your technology. Moreover, a patent portfolio that focuses only on such solutions may not be worth much. Patents only protect your place in the market and are only valuable if other companies need your protected intellectual property. This means that the patents are assertable and that they encompass alternative technologies to the particular solutions that your company is pursuing—alternatives that your competition may use. It is important that your patent portfolio be developed to enable your company to own the entire problem, if possible, rather than specific solutions to the problem. If your company cannot own the entire problem, it is certainly desirable to own sufficient portions of the problem so that other companies have to negotiate patent exchange agreements with your company or they risk being frozen out of the market. Portfolios that achieve this goal do not come about by accident. Rather, they are the result of careful planning, often directed by a patent engineer who will be working with your technical team members, management, and legal advisors to make sure that your patent portfolio is, in fact, a valuable product of your company.

Patents are or should be part of your business. In some ways, they present opportunities that can enhance your business. In other ways, they pose challenges to your business. Patents do exist and you will have to work with them. How you choose to work with them and the future of your business are within your control.

References

1. K. G. Rivette and D. Kline, *Rembrants in the Attic*, Harvard Business School Press, Boston (2000).
2. L. G. Bryer, S. J. Lebson, and M. D. Asbell, *Intellectual Property Strategies for the 21st Century Corporation*, John Wiley and Sons, Hoboken (2011).

3. M. A. Gollin, *Driving Innovation*, Cambridge University Press, Cambridge (2008).
4. Adam Smith, *The Wealth of Nations* (1776). Modern Library, New York (1937).
5. S. E. Morison, H. S. Commager, and W. E. Leuchtenburg, *The Growth of the American Republic*, Vol. II, 6th edition, Oxford University Press, New York (1969).
6. D. Marinucci, *Motor*, pp. 10–12 (August 2012).

Index

Printed in the USA/Agawam, MA
September 16, 2026

910661.004